Resistant Structures

Particularity, Radicalism, and Renaissance Texts

Richard Strier

UNIVERSITY OF CALIFORNIA PRESS

Berkeley / Los Angeles / London

University of California Press
Berkeley and Los Angeles, California

University of California Press, Ltd.
London, England

Earlier versions of some of the essays in this book have been
previously published as follows:
Chapter 3: "Shakespeare and the Question of Theory," *Modern
Philology* 86 (1988): 56–76. © 1988 by The University of Chicago.
All rights reserved.
Chapter 5: "Sanctifying the Aristocracy," *Journal of Religion* 69
(1989): 36–58. © 1989 by The University of Chicago. All rights
reserved.
Chapter 6: "Radical Donne: Satire III," *ELH* 60, no. 2 (Summer
1993): 283–322. Reprinted by permission of The Johns Hopkins
University Press.
Chapter 7: "Faithful Servants," *The Historical Renaissance: New
Essays on Tudor and Stuart Literature and Culture*, ed. Heather
Dubrow and Richard Strier (1988), 104–33. © 1988 by the
University of Chicago. All rights reserved.

First Paperback Printing, 1997

Library of Congress Cataloging-in-Publication Data

Strier, Richard.
 Resistant structures : particularly, radicalism, and Renaissance
texts / Richard Strier.
  p. cm.—(The new historicism ; 34)
 Includes bibliographical references and index.
 ISBN 0-520-20905-2
  1. English literature—Early modern, 1500–1700—History and
criticism—Theory, etc. 2. Literature and history—England—
History—16th century. 3. Literature and history—England—
History—17th century. 4. Particularly (Aesthetics)
5. Radicalism in literature. 6. Renaissance—England. I. Title.
II. Series.
PR428.H57S77 1995
820.9′003—dc20   94-35106
                                                           CIP

Printed in the United States of America
9 8 7 6 5 4 3 2 1

For Camille, and in memory of John

"Don't think, but look!"
Wittgenstein

"No method nor discipline can supersede the necessity of being forever on the alert."
Thoreau

Contents

Acknowledgments

Many friends and colleagues helped make this book actual and encouraged me to persevere. Gerald Graff and Jay Schleusener made extremely helpful comments on the theoretical essays in the book.

In reflecting on my work, I find that there are a handful of friends and colleagues who not only read and comment helpfully on almost everything I write, but who are always presences to me even when I am working on pieces that any particular one (or all) of them have not seen. I find that I am in dialogue with them even when they do not know it. Imagining their voices and reactions has simply become part of what serious writing means for me. The friends and colleagues with whom I am always in dialogue in this way (and usually literally as well) are Frank Whigham, Stephen Greenblatt, Michael Murrin, and David Bevington. I am grateful to Stephen Greenblatt in concrete ways as well, for encouraging this project and (somewhat to my surprise, but much to my delight) wanting it to be part of his series.

I am also deeply grateful to the two readers of this book for the University of California Press, and to my wonderfully prompt and encouraging editor there, Doris Kretschmer, for finding me these excellent readers, and for much else. Debora Shuger read a draft of this book that I now shudder to think about, and made extraordinarily intelligent and helpful comments, both structural and substantive, almost all of which I simply adopted and have ever after mendaciously claimed as things that I wanted to do on my own in any case. I have no doubt that a less intelligent, sympathetic, and learned reader could have killed off this project in its semiformed, embryonic stage. Instead, Debora was a nursing father to it. Paul Alpers read the penultimate version of the manuscript with characteristic rigor and wit. His comments were shrewd, bracing, and tonic, and the book is much the better for them. I am deeply grateful for the time and effort that both of these busy and productive scholars put into helping me with this book (and I'm also glad that they liked it!). I am deeply grateful as well for the superlative set of comments, queries, and suggestions that I received from the anonymous member of the Press Editorial Board who presented my manuscript at the board meeting.

Many friends and colleagues have made important contributions to particular essays. William Veeder helped with the introduction (and with general conversation about the whole project). Paul Fry responded generously and brilliantly to an early version of the first essay and sent me a xerox of the unpublished correspondence between Tuve and Empson. Tom Mitchell and Wayne Booth commented very helpfully on the piece on Stanley Fish. Together with Schleusener and Graff, Beth Sharon Ash, Loy D. Martin, and Robert von Hallberg commented helpfully on the third essay. For comments on the French contexts of the "Devout Humanism" essay, I am very grateful to my colleague Philippe Desan, and for superb and helpful comments on the whole essay I am grateful to Michael Schoenfeldt. My colleague Joshua Scodel was writing his wonderful essay on Donne's third Satire at the same time that I was working on the poem, and dialogue with him on this extraordinary text was interesting and productive in ways that my notes are only partially able to capture. The Donne essay also benefited from the flavorful combination of appreciation, learning, and mordant wit that I have come to expect from my friend Ken Gross. The Shakespeare and disobedience essay benefited greatly from comments by Louis Montrose, Quentin Skinner, and, most recently, James Holstun, with whom I have discovered many intellectual affinities. The essay on Tate's *Lear* was the subject of the last scholarly conversation I was able to have with the codedicatee of this book, the late John M. Wallace, who was typically helpful and generous about the essay, including its discussion of his work. This essay also benefitted from reactions and suggestions from Steven Pincus, Edward W. Rosenheim Jr., James K. Chandler, and John Morillo. I am especially grateful for the learned, detailed, and generous comments of Philip Harth (who will, I am afraid, still not be fully satisfied).

I would like to take this occasion to say a few words to those few, those happy few, who have read the publications on which some of these essays (numbers 3, 5, 6, and 7) are based. I can say two things to such persons (blessed be they). First, it is my hope that these pieces have a somewhat different feel and weight in this book than they did as separate effusions. And second, they actually are different. The essays that are based on previously published pieces are not identical with those pieces. There are, in all cases, significant changes, and in the cases of the historical essays, significant additions. I hope that the experience of reading these essays for such readers will not be "déjà vu all over again" but rather an experience of seeing some familiar points more deeply, richly, and reflectively developed.

Andrew and Sonja Weiner, beloved friends and owners of Spaightwood Galleries in Madison, responded to my impossible demand for a work of art illustrating the argument of this book by finding the wonderful Alechinsky litho reproduced (with kind permission of the artist) on the cover. I read this image as showing the critic as Fool attempting to impose a scheme on a resistant text.

Finally, I want to thank my wife, Camille E. Bennett, not only for help with many of these pieces, especially the introduction (to which she contributed Groucho Marx), but for helping to create a life for us in which productivity is possible. I can't imagine scholarship, or anything else, without her.

Introduction

Resistant Structures

In describing his experience in teaching Humanities 6 at Harvard, Paul de Man spoke of the power of "mere reading" prior to any theory. He spoke of "the bafflement" that "singular turns of tone, phrase, and figure were bound to produce in readers attentive enough to notice their non-understanding behind the screen of received ideas."[1] This book is a defense of the possibility and the desirability—though not the inevitability—of such bafflement. I take seriously the idea that "reading" prior to any theory is, as de Man suggests, a strong and distinct experience. The "resistant structures" in the title of this book are, in the first instance, the structures of and in particular texts that produce "bafflement," that surprise or puzzle the reader on a large or small scale, and that in some sense resist assimilation to totalizing interpretive strategies or methods. I agree with de Man's view that such structures are, in a perfectly intelligible and defensible sense, *in* the texts, that texts are "bound to produce" them in readers, as Dr. Johnson would say, "uncorrupted with literary prejudices." Where I disagree with de Man is that I do not believe that the resistance of particulars to theories can itself be theorized; I do not believe that this resistance always points to the same scandal or deep truth that "it is the more or less secret aim of literary teaching to keep hidden."

---

1. Paul de Man, "The Return to Philology," *The Resistance to Theory*, with a foreword by Wlad Godzich (Minneapolis: University of Minnesota Press, 1986), 23. The quotations from de Man in this paragraph all occur on pp. 23–24.

I do not believe, in other words, that we can know in advance what sort of bafflements texts will produce, or even that texts will produce them. What this book is against is any sort of approach to texts that knows in advance what they will or must be doing or saying, or, on the other hand, what they cannot possibly be doing or saying. De Man's knowledge of the nature of the bafflement that texts will inevitably produce is, in my view, one of the a priori approaches that dictate to particulars how they must behave, that tell critics what they must find when they look closely at texts. I want to argue for the desirability of approaching individual texts with as few presuppositions—theoretical and historical—as possible.[2] The more that the critic knows in advance what a text must or cannot do, the less reading, in the strong sense, will occur. I have taken Wittgenstein's "Don't think, but look" as the guiding motto of this book.[3] I want to be as skeptical as possible toward general claims about literature, authors, or periods, while being, on the other hand, extremely nonskeptical, as I have already suggested, about the "objective" existence of facts and structures prior to theories. "Don't think, but look" makes no sense as an exhortation if "looking" can never reveal anything that "thinking" does not.

It is sometimes said that there are no facts independent of theories. Something like this may—with enough of an account of "theories"—be true, and it is certainly true that there is no "world" without language. But this does not mean that there are no facts independent of particular theories, or that there are no facts that many different "theories" all presuppose. Literary approaches, with the exception of deconstruction, are often not "theories" in any very strong sense, and certainly particular interpretations are not "theories." There are many features of literary

2. It has been pointed out to me that this sentence could be read as a plea for ignorance, for, as one colleague put it, "know nothingism." I understand this possibility, but I mean to be arguing for a methodological principle of something like "*docta ignorantia*" ("learned ignorance"), a procedure that suspends many things that one knows (or thinks one knows) in favor of an initial experience of "mere reading." Only after this has been done, I would argue, can knowledge be brought fruitfully to bear on the text (and also, I would add, be tested by it). I return to this point of procedure toward the end of Essay 1. For an application of this procedure to two historical "documents" (and a defense of this application), see Richard Strier, "From Diagnosis to Operation: The Roots and Branches Petition and the Grand Remonstrance," in David L. Smith, Richard Strier, and David Bevington, eds., *The Theatrical City: London's Culture, Theatre and Literature, 1576–1649* (Cambridge: Cambridge University Press, 1995).

3. Ludwig Wittgenstein, *Philosophical Investigations,* ed. and trans. G. E. M. Anscombe (New York: Macmillan, 1953), 31e. The German is "*denk nicht, sondern schau!*" (31).

texts that all "theories" would agree on. Agreeing to these does not mean subscribing to a theory but merely being a competent user of the language in which the texts are being discussed. These features may be thought to be trivial or obvious, but that is neither here nor there. Or rather, I would argue, it is very much here. Claims about texts that get these features wrong, that misquote, miscount, etc., are never taken to be viable. Differing interpretations of a text generally share a large number of particular agreements before they part company. And when they part company, they are still responsible to the features—I would call them facts—that they share. Interpretive conclusions, even widely held ones, do not become facts. That Hamlet delays in killing Claudius is a fact; that Hamlet is neurotic (or whatever) in doing so is not. This book means to defend the importance of the obvious, the surface, and the literal as well as the particular. It means to look very hard at moments when a critic or scholar dismisses or downgrades (or misrepresents) the obvious, the "surface," or the literal. Since I believe that these features of texts have, and ought to have, a privileged place in interpretation, and that these features have a reality independent of (particular) theories, the moments when they are denigrated are often, I will argue, moments when an a priori scheme or conception can be seen at work.[4]

---

4. I have quite consciously written this paragraph (until now) without footnotes. I want to take full responsibility for the position that I have enunciated, and I want the positions that I have attacked and defended to stand or fall on their own, without being tied to competing authorities. Too often, I think, in discussions of this sort, names of holders of positions stand in for the substance of positions. The reader who is familiar with these discussions will certainly have recognized the relations of the assertions in this paragraph to the following (and the reader who is unfamiliar with these discussions may wish to consult the following). For an application of (something like) the skeptical position that I am attacking to matters of textual interpretation, see the essays in Stanley Fish, *Doing What Comes Naturally: Change, Rhetoric, and the Practice of Theory in Literary and Legal Studies* (Durham: Duke University Press, 1989), and for the philosophical basis of the position, see the essays in Richard Rorty, *Consequences of Pragmatism* (Minneapolis: University of Minnesota Press, 1982); for (something like) the position that I am defending, see the essays in Donald Davidson, *Inquiries into Truth and Interpretation* (Oxford: Clarendon Press, 1984). It should perhaps be noted that Davidson has been cited on both sides of this controversy. For reflections on this apparent paradox, see Christopher Norris, "Reading Donald Davidson: Truth, Meaning, and Right Interpretation," in *Deconstruction and the Interests of Theory* (Norman: University of Oklahoma Press, 1989), 59–83. Davidson has responded (negatively) to Rorty's use of Davidson's work in "A Coherence Theory of Truth and Knowledge," in Ernest LePore, ed., *Truth and Interpretation: Perspectives on the Philosophy of Donald Davidson* (Oxford: Blackwell, 1986), 307–19. For some other essays suggesting the relevance of Davidson's work to literary criticism, see Reed Way Dasenbrock, ed., *Literary Theory after Davidson* (University Park: Pennsylvania State Press, 1993). Also in the background of my thinking is an essay by

I do not mean to suggest that we should (or could) read without hypotheses or that hypotheses cannot reveal hitherto unnoticed features or aspects of texts. I am interested in moments when texts resist even very brilliant, illuminating, and well-founded hypotheses. I believe that these moments are often marked in criticism by a rhetoric of discounting: "This seems to be doing or saying X, but it is really doing or saying Y," or "It doesn't matter that the text seems to be doing X because," etc. My aim is not to discourage critics and scholars from forming hypotheses and from finding confirmatory evidence for them. My aim is to encourage a certain modesty in the scope that is claimed for critical or historical insights. A valid insight, an insight that explains or illuminates a great deal in a text or a period, does not have to explain everything and be everywhere valid. I do not wish to encourage critics to work less hard or to know less but only to resist the final turn of the screw, the moment when resistance in the text is overcome rather than acknowledged. The thrust of this book is to be monitory rather than negative. Tempting as I find the position, I do not mean to assert with Groucho Marx that "Whatever it is, I'm against it." I am wary of the totalizing impulse that tempts interpretive and explanatory hypotheses. By resisting our totalizing impulses and acknowledging where texts offer resistance to us, we gain the possibility of surprise and, most of all, the experience of variety. That all texts, or all texts from a particular period or of a particular kind, do not always mean or do the same thing has got to prove, ultimately, a more deeply satisfying and humanizing pleasure than that which derives from finding the same thing—the thing we expected—everywhere. That the recognition of genuine variety is ethically (and politically) more admirable than the denial of difference does not, of course, make the position that produces the admirable recognition true, but it is a happy consequence.

As I have already suggested, a priori views of texts can be divided, roughly speaking, into two groups: those which derive from general schemes and those which derive from particular assertions. This division corresponds to the two sections of this book. The first section, comprising Essays 1 through 4, deals with general schemes that mandate what a text (or a valuable text) from a particular period must or must not

---

William C. Wimsatt on "Robustness, Reliability, and Overdetermination," in M. Brewer and B. Collins, eds., *Scientific Inquiry and the Social Sciences* (San Francisco: Jossey-Bass, 1981), 124–63.

do or mean. The section moves from examining a preemptive appeal to scholarship to settle issues ("Tradition") to two essays that examine closely related general schemes for how texts (or valuable texts) work ("self-consumption" and deconstruction) to an essay on an approach or praxis, "New Historicism," that falls into an untenable behaviorism.

The second section, "Against Received Ideas," deals with specific ideas that work against seeing or reading particular texts or specific themes in particular texts of the early modern period. The first essay in the section ("Devout Humanism") deals primarily with figures who have been obscured with an aura of sanctity, so that their texts have not, in any strong sense, really been read. This is especially true of St. François de Sales and the *Introduction to the Devout Life* (1609), but it has, until very recently, also been true of George Herbert's "The Church-porch." Both of these texts (with some by Donne) and the movement with which they have been associated ("devout humanism") are shown to be quite disturbing when read along a sociological rather than a diffused religio-moral axis. My claim is not to have discovered anything about these texts but simply to be reading them for their social attitudes, reading them literally and on the surface. What is interesting is not only what is there in these texts but why this obvious feature of their content has not been widely recognized. An appendix to this essay takes the argument in a thematically, though not methodologically, opposite direction. It asserts, in Herbert's case, the possibility of transcending the ideology of "devout humanism." This appendix continues the discussion of New Historicism, seeing it as a view that would deny the possibility of such transcendence. As a whole, therefore, Essay 5 argues that it is as inappropriate to deny as it is to assert the possibility of saintliness a priori.

Essays 6–8 form a unit. As their titles indicate, they argue for what I am calling "impossible radicalism" in the sixteenth and seventeenth centuries. They set themselves against a significant body of scholarly opinion—to which both old and new historicism have contributed—that sees conceptions like freedom of conscience, justified individual disobedience, and justified popular rebellion as "unthinkable" in the Renaissance or "early modern" period.[5] This notion of "unthinkability" seems

5. These terms are interestingly at variance, and each has its advantages and disadvantages. "Renaissance" has the advantage of capturing the claim of many intellectuals in the (let's call it) period that something that had (supposedly) been lost was being consciously revived: good Latin; good letters; the art of perspective; the true church. "Early modern" has the advantage of neutrality with regard to privileging the arts and "high" culture, so that an account of "early modern" culture does not necessarily flatter or idealize

to me a very dangerous one. It is another sort of a priori. It makes it necessary for a critic or scholar to explain away—or simply not see—moments in texts where the "unthinkable" is actually thought. The view in which "unthinkability" prominently figures tends, I argue, to present periods or "discursive formations" as too homogeneous, dominant discourses as too successfully dominant (and too homogeneous in themselves), and to overemphasize breaks or ruptures between periods or discursive formations. I discuss this problem in Essay 6 (on Donne's third Satire), but the problem of acknowledging the existence and representation of genuinely radical or oppositional discourse dominates all three of the essays with which this book closes.

But what about the problem of anachronism and of "Whig" historiography? Obviously the avoidance of anachronism is important (and a historical achievement), but I would urge great circumspection in the application of the notion. Often conceptions are said to be "anachronistic" merely because they are nonhegemonic or unusual in a period. The cry of anachronism, I suggest, almost always serves the interests of a conservative picture of the past. A recent essay on *King Lear*, for example, devotes a great deal of useful and important scholarship to "proving" that when the mutilated and abandoned Gloucester prays that "distribution should undo excess" so that "each man have enough," Gloucester is merely saying something normal and completely familiar. To think anything else would be—and this is the normal tone and stance of such claims—"totally ahistorical."[6] Even in imagining extreme situations, Shakespeare cannot be seen as imagining radical solutions. Surely there was no such book in the sixteenth century as More's *Utopia*.[7]

As for "Whig" historiography, when it is false and distorting it is certainly a problem, but the revolt against the "Whig" historiography of seventeenth-century England has produced a view of the culture that makes the most dramatic historical event of the century virtually unin-

---

the culture in question and does not restrict its scope or focus to cultural production in the Humanities sense of the term (invented by "the Renaissance"). The term "early modern" does, however, flatter and perhaps idealize us—the earlier period is seen to take its orientation from how it leads to "modern" culture. This too seems to be a historiographic myth. So one is left with a choice of myths—theirs or ours.

6. Judy Kronenfeld, "'So Distribution Should Undo Excess, and Each Man Have Enough': Shakespeare's *King Lear*—Anabaptist Egalitarianism, Anglican Charity, Both, Neither?" *ELH* 59 (1992): 755–84. The quotation is from p. 757. This article is discussed in note 90 to Essay 8 below.

7. For the "surely there [was] no such" formulation, see Essay 1, p. 25 below.

telligible. The culture somehow inadvertently or accidentally gave rise to (or allowed) the first modern revolution, an event in which a king was formally brought to trial and executed for offenses against "the people" and "the laws."[8] It may be misleading to see England in the early seventeenth century as a "prerevolutionary" society in any but a technical sense, but it certainly seems important to acknowledge the possibilities in that culture for thinking as well as enacting resistance. The texts that the last three essays treat are "resistant" in the political as well as the epistemological sense.

The ghosts of two past critics haunt these pages. The first is a spirit I have quite consciously conjured, and who stands as the guiding figure for both parts of this book, namely, William Empson. Empson's controversy with Rosemond Tuve is the subject of the first essay of the book—in which I argue that Empson is a better model for historical criticism than Tuve—and the essay on Donne and freedom of conscience (Essay 6) is explicit in its commitment to carrying on Empson's project of seeing Donne (and others in the period) as capable of genuinely radical thought. Empson is a model for me by virtue of his verbal and philosophical alertness, his nonprogrammatic curiosity and bafflement, and his complete lack of theoretically imposed inhibitions in approaching texts. The other figure who haunts these pages comes largely unbidden. At moments in this introduction and elsewhere, I found myself echoing R. S. Crane on the "high priori road" and on hypotheses in historical criticism.[9] I discovered to my astonishment that, without ever having been trained as such, I was a member of the "Chicago school" in a stronger sense than merely teaching in the department in which Crane taught. I felt like the protagonist of one of those remarkable Islamic narratives in which choice is revealed to be predestined fate.[10] Despite Crane's lucidity and perspicacity, I am less happy with Crane

8. For a discussion of "revisionist" (anti-"Whig") historiography of seventeenth-century England and the reaction against such "revisionism," see the "Introduction: After Revisionism" and the essays in Richard Cust and Ann Hughes, eds., *Conflict in Early Stuart England: Studies in Religion and Politics, 1603–1642* (London: Longman, 1989). See also Derek Hirst, "Revisionism Revised: Early Stuart Paliamentary History—The Place of Principle," *Past and Present* 92 (1981): 79–99.

9. R. S. Crane, "Criticism as Inquiry; or, The Perils of the 'High Priori Road,'" and "On Hypotheses in 'Historical Criticism': Apropos of Certain Contemporary Medievalists," in *The Idea of the Humanities and Other Essays* (Chicago: University of Chicago Press, 1967), 2: 25–44, 236–60.

10. See the discussion in Rudolf Otto, *The Idea of the Holy*, trans. John W. Harvey (London: Oxford University Press, 1950), 88–90.

than with Empson as a guiding spirit here, however, because Crane (like de Man) seems to me to have had a dogmatic as well as a critical side. I do not believe that nature and Aristotle are the same. And I share Empson's puzzlement at why, for instance, "because *Macbeth* is 'imitative,' it can't be 'didactic' as well."[11]

The question obviously arises as to how I can avoid the *tu quoque*. Do not I have my own presuppositions and schemes? In one sense, I cannot answer this. It is not for me to say. I can say that I have tried never to brush aside the obvious and the "surface." When I have said "Yes, but," I have tried to give weight to the affirmative as well as to the adversative. I can also say that I have tried to keep my own claims methodologically modest (other forms of modesty I do not aspire to). When arguing for the presence of a theme in a work, I have not argued that the theme in question is the only one in the work or even the "central" one. Similarly, in arguing for the existence of genuine radicalism in the early modern period, I have not argued that such radicalism is the spirit or the essential spirit or the true spirit of the age. I have only argued that the features to which I point are "there," in a quite strong sense, and that they matter, not that they are the only things that are or do. I have tried to make my orientations explicit, and though I do a good deal of polemicizing against various critical and historical schemes, I hope not to have put forth any dogmas.

But is "not having dogmas" itself a dogma? I cannot say that I find the claim that it is such interesting or powerful—or even fully intelligible. The attempt to present "pluralism as dogmatism" involves treating all founding principles as dogmas and, in its desire to present a "benign" picture of dogmatism, involves ignoring historical evidence that the function of the promulgation of dogma was always to repress heresy, to shut down or narrow rather than to expand or encourage public discussion.[12] It is certainly, however, worthwhile to be reminded that "pluralism" can be a cover for arrogance and for setting oneself "above the fray" (there is indeed an element of this in R. S. Crane). It is also useful to be reminded that, in the world of international politics, pluralism can be used as a cover for and justification of aggression and suppression,

11. "Still the Strange Necessity," in William Empson, *Argufying: Essays on Literature and Culture*, ed. John Haffenden (London: Hogarth, 1988), 122.

12. See W. J. T. Mitchell, "Pluralism as Dogmatism," *Critical Inquiry* 12 (1986): 494–502. For the "benign" picture, see p. 496; for an assertion of the point that dogmas were first formulated against heretics, see the paragraph from the *Encyclopedia of Religion and Religions* that Mitchell quotes (495).

though it should be noted that even the author of this attack on pluralism (W. J. T. Mitchell) distinguishes between "real tolerance" and "the use of tolerance as a code word for repression."[13] To this distinction, of course, I can only say "Amen." Mitchell's need for it implies that his presentation of "pluralism as dogmatism" is not truly in good faith. "Real tolerance" (to Mitchell's credit) escapes unscathed. As to location with regard to "the fray," I hope to have located myself in rather than "above" it. Finally, I want to note that it is no longer as clear as it may have seemed in 1986 (the date of Mitchell's essay) that "pluralism is the reigning ideology of American politics on both the Right and Left." If this has changed, it may be especially important now to argue for pluralism—in the fray, and inside and outside the academic world.

13. Mitchell, "Pluralism as Dogmatism," 502.

Against Schemes

"Tradition"

In the collective memory or mythology of literary studies in America, the clash between Rosemond Tuve and William Empson in the early 1950s is an episode in the conflict between "history" and "formalism." My strong impression is that most scholars of English Renaissance literature still think of Tuve as having "won" the debate with Empson. It is my further impression that Rosemond Tuve is still regarded as an excellent model of true (or at least, solid) scholarship and—depending on one's attitudes toward the current scene—of either "old" or "real" historicism. Empson, of course. . . . Well, everyone knows about Empson.

I mean to argue that this episode is improperly described as a conflict between "formalism" and "history." I will try to show that what was really at issue was a particular conception of historical knowledge and its role in literary studies. My main concern is not to praise Empson in this essay—though I will do so—but to criticize in some detail the position in the controversy taken by Tuve. I will praise Empson not just as the better "reader," but as the better historicist—as if these virtues could truly be separated. I will argue that Tuve is a bad model for historicism, that her appeal to historical data, and especially her appeal to and understanding of "tradition," are actually quite pernicious. Kenneth Burke, with typical wit and typical generosity, has a brilliant joke about the controversy, a joke that capaciously embraces both Empson and Tuve. "Criticism," concludes Burke, "should be for both Dis-a and

Data.''[1] Brilliant as it is, I am afraid that I think Burke's joke grants too much to Tuve. I will show that Empson's joke about the controversy, which I will recount and discuss later, is as profound (and as funny) as Burke's and points to a serious problem with Tuve's conception of Data. Tuve, of course, does not make jokes. She is much too busy, as we shall see, holding the fort against modernity.

Before turning to the details of the controversy, let me say a few words about Empson. It may seem outrageously paradoxical to suggest him as a model for historical criticism. Tuve attacked the final analysis in *Seven Types of Ambiguity*, and "everyone knows" about Empson and ambiguity.[2] Everyone feels secure in the knowledge of what *kind* of critic Empson was, and what sort of book *Seven Types* is. Empson was a New Critic, and *Seven Types* is a book of "readings." To call Empson a New Critic is to ally him with Cleanth Brooks and *Seven Types* with *The Well Wrought Urn*.[3] Empson's practice is formalist, internalist, anti-intentionalist, and antihistoricist. This view of Empson, though I think still widely held, is entirely, even spectacularly wrong.[4] The best readers of Empson, whether they approve of him or not, have long recognized that to view him as a doctrinaire or normative New Critic is wrong. To take two important cases, René Wellek, who disapproved of Empson, and Paul de Man, who highly approved of him, both recognized this.[5] The difference between Empson and the other "formalists," especially I. A. Richards and Roland Barthes, is the central argument of de Man's famous essay on "The Dead-End of Formalist Criticism." In the Hegelian language of his early thinking, de Man credits Empson with philosophical correctness—with understanding "the deep division of

1. See Kenneth Burke, "On Covery, Re- and Dis-," *Accent* 13 (1959): 225. For those to whom the Brooklyn pronunciation of "this" and "that" as "dis" and "dat" is not immediately familiar, the joke is thereby explained. "Dis-a" stands for the particular; "Data," presumably, needs no explanation.

2. William Empson, *Seven Types of Ambiguity: A Study of Its Effects in English Verse* (1930; 2d ed., rev., 1947; 3d ed., New York: Meridien Books, 1955). I have used the third edition.

3. Cleanth Brooks, *The Well Wrought Urn: Studies in the Structure of Poetry* (New York: Harcourt Brace, 1947).

4. This is also observed in Paul H. Fry, *William Empson: Prophet against Sacrifice* (London: Routledge, 1991), 7.

5. René Wellek, "Literary Theory, Criticism, and History," in *Concepts of Criticism*, ed. Stephen G. Nichols Jr. (New Haven: Yale University Press, 1963), 8–9; Paul de Man, "The Dead-End of Formalist Criticism" (1954), in *Blindness and Insight: Essays in the Rhetoric of Contemporary Criticism*, 2d. ed., rev. (Minneapolis: University of Minnesota Press, 1983), 229–45.

Being itself "—and with opening the way to genuine historicism, to "the sorrowful time of patience, i.e., history."[6]

Empson's historicism will be treated at some length in this essay, but it might be well to say a word here about his supposed obsession with the "purely verbal," and about his supposed anti-intentionalism.[7] Elder Olson's 1952 essay, "William Empson, Contemporary Criticism, and Poetic Diction," is the classic attack.[8] Olson severely rebukes the myopia of Empson's focus on "diction." This attack, however, founders on the recognition that Empson was interested in "ambiguity" only because he saw this feature of language as a probable indicator of something else—namely, of "interesting and valuable situations" being addressed or embodied in a text.[9] It was these "situations" in which he was really interested. Olson mocks this talk about situations, but then goes on himself to speak of the importance of seeing speeches in plays as by "a certain character in a certain situation."[10] In response to Olson, Empson remarks, somewhat bemusedly (and correctly), that what Olson means by "literary effect" is included in what he, Empson, means by "meaning."[11] As for anti-intentionalism, Empson notes in his generally positive review of *The Well Wrought Urn* that he finds Brooks overly concerned with purely formal qualities to the exclusion of political and biographical realism.[12] And in a review of William K. Wimsatt's *The Verbal Icon* in

6. "The Dead-End of Formalist Criticism," 237, 245. In his later essay on "Wordsworth and the Victorians" (1979), de Man praises Empson as an ethical model for deconstructionists, as someone whose work shows "the tact with which such a potentially mischievous task should be carried out." See *The Rhetoric of Romanticism* (New York: Columbia University Press, 1984), 88.

7. On Empson as an anti-intentionalist, see E. D. Hirsch, *Validity in Interpretation* (New Haven: Yale University Press, 1967), 224–25. Hirsch bases his sense of Empson and "the critical school Empson founded" on a phrase ("piece of language") in the first paragraph of *Seven Types of Ambiguity* (!), and on the understanding of Empson produced by the Chicago Aristotelians (see n. 8 below).

8. Elder Olson, "William Empson, Contemporary Criticism, and Poetic Diction," in R. S. Crane, ed., *Critics and Criticism, Ancient and Modern* (Chicago: University of Chicago Press, 1952), 45–82. Olson's critique of Empson depends on viewing Empson as a typical "new critic," essentially identical with Cleanth Brooks. In the context of *Critics and Criticism,* Olson's essay stands between and links Crane's critiques of Richards and of Brooks.

9. Olson, "William Empson," 50; Empson, *Seven Types,* 266.

10. Olson, "William Empson," 56.

11. "The Verbal Analysis," *Kenyon Review* 12 (1950); reprinted in William Empson, *Argufying: Essays on Literature and Culture* , ed. John Haffenden (London: Hogarth, 1988), 107.

12. "Thy Darling in an Urn," *Sewanee Review* 55 (1947); reprinted in *Argufying,* 282–88.

1955, Empson strongly reprehended Wimsatt's anti-intentionalism, making the point that since "estimating other people's intentions" is an ordinary feature of social life, and is crucial in many legal contexts, it seems bizarre that "only in the criticism of imaginative literature, a thing delicately concerned with human intimacy, we are told that we must give up all idea of knowing [a person's] intention."[13] This passage is pure Empson. What "we all know" about him needs to be revised.[14]

But let me return to my story. In the battle between Tuve and Empson, it is not exactly clear who fired the first shot. One might think that Empson did, since his review of *Elizabethan and Metaphysical Imagery* ("Donne and the Rhetorical Tradition") appeared in the volume of the *Kenyon Review* preceding the volume in which Tuve's attack on him appeared, but the editors of the *Review* are at pains to assert in a prefatory note to Tuve's essay that her piece was received before the publication of Empson's review.[15] If this is true (and I see no reason to doubt it), we have a situation in which Empson was troubled by Tuve's recent readings of English Renaissance poetry, especially that of Donne, at the exact same time that Tuve was troubled by Empson's rather old readings of English Renaissance poetry, especially that of Herbert. Each of these critics, in other words, took up the cudgels spontaneously and

13. "Still the Strange Necessity," *Sewanee Review* 63 (1955); *Argufying*, 124. Empson's view of the ordinariness of "estimating other people's intentions" is uncannily close to Donald Davidson's view of the "commonplace" quality of "radical interpretation" among persons (see Essay 3, n. 36 below).

14. Paul Fry's book (cited in n. 4 above) should help, but the most tireless contemporary defender and expositor of Empson is undoubtedly Christopher Norris. Norris's work on Empson is indispensable for anyone interested in the history and state of literary theory and criticism in our century. Among Norris's writings on Empson are *William Empson and the Philosophy of Literary Criticism* (London: Athlone Press, 1978); "Introduction: Empson as Literary Theorist," in Christopher Norris and Nigel Mapp, eds., *William Empson: The Critical Achievement* (Cambridge: Cambridge University Press, 1993), 1–120; and "For Truth in Criticism: William Empson and the Claims of Theory," in *The Truth about Postmodernism* (Oxford: Blackwell, 1993), 100–81. This is by no means an exhaustive list of Norris's writings on Empson.

15. Empson's review of Tuve's *Elizabethan and Metaphysical Imagery: Renaissance Poetic and Twentieth-Century Critics* (Chicago: University of Chicago Press, 1947) appeared as "Donne and the Rhetorical Tradition," *Kenyon Review* 11 (1949): 571–87; Tuve's "On Herbert's 'Sacrifice'" appeared in *Kenyon Review* 12 (1950): 52–75. The note by the editors appears at the bottom of the first page of Tuve's essay. Tuve greatly expanded this essay into "'The Sacrifice' and Modern Criticism," part one of *A Reading of George Herbert* (Chicago: University of Chicago Press, 1952), 19–99 (hereafter cited as *A Reading*). "Donne and the Rhetorical Tradition" is now available in William Empson, *Essays on Renaissance Literature*, vol. 1, *Donne and the New Philosophy*, ed. John Haffenden (Cambridge: Cambridge University Press, 1993), 63–77.

unprovoked. They each felt moved to attack the other *on principle*— which makes the controversy particularly interesting.

Since the chronology leaves us free to proceed in any order, I will begin with Tuve on Empson, since her attack is avowedly theoretical and since, in this case, we have a response as well. Tuve is defending the idea that "there is such a thing as misreading," and especially the idea that "meanings have histories," that meanings of elements in poems are "clarified by knowledge of meanings those elements have carried before the poem was written, and, as we say, 'outside' it."[16] Most generally, Tuve sees herself as defending "the value of knowledge to criticism."[17] She means by this the value of knowing the sorts of things than an author can reasonably be taken to have known and to have assumed that his or her audience knew, though this is already a more cautious formulation than Tuve's. "Tradition" is Tuve's favorite word. Above all, Tuve sees her role as making sure that traditional elements in texts will be seen as such, and that inappropriate notions of novelty will not be applied to highly "traditional" poetry. Herbert's poetry, in other words, must be praised for the right things in the right way. "Illegal" critical practices (her word) and "illegitimate" readings must be detected and rebuked (OHS, 71). Tuve sees herself as policing the borders of the past, so that no anachronistically modern element can falsely enter and so that the massive outlines of "the tradition" can be clearly discerned by the (not so humble) seeker after truth.

There are many problems with all this. The first of them is that Empson does not deny that there are "such things as misreadings"— though he persists (like Richards) in being interested in them.[18] Even more damaging to Tuve's polemic is the fact that Empson, as we have already seen, does not hold an "internalist" point of view. He constantly brings in historical and biographical material, and he is a passionate devotee of the *OED*. Other critics of *Seven Types,* in fact, accused Empson of bringing in too much "outside" material, of assuming that the reader could carry too much "baggage" with him. He was attacked for con-

---

16. "On Herbert's 'Sacrifice,'" 54. Hereafter references to this essay will appear in the text as "OHS" followed by a page number.

17. *A Reading,* 9–10. Subsequent page references in text.

18. The most spectacular (and spectacularly good-humored) instance of this is Empson's discussion of a misreading he had cherished of a line from Rupert Brooke. See *Seven Types,* 232 (subsequent page references in text). I. A. Richards's interest in "mis-" and other bad readings is fully manifested in the analyses of the protocols in *Practical Criticism* (1929; pap. rpt., New York: Harcourt Brace, 1966).

necting "bare ruined choirs" to the Reformation on the one hand and to Shakespeare's sexual predilections on the other.[19] Like Burke, Empson was radically uninhibited in what he would bring to or say about a text. Like Burke, he was a pragmatic, "kitchen-sink" sort of critic, bringing in *anything* that seemed to him relevant to the meaning of the text in question. But the meaning *to whom,* Tuve would—and did—ask. She sees Empson as interested only in the meanings that an older text might have to a modern reader who is interested only in modern ideas. This is the heart of Tuve's attack on Empson's reading of "The Sacrifice." Tuve is certain that "modern" ideas are necessarily irrelevant to "traditional" ones.

The section on Herbert's "The Sacrifice" is the longest reading in *Seven Types* and, as the final reading in the final substantive chapter, it is meant to cap the argument of the book. Empson sees the "ambiguities" that he explores as ordered (loosely) on a scale of increasing psychological complexity. He gives "The Sacrifice" the crowning place because he sees this poem as powerfully and beautifully presenting (in the final words of the chapter) "the most complicated and deeply rooted notion of the human mind."[20] This notion is "the idea of sacrifice," and Empson praises the poem for imagining this idea so fully "that all its [the idea's] impulses are involved." That the impulses involved are contradictory is what makes this idea an especially interesting "type of ambiguity" for Empson. The central contradiction in "the sacrificial idea" is between submission and aggression. Empson values the Herbert poem so highly for the intricate mixture of vindictiveness and tenderness it projects into the voice of the crucified Christ. Empson is particularly insistent that the vindictiveness in the voice be heard.[21]

Interestingly, Empson was quite concerned about the historical and intentionalist plausibility of this reading. "You may say," he notes, "that

19. See the "Note for the Third Edition" of *Seven Types,* xviii. This refers to a discussion with F. W. Bateson; see "Bare Ruined Choirs," *Essays in Criticism* 3 (1953): 357–63.

20. *Seven Types,* 263. The analysis of "The Sacrifice" occupies pp. 256–63. I will not give specific page citations for quotations from this analysis.

21. These pages in *Seven Types* can be seen as the beginning of Empson's lifelong agon with the central doctrine of western Christianity, the Atonement. *Milton's God* (1961; rev. ed., London: Chatto and Windus, 1965) is the culmination of this agon. Even *Milton's God,* though certainly a polemic, is not entirely ahistorical. As Empson well knew, many of the Gnostics saw God the Father in much the same way Empson (and Shelley) did. It is true, however, that what is central to *Milton's God* is its moral passion, its sense of justice and hatred of cruelty, rather than either its historical or its literary dimension. Its deepest kinship is perhaps with Voltaire.

the pious Herbert could not have intended such a contradiction, because
he would have thought it blasphemous, and because he took a 'sunny'
view of his religion." In a typically brilliant, offhanded, and telling joke,
Empson suggests that a fog of piety has obscured "the pious Herbert,"
and that actually looking at his work (or almost anything else) produces
surprising results: "It is true George Herbert is a cricket in the sunshine,
but one is accustomed to be shocked on discovering the habits of such
creatures; they are more savage than they seem." Empson suggests,
moreover, not only that "the pious Herbert" is more savage than he
seems, but that the whole orthodox tradition is. His main strategy is to
appeal first to orthodoxy ("it is merely orthodox to make Christ insist
on the damnation of the wicked") and then, above all, to the Bible: "a
memory of the revengeful power of Jehovah gives resonance to the voice
of the merciful Jesus." The achievement of "The Sacrifice," for Empson,
is its ability to sustain this doubleness. "Only the speed, isolation, and
compactness" of Herbert's method in this poem, Empson says, could
handle in so sustained a way "impulses of such reach and complexity."
He sees this poem as unusually impersonal for Herbert. He sees it as a
poem in which "the theological system is accepted so completely that
the poet is only its mouthpiece," and he speculates that this kind of
impersonality and systematicity might be psychologically necessary "if so
high a degree of ambiguity is to seem normal."

One can see why Tuve would have wanted to attack this reading and
why she found herself so frustrated in the course of doing so. On the one
hand, Empson clearly relies on a Freudian-Frazerian framework; on the
other hand, he fully recognizes the "traditional" basis of the poem. But
not the right tradition—and besides, Freud must go. Tuve particularly
singles out two of Empson's readings of lines as "impossible." This kind
of claim particularly worries me, and I think that it should always be a
red flag. Tuve is insistent that when Herbert's Christ says "Man stole the
fruit, but I must climb the tree," Empson is completely misguided in
thinking that "this makes Christ smaller, more childlike than Eve, who
could reach the apple without climbing," and Tuve is sure that there
cannot possibly be any implication in the phrase that Christ himself is
"doing the stealing." Tuve insists that the phrase "*could not have* implied
this for Herbert" because—because what?[22] Because such a meaning
could not have existed in "the tradition." Yet in the course of making
this suggestion, Empson cited the gospel privileging of little children,

22. OHS, 56, emphasis mine; *Seven Types*, 262.

surely a relevant part of "the tradition." He could also (as Burke would) have cited the famous pear-stealing episode in Augustine's *Confessions* as relevant.[23] As we shall see, "the tradition" turns out to mean something very specific for Tuve.

The suggestion that Christ is stealing the apple like a mischievous boy leads Empson to see a hint of incest here; "the son stealing from his father's orchard is a symbol of incest," he says. This seems hopelessly arbitrary, though not, when one considers the imagery and plot of *Pericles,* where Antiochus's abused daughter is strikingly referred to as fruit on a tree, hopelessly anachronistic.[24] But immediately Empson pulls back to his major point, that "in the person of Christ the supreme act of sin is combined with the supreme act of virtue." Tuve warns that supposed "primeval" meanings should not be substituted for "layers upon layers of consciously apprehended significance" (OHS, 73). But this is precisely what Empson does not do. He fully integrates the "primeval" into the theological. His "digression" into Freud and Frazer only seems to deepen the "traditional" meaning for him. Oddly and significantly enough, it is Tuve who seeks refuge in a notion of the literary, wanting to separate out "literary" from psychological or anthropological facts (OHS, 72–73). It she who is defending "the poem itself." This is no accident, I think. Her view is much more restricted and restrictive than Empson's.

Let us examine another moment when Tuve simply rules out one of Empson's readings. The lines in question are these:

> Why, Caesar is their only King, not I:
> He clave the stonie rock, when they were drie;
> But surely not their hearts, as I well trie.[25]

Empson sees this stanza as contrasting both "the earthly power of the conqueror" and "the legal rationalism of the Pharisees" to "the pro-

23. See "Adolescent Perversity," section 8 of "Verbal Action in St. Augustine's *Confessions,*" in *The Rhetoric of Religion: Studies in Logology* (Berkeley and Los Angeles: University of California Press, 1961), 93–101.

24. See William Shakespeare, *Pericles,* ed. F. D. Hoeniger (London: Methuen, 1969), 1.1.22 and 29. With regard to Christ as a "mischievous boy" who is executed on a tree, Paul Fry has suggested (in a superb commentary on an earlier draft of this essay) that Ralegh's poem on "the wood, the weed, the wagg" might provide some relevant contemporary context; see *The Poems of Sir Walter Ralegh,* ed. Agnes Latham (Cambridge: Harvard University Press, 1962), 49.

25. "The Sacrifice," lines 121–23, in *The Works of George Herbert,* ed. F. E. Hutchinson (Oxford, 1945).

founder mercy of the Christ and the profounder searching of the heart that causes" (*Seven Types,* 260). Tuve again points out an "impossibility": Herbert could not have identified Moses with Caesar. And why? Because of "the tradition," because of the "traditional" way of reading the bible. Herbert could not have identified Moses with Caesar because—and here comes the big gun—*typologically* Moses is identified with Christ. Tuve considers this a knock-down argument (OHS, 54–56). She is jubilant. Empson does not know typology!

In his printed reply to Tuve, Empson acknowledged that perhaps he should have noted the contrast between Caesar and Moses in the second line of this stanza. He insists, however, that there is a shift in the stanza, so that where the second line differentiates Moses (and Jesus) from Caesar, the third line differentiates Jesus from both Caesar and Moses. For Tuve, the third line simply cannot be saying something different from the second. "The tradition" will not allow it. But Empson holds the not implausible view that Herbert was stressing the special inwardness of Christ's teachings. Empson rather dryly notes that "surely it is also traditional to regard the Old Testament dispensation as different from the New."[26] Empson is right about both the stanza and "the tradition." But what is most important to recognize is that there is no such thing as "the tradition," in this and probably any regard. "The tradition," even when—after a historical evolution that needs to be traced—it assumes a dominant and relatively stable form, is complex, multifaceted, and internally conflicted; it is always the product of contestation and the repressed or suppressed positions are never totally extinguished.[27] "The tradition" is a deeply misleading (and coercive) form of speech. Typology, to return to our particular case, was used to establish differences as well as continuities between the Testaments.[28] Tuve is using her construction of "the tradition," backed up by massive but very selective erudition, as a bludgeon with which to browbeat a less learned but more adventurous and not necessarily less accurate critic. Perhaps we can derive a first lesson from the controversy: Beware of all

26. William Empson, "George Herbert and Miss Tuve," *Kenyon Review* 12 (1950): 736; *Argufying,* 252.

27. For a very clear and cogent exposition of this view, see Raymond Williams, *Marxism and Literature* (Oxford: Oxford University Press, 1977), chaps. 6–8.

28. For clear accounts of this see, for instance, Thomas M. Davis, "The Traditions of Puritan Typology," and Richard Reinitz, "The Separatist Background of Roger Williams' Argument for Religious Toleration," in Sacvan Bercovitch, ed., *Typology and Early American Literature* (N.p.: University of Massachusetts Press, 1972), 11–45, 107–37.

talk of "the tradition." This has an immediate relevance to our current pedagogical situation in the United States. It means that, in curricular debates, attacks on and defenses of "the tradition" or "the Western tradition" or "the great tradition" are equally misguided.

It is important to look hard at what any scholar puts forth as "the tradition." Tuve's "tradition," like all such hypostases, is produced by special pleading. This becomes quite clear when we examine another moment in Tuve's discussion of Herbert's Caesar-Moses stanza. Tuve mocks Empson (OHS, 55; *A Reading*, 28) for paraphrasing "Caesar is their only King, not I" as "I am not a political agitator." Empson's phrasing is deliberately provocative here, but his viewpoint on the line is a profoundly *historical* one. He is showing his normal feeling for historical and narrative situations (he was especially impatient with critics "too proud to attend to the story").[29] Empson's viewpoint is directly relevant to the trial of Jesus, which took place in the context of the Maccabean-Zealot revolts.[30] Milton's Satan, we recall, propounds the Maccabean model to Jesus in *Paradise Regained*.[31] The point would seem to be unimpeachably historical. This does not, however, make it properly "traditional" for Tuve. "Traditional," for Tuve, means medieval. Empson, though he does acknowledge a medieval quality in the poem, goes directly from Herbert to the Bible. This, for Tuve, is illicit. In regard to the refrain of "The Sacrifice" ("Was ever grief like mine?") Tuve explicitly rebukes Empson's recourse to the Bible. "We must be chary," she says, of interpretations of these words "based on a lively sense of their being rather said by the sinful city of Jerusalem 'in the original'" (*A Reading*, 34). As her scare quotes indicate, Tuve heaps scorn on the notion of "in the original." From the height of her erudition, she contemptuously explains that "Herbert's 'original'" was not a verse in Lamentations but "a well-known and effortlessly accepted" liturgical tradition.

But is the picture of Herbert harking back to the biblical context of a phrase widely used in Latin liturgies absurd and unhistorical? Didn't the Reformation send everyone, especially every Protestant, back to their

---

29. See "Rhythm and Imagery in English Poetry," *British Journal of Aesthetics* 17 (1962); *Argufying*, 162.

30. See, inter alia, Paul Winter, *On the Trial of Jesus*, 2d ed. (Berlin and New York: de Gruyter, 1974); and especially S. G. F. Brandon, *Jesus and the Zealots: A Study of the Political Factor in Early Christianity* (New York: Scribner's, 1968).

31. See *Paradise Regained*, 3.165–80, in John Milton, *Complete Poems and Major Prose*, ed. Merritt Y. Hughes (New York: Odyssey, 1957).

bibles? And wasn't the great triumph in the North of the humanist call for a textual and moral return *ad fontes* the encouragement of the study of the bible "in the original"—in the original languages and not in the Latin translation?[32] Again, Tuve's "tradition" reveals itself as special pleading. In a private letter to Tuve (dated February 25, 1953), Empson made the crucial point about Tuve's notion of "the [Christian] tradition": it is an abstract hypostasis that does not allow for actual history, for a rupture like the Reformation or a ferment like the Renaissance. With an exasperation that was clearly not directed only at Tuve, Empson exclaimed: "I can never understand why critics who claim to be historical think they show expertise by getting their date wrong and claiming that Renaissance writers were really medieval ones."[33]

It was in fact the limits and peculiarities of her notion of tradition for which Empson criticized Tuve in "Donne and the Rhetorical Tradition" (Burke, it should be noted, very gently criticized her for the same thing).[34] Empson did not criticize Tuve for believing in "the value of knowledge to criticism" or for going "outside" the text. Empson criticizes the way in which Tuve relates knowledge to interpretation and the peculiar qualities of what she counts as knowledge. In *Elizabethan and Metaphysical Imagery*, the tradition in question is "the rhetorical" rather than "the Christian" tradition, but here too there is an enormous amount of special pleading. Empson points out the limits of what the English rhetoricians actually say about tropes, and the distance between the "system" that Tuve expounds and anything that is actually in the rhetoricians.[35] Even more significant, however, is Tuve's outright rejection of historical evidence when it does not coincide with her general presuppositions.

One of Tuve's deepest working presumptions is that nothing in past literature ever struck a learned contemporary of that literature as strange

---

32. See, for instance, E. Harris Harbison, *The Christian Scholar in the Age of the Reformation* (New York, 1956), esp. chap. 3; and Jerry H. Bentley, *Humanists and Holy Writ: New Testament Scholarship in the Renaissance* (Princeton, 1983).

33. I am grateful to Paul Fry for a copy of this letter and the whole Empson-Tuve correspondence. Empson's most sustained meditation on conservative, pseudo-historical presentations of "the Christian tradition" is "Literary Criticism and the Christian Revival" (1966), in *Argufying*, 632–37.

34. See "On Covery, Re- and Dis-," 223, for what Burke calls the "latitudinarian" (that is, liberating and liberalizing) effect of reading "The Sacrifice" in the context of Herbert's corpus rather than in the context Tuve provides.

35. "Donne and the Rhetorical Tradition," in Empson, *Essays on Renaissance Literature*, 1:65. Hereafter cited as DRT.

or odd. To see a literary work as strange means, for Tuve, that one has not properly understood it. A work couldn't actually *be* strange or odd. The aim of criticism is to eliminate strangeness. This is where Empson strongly demurs. He points to the elitism as well as the insensibility of this view when he asserts that "if you make yourself really servile about accepting a 'convention,' if you insist on taking it as a matter of course for us few who are in the know, you are at bottom refusing to let it give you the shock which it was intended to produce, even in its prime."[36] A "convention" may have been intended to shock—"even in its prime." Empson takes the central conceit of Donne's *Anniversaries*, the deceased teenage girl as the world, as an example of this. He points out what a serious embarrassment for Tuve it is that Ben Jonson, a contemporary of Donne's as learned and as well-disposed to Donne as possible, thought that Donne's *Anniversaries* were very odd indeed.[37] Jonson thought that the poems were, in fact, so shocking as to be blasphemous.[38] If the educated reader was supposed to see exactly what familiar thing Donne was doing, it is odd that a learned and well-disposed contemporary did not take the poems in this way. Again, Empson emerges as the better historicist. He spends a number of pages giving a fully and convincingly historical account of why Jonson would legitimately have thought that Donne's hyperboles were, as the later Johnson said, enormous and disgusting.[39] Empson takes as central to Donne's historical context not "the tradition" but the great division between the churches that dominated the consciousness of European intellectuals in the post-Reformation period. Empson sees Donne as using an essentially Catholic and Spanish rhetorical trope, the identification of an individual with the Logos, in the consciously Protestant English context, so that "the Protestant treatment gave an extra gaiety to his defiantly Catholic

36. Empson, "Last Words on George Herbert," *TLS* December 31, 1993, 11. This is a posthumously published essay that Empson wrote in the early 1950s in response to Tuve's *A Reading of George Herbert* (see n. 15 above).

37. Modern critics occasionally assert or assume that Jonson was not well disposed toward Donne's poetry (and vice versa). This is a mistake. There was admiration on both sides. For a discussion, see Richard Strier, "Lyric Poetry from Donne to Philips," in Carl Woodring, ed., *The Columbia History of British Poetry* (New York: Columbia University Press, 1993), 236–37.

38. For Jonson's remark that "Dones Anniversarie was profane and full of Blasphemies," see Jonson's "Conversations with William Drummond of Hawthornden," in *Ben Jonson*, ed. C. H. Herford and Percy Simpson (Oxford: Clarendon Press, 1925), 1:133 (see DRT, 70).

39. For "enormous and disgusting hyperboles," see Samuel Johnson, "Abraham Cowley," *Lives of the English Poets* (London: Dent, Everyman's Library, 1925), 1:17.

but startlingly displaced trope" (DRT, 75). Empson speculates that Donne's use of this trope might well have seemed nearly as strange and strained to his English contemporaries as it does to most readers now.[40]

So another moral may emerge from this confrontation: a work of art in the past can be doing something that would have struck its own educated contemporaries as strange. Lots of different ideas were available in the past, especially in so yeasty a period as the Renaissance, and there has never been a homogeneous and self-consistent "tradition" or dominant discourse. A work might be using heterodox ideas. This was a point that was very dear to Empson.[41] And even with regard to works using traditional and familiar ideas we cannot just read off their meanings by identifying their apparently traditional elements. Empson's joke, which I promised to recount, is that Tuve's attitude toward tradition reminds him of "an Emperor of China who returned a poem to its author with a somewhat embarrassed air and said, 'But surely there is no such poem,' meaning that he could not recall the classical poem that it must be presumed to imitate."[42]

We must strive to see traditional works against the backdrop of their traditions, not as merging indistinguishably into them. All the "elements" of a poem can be familiar, yet the poem can be startlingly original. We must, in Empson's wonderful phrase, taste each text with "as clean a palate" as we can—rather than, following Tuve, with as full a mouth as possible.[43] To do what Empson recommends does not mean making believe that each text is the first thing ever written, or the first thing ever written on its topic, but it does mean trying to appreciate each text's distinctive qualities, however strange or familiar. It means letting the historical chips fall where they may. Ultimately this is why Empson is a better guide to historical criticism than Tuve, since Empson keeps the particular in focus rather than letting it dissolve into its (supposed) component elements. In his essay on "The Verbal Analysis," written in the same period as his controversy with Tuve, Empson asserts that "a

40. Barbara K. Lewalski's treatment of the *Anniversaries* within a Protestant context has the advantage of centrally acknowledging the Reformation, but is liable to the same critique of "normalizing" the poems and dissolving them into a relatively homogenized tradition; see *Donne's "Anniversaries" and the Poetry of Praise: The Creation of a Symbolic Mode* (Princeton: Princeton University Press, 1973). For Lewalski too, Jonson's remarks are an annoyance (see pp. 3, 140–41, and 193).

41. For a consciously Empsonian reading of a Donne poem ("Satire III") along these lines, see Essay 6 below.

42. "George Herbert and Miss Tuve," 736; *Argufying*, 253.

43. "George Herbert and Miss Tuve," 738; *Argufying*, 254.

profound enough criticism could extract an entire cultural history from a single lyric."[44] Tuve might well have agreed with this, but, as we have seen, the directionality implied here is important. To put the point in Burke's wonderfully funny and cogent terms, Empson is a better model for historical critics because Empson, as Tuve does not, lets the Dis-a lead him to the Data.

44. "The Verbal Analysis," 599; *Argufying*, 107.

ESSAY 2

"Self-Consumption"

Bacon opens his *Essays* with an attack on skepticism. He sees it as a form of impatience: "*What is Truth?* said jesting Pilate; and would not stay for an answer."[1] In his next sentence, Bacon notes, disapprovingly, that there are some persons who are Pilates (in this sense) by nature, who "delight in giddiness, and count it a bondage to fix a belief." At least in his critical persona, the author of *Self-Consuming Artifacts* seems to be such a person.[2] He delights in "giddiness," in showing that in texts that he values there are no stabilities, no certainties, no positions, no place in which the mind can legitimately rest. The good reader of these works, according to Stanley Fish, learns to count it a mistake, if not a bondage, to fix a belief. Ultimately, for Fish, the writers that he admires in *SCA* all "affirm nothing" in both senses of this phrase: they do not make definite particular assertions, and they affirm a sort of nihilism with regard to normal conceptual, ontological, and moral distinctions. A truly self-consuming text, for Fish—a valuable text, for him—leaves itself and its reader literally nowhere.[3]

1. "Of Truth," in *Essays or Counsels, Civil and Moral* (1625), in *Selected Writings of Francis Bacon,* ed. with an introduction by Hugh G. Dick (New York: Random House, Modern Library, 1955), 7. Unless otherwise noted, all citations of the *Essays* are to this edition.

2. Stanley E. Fish, *Self-Consuming Artifacts: The Experience of Seventeenth-Century Literature* (Berkeley and Los Angeles: University of California Press, 1972). Unless otherwise noted, all quotations from Fish are from this book (hereafter cited as *SCA*). Page references will hereafter be included parenthetically in the text.

3. On the question of value, see chap. 7 of *SCA* ("The Bad Physician: The Case of Sir Thomas Browne," and the Epilogue ("The Plain Style Question").

I believe this view of the seventeenth-century texts in question to be brilliant, seductive, and deeply misleading, a bewitching scheme. Fish's nihilism is just as misleading as Tuve's "tradition"; the low priori is just as misleading as the high.[4] I have argued elsewhere that, with regard to Herbert's poetry, Fish mistakes a theological distinction for a philosophical one, and by overgeneralizing the point loses its specific content and force.[5] Here I will focus on Fish's treatment of two primarily secular writers, Francis Bacon and Robert Burton, though we shall see that Fish's treatment of all three writers (discounting some special strategies for dealing with religion) are very similar. I mean to attack Fish at his strongest. The chapter on Bacon's *Essays* is the longest in *Self-Consuming Artifacts*, and the chapter on Burton is the one that seems least assailable, the essay that has the most obvious plausibility and the most straightforward evidentiary base. I will try to demonstrate that the readings that Fish offers are *systematically* skewed, skewed in a way that produces not "plausible readings from a particular point of view"—the best that pluralism can hope for—but mistaken readings, readings that call into question the validity of the point of view from which they are produced. I will argue that Fish's readings systematically (as with Herbert) *eliminate the particular content* from the texts in question and equally systematically assert a generalized (negative) content for them. I will argue both for the importance of particular assertions and positions in these texts and against the ascription of extreme moral or epistemological negativity to them. I will try to show, in brief, not that the texts could not work in the ways that Stanley Fish says they do but that they do not do so, and I am happy to agree that this is equivalent to saying that they do not mean what he says they do, and what he says they don't.

I will begin, as Fish himself does, with Bacon's *Essays*. As Fish acknowledges, he is one with many other recent scholars in accepting R. S. Crane's linking of the *Essays* to Bacon's larger project for "the advancement of learning."[6] This means seeing the *Essays* as in some sense "scientific." Fish claims that what is "scientific" about the *Essays* is not a matter of the views they express but of the way in which they express

---

4. For the "high priori road," see the Introduction, n. 9 above.

5. See "Interlude: Theology or Philosophy?" in Richard Strier, *Love Known: Theology and Experience in George Herbert's Poetry* (Chicago: University of Chicago Press, 1983), 61–83. "The Holdfast" and "Love" (III) are the central poems for this discussion.

6. Ronald S. Crane, "The Relation of Bacon's *Essays* to his Program for the Advancement of Learning," in Brian Vickers, ed., *Essential Articles for the Study of Francis Bacon* (Hamden, Conn.: Archon, 1968), 272–92; *SCA*, 78–79.

their views: "Bacon's concern as a scientist *is wholly with the form* of his presentation" (81; emphasis mine). The essential point of the *Essays* is not to put forth any particular views—"Machiavellian," traditional, or other—but to question all strongly asserted views. This thesis about what is "scientific" about the *Essays* is not one that Fish sticks to consistently, but it does lead him into a number of important premises and procedures. It allows him, first of all, to treat the announced topic of any essay as of no real interest to either Bacon or his (proper) reader. The topics are merely occasions for providing a certain kind of epistemological experience: the generation of skepticism about generalizations. All the essays, for Fish, do the same thing; they are actually, from a "formal," philosophical point of view, identical. Seeing the essays in this way affects Fish's readings on both the macro and the micro levels. On the macro-level, it leads Fish to a generalized model of how the essays *must* proceed; on the micro-level, it leads him to view certain kinds of sentences as always intended to be objects of suspicion.

The pattern that Fish sees in the best of Bacon's *Essays* is very similar to that which Helen Vendler sees in the poems of Herbert that she likes best; it is the pattern of what Vendler calls "re-invention."[7] The writer initially puts forth a dull, commonplace, or standard view, which is then repudiated, undermined, or complicated in the course of the work. This is a perfectly possible pattern. The trouble begins when it is taken either as a general procedural model or as the criterion for value. The critic who does this, whether it be Vendler or Fish, is thereby committed to showing that the opening move of every significant or successful text by the writer in question is a jejune commonplace that we are meant to recognize as such. The model allows only for dialectical and not at all for linear development. A text that is highly valued cannot proceed either by apprehending the truth of a truism or by beginning with a complex or unfamiliar view.[8] For Fish, it is impossible that Bacon could not be mocking the "high speech" quoted at the opening of the essay on

7. See Helen Vendler, "The Re-invented Poem: George Herbert's Alternatives," in Reuben Brower, ed., *Forms of Lyric* (New York: Columbia University Press, 1970), 19–45; and *The Poetry of George Herbert* (Cambridge: Harvard University Press, 1975), chap. 2. I have commented on this schema in Vendler in "'Humanizing' Herbert," *Modern Philology* 74 (1976): 78–88.

8. On apprehending the truth of a truism as a model for great lyric poetry, see Yvor Winters, "The Sixteenth-Century Lyric in England: A Critical and Historical Reinterpretation," in Paul Alpers, ed., *Elizabethan Poetry: Modern Essays in Criticism* (New York: Oxford University Press, 1967), 95–96.

adversity; it is equally impossible for the first sentence of the essay on "Simulation and Dissimulation" to be simply pejorative about dissembling and dissemblers (*SCA*, 102). The pattern of development must always be dialectical. This model determines Fish's view of the opening sentences of all the final versions of the essays; it also determines his view of the revision of the essays. Here too, with regard to the revisions, the movement must always be from simplicity and optimism to complexity, confusion, and darkness. Although Fish reprehends another critic for taking the moral attitudes of the 1612 *Essays* to be "uniformly clear" (*SCA*, 127), Fish's schema for describing Bacon's revisions requires Fish himself to hold the view that he reprehends. And, of course, he does so; he is relentlessly true to his scheme. The 1612 version of the essay on ambition is said to be utterly "high-minded and highly moral" (119); the 1612 "Of Love" is said to be "a perfectly straightforward piece of conventional moralism" (109). It has to be this, since it has not yet been "reinvented" into its mature (1625) form. Yet the 1612 essay sees love as "ever rewarded" either with reciprocity "or with an inward and secret contempt," and ends by worrying that love interferes with the proper pursuit of self-interest—views that are hardly "conventional moralism."[9]

When a critic as intelligent as Stanley Fish falls into embracing a view that he correctly reprehends others for holding, one can say with some confidence that there must be systemic pressures at work. We can see this even at the micro-level of analysis. Fish falls into a theoretical fallacy that he has written a strong essay cogently attacking. In "What is Stylistics and Why are They Saying Such Terrible Things About It," Fish argues—completely convincingly, I believe—that one must never attribute a fixed meaning to a particular linguistic feature.[10] Yet in his work on Bacon, Fish assumes that a certain linguistic form, regardless of its context or content, always has a particular meaning or effect. Fish's view is that aphoristic utterances, especially "Senecan" ones with highly foregrounded parallel members and pointed schemes, are always to be seen as attempting "to secure the kind of facile assent Bacon is always warning against" (100). In the world of Bacon's essays, as Fish sees it, aphoristic or Senecan form always signals simplicity, falsity, or patness of content. But is it clear that Bacon intended the reader's response to the final

---

9. For the 1612 versions of the essays on ambition and on love, see *A Harmony of the Essays, etc. of Francis Bacon,* ed. Edward Arber (London: English Reprints, 1871), 222–28, 444–46.

10. See *Is There a Text in This Class?* (Cambridge: Harvard University Press, 1980), 77 et passim. "What is Stylistics" was originally published in 1973.

maxim in the 1625 essay on adversity ("Prosperity doth best discover vice, but Adversity doth best discover virtue") to be, as Fish puts it, "That's all very nice, but . . ." (101)? Isn't it possible that we are supposed to contemplate the *truth* of the maxim?

An even clearer example of the non-pat and non-false aphorism is the sentence with which "Of Suitors" begins in both 1597 and 1612: "Manie ill matters are undertaken, and many good matters, with ill mindes." Fish points to the rhetorical figures employed and concludes that this highly wrought sentence necessarily leaves the reader "little, if anything, to do" (120). But this is to ignore content altogether. The interjection of "and many good matters" is shocking and puzzling. The reader of this aphorism is left with a lot to do, namely, to try to understand and come to terms with *what it is saying,* with its content. What does it mean to say that many good matters are undertaken "with ill mindes"? Does it eliminate the distinction between good and ill "matters," or does it merely locate this distinction elsewhere, outside the realm of the intentions or motives of the agent? Can this latter view be made coherent? There seems to be much "to do" here, though it all involves coming to terms with, not rejecting, the content of the maxim.

Moreover Bacon, as opposed to Fish, always praised aphorisms. Fish sees Bacon's preference for aphorisms over "methods" as purely a matter of "psychological effect" and not at all a matter of content. "The content of aphorisms," says Fish, "is not necessarily more true than the content of methodological writing" (87). This is a trick sentence: not "necessarily" but usually. Bacon's main praise for aphorisms, in the passage that Fish quotes from the *Advancement,* is that, since they are shorn of so much ornamentation, they "cannot be made but of the pith and heart of sciences," that is, from solid truths. In order to have any chance of success, the author of aphorisms must have "some good quantity of observation," that is, of true observations. Such an author must be, as Bacon puts it, "sound and grounded." Bacon's emphasis on the importance of content to aphorisms could hardly be more explicit. Bacon sees "methods," on the other hand, as merely having to be internally consistent (and Bacon distinguished sharply between truth and mere consistency), and he sees methods as dangerous in their "carrying the shew of a total." The complete disjunction between the way in which Bacon sees aphorisms and the way in which Fish does becomes apparent a few pages after Fish's discounting of the importance of the content of aphorisms. Whereas Bacon distrusted methods and praised maxims, Fish soon starts to use "method" as a positive term (94), and "aphorism" as negative. In doing this, he entirely reverses Bacon's usage and supplants it with his own.

With these caveats in mind, it might be worthwhile to examine Fish's work on some individual essays. Every reader of Bacon's *Essays* would agree that "Of Goodness, and Goodness of Nature" and "Of Friendship" are major pieces. It is not surprising, therefore, that Fish singles them out for analysis, but I do not believe that Fish chose these essays, or most of the others that he analyzes at length, purely (as he pretends) on the basis of their formal characteristics. I believe that Fish was actually attracted to what he takes to be the content of these pieces, namely their (supposed) moral skepticism or cynicism, rather than merely to their form. And I believe that he misconstrues both their content and their "form" or effect. There is no doubt that, as Blake sardonically pointed out, Bacon was in fairly full retreat from the gospels in the "Goodness" essay, but Fish misdescribes the nature of Bacon's anxiety.[11] Bacon insists that self-love is "the pattern" for all love and "Love of our neighbors but the portraiture." In response to the gospel injunction to "sell all thou hast, and give it to the poor," Bacon, as a proper devout humanist, cautions that this makes sense only if "thou mayest do as much good with little means as with great."[12] Fish sees in this passage "more than a hint" that "the lessons and sayings of the Bible may be too 'high' for its intended pupils who are for the most part naturally malign" (116). This sounds reasonable, and appeals to our complicity in natural low-mindedness, but it is important to see that the question of whether the gospel commands are too "high" for human nature is entirely imported into Fish's analysis. It comes from Fish's very dubious ironic reading of the phrase "high speech" at the beginning of the essay on adversity. This question or image of moral "height," in other words, does not exist in the essay on "Goodness"; it is entirely imported by Fish. What Bacon is worried about is not that men can't or won't follow the gospel but that they will. Fish gets the matter exactly backward. The view that he ascribes to Bacon is the familiar kind of cynicism that we tend (for reasons that it would be interesting to explore) to equate with sophistication. But Bacon is doing something less easy and familiar.

The major effort of the "goodness" essay is to warn men against the temptation to excessive goodness, not to suggest that goodness is im-

11. See Blake's annotations to Bacon's *Essays* in *The Poetry and Prose of William Blake*, ed. David V. Erdman (New York: Doubleday, 1965), 613.

12. For a consideration of the role of this and similar arguments in early seventeenth-century moral and religious thinking in England and France, see Essay 5 below.

possible. Unlike Fish, Bacon does not say or seem to think that persons "are for the most part naturally malign." Fish does not quote Bacon's description of the "deeper sort" of naturally malign men as "like flies that are still buzzing upon anything that is raw."[13] Bacon seems to mean it when he describes persons with such dispositions as "the very errours of human nature." So we are, as Fish notes, surprised when Bacon adds, "and yet they are the fittest timber to make great politiques; like to knee timber, that is good for ships, that are ordained to be tossed." What is unjustified is Fish's conclusion that "we are all, of course, such 'knee timbers' [*sic*], for we are all ordained to be 'tossed'" (117). "Of course"—this is another bullying and preemptive move. And it is worth pausing for a moment over Fish's misquotation: the shift from an abstract category, "knee timber," that is clearly one kind among many, to an infinitely and easily expandable plural, "all such knee timbers." Extension of a special case into a general rule is one of Fish's (and deconstruction's) most characteristic procedures (let's call it the technique of illegitimate extension). The authorization that Fish provides for such extension ("for we are all ordained to be 'tossed'") is entirely noncontextual; it comes close to relying on "the tradition." Moreover, Fish gives the impression that Bacon's sentence ends after "tossed." He suppresses the fact that the sentence goes on to qualify seriously the usefulness of the rather unusual species of *misanthropi*; they are "good for ships, that are ordained to be tossed, *but not for building houses, that shall stand firm*."[14] Fish entirely suppresses this contrast between ships and "houses, that shall stand firm" (of which, Bacon certainly counts on us to think, there are many more than there are ships in the world). Fish does not want anything to "stand firm," but Bacon sees the crooked ("knee timber"), who make "great politiques," as a special and not especially admirable case. The examples of goodness that Bacon lists are not conditional.

Fish's reading of the 1625 essay "Of Friendship" is similar. He uniformly darkens—and therefore simplifies—the picture that Bacon presents. A very complex and nuanced sentence is described as "disorienting" to Fish's postulated reader, a figure who is oddly sensitive in some respects and oddly obtuse in others. The important claim is Fish's suggestion that when Bacon says that it is "solitude to want true friends," Bacon might be saying that it is solitude to *desire* true friends, and that the world may in fact be without true friendship. In context,

---

13. Bacon, *Selected Writings*, ed. Dick, 35.
14. Bacon, *Selected Writings*, ed. Dick, 36; italics mine.

however, there is no ambiguity. Grammatically, the objective sense, "to want" as "to lack," is the normal seventeenth-century usage; the suggestion about the nonexistence of true friendship is entirely unwarranted. Fish has to postulate a special rhetorical situation for this essay. He postulates a naive speaker for it, one who intended simply to praise friendship but who somehow failed to notice "the unsettling implications of his examples" (142), various "Roman Villains," as Blake said.[15]

But why should we assume a foolish persona rather than a competent author? Isn't it simpler and more plausible to assume that the aim of the essay never was simple praise? The examples then become proof of the strange extent of the human need for friendship, even at the hazard "of safety and greatness." Fish treats the explicit logic of the essay as mere "surface rhetoric" (139). I think we should be wary of such locutions even though they are extremely common in interpretive literary criticism. They are common because their major function is to create the authority of the critic ("this text may seem, to the uninitiated, to be saying X, but the true professional will see that it is *really* saying Y"). And they are based on a "surface/depth" dichotomy that is by no means self-evidently intelligible. What justifies dismissing the "surface"? I think that one needs a very good reason—which in some cases can certainly be provided—for dismissing the "surface" of a text, its obvious syntactic, logical, and semantic structure. Fish is always ready to dismiss "surface" meanings (and thereby to enhance the authority of the critic). In this case, he creates a hidden structure that makes the ideal of the essay not true friendship—which Fish, not Bacon, declares chimerical—but Stoic self-sufficiency. This is a historically intriguing suggestion, though Fish does not present it as such. The psychological and social thinking and feeling of many figures in the Renaissance was deeply and incoherently divided between Stoic ideals of self-sufficiency on the one hand, and Christian and other ideals of mutuality and community on the other. As Lacey Baldwin Smith puts it, the idea of the friend both "fascinated and repelled Tudor society."[16] Yet in Bacon's essay, the ideal of self-sufficiency exists only as a possible implication of Bacon's stress on the hazards of friendship. Bacon cites Trajan and Marcus Aurelius as examples of "goodness of nature," but Fish insists that they *must* be examples of "the Stoic doctrine of self-sufficiency" and therefore of

---

15. Blake, *Poetry and Prose*, 618.
16. Lacey Baldwin Smith, *Treason in Tudor England: Politics and Paranoia* (Princeton: Princeton University Press, 1986), 45.

persons "presumably . . . independent of outside supports" (144). This presumption is then deployed by Fish, in a manner that we would now call deconstructive, to counteract all the assertions—that is, the "surface rhetoric"—of the essay about the importance and the usefulness of the true friend.

A noncontextual association imported by the critic is brought forth as the central point of the text (compare "we are all ordained to be 'tossed'"). We might call this the technique of noncontextual importation. It is a powerful and, I think, pernicious technique—if, that is, we are interested in understanding what a text might actually be saying or doing rather than merely in having it confirm what we already "know." This technique is often used together with that of illegitimate extension. In Fish's analysis of the 1625 essay on friendship, this occurs when Bacon's warning against taking counsel from too many is seen as "finally a warning against taking any counsel at all" (146). The "true moral" of the section is found, according to Fish, "buried in a parenthesis." This is perfectly possible if we disregard all "surface rhetoric," but to do so cuts against the "affective stylistics" that Fish claims to be practicing, since it is not clear that a reader could experience something so buried as "the true moral" of the passage.[17] Affective stylistics would seem, in fact, to lead one to respect the surface of a text. In any case, the true moral regarding counsel in "Of Friendship" is said to be the phrase, "better perhaps . . . if he asked none at all" (147). Fish creates this moral by sheer sleight-of-hand, not to say deception. What Fish elides from the quotation is a single word, the word "than." The passage actually reads, "better perhaps than if he asked none at all."[18] Bacon's claim is not that asking counsel is a mistake but that any counsel is probably better than none, despite the dangers involved. Fish elides Bacon's point into its opposite. A complex concession is turned into a simple negative. Complexity disappears into generalized cynicism.

The same process occurs in Fish's reading of the end of the essay. In Fish's paraphrase, Bacon is there saying that a person "may rely on a friend to do those things that might better have been left undone" (148). What Bacon actually says is that a person may rely on a friend to do those "many things" which a person "cannot, with any face or comeliness, say or do for himself." There is no suggestion of "things that

---

17. For "Literature in the Reader: Affective Stylistics," see the Appendix to *SCA*, 383–427; *Is There a Text*, 22–67.
18. Bacon, *Selected Writings*, ed. Dick, 74.

might better have been left undone." Fish entirely ignores Bacon's emphasis on "face or comeliness," on decorum. This allows Fish to read the final maxim of the essay ("where a man cannot fitly play his own part; if he have not a friend, he may quit the stage") as suggesting that the ideal is to play one's own part successfully, to which there is no real alternative. Yet Bacon is still, with perfect continuity, discussing how useful friends are in the many practical situations in which, not from incompetence or lack of opportunity but from the very nature of normal social life, "a man cannot fitly play his own part." Again, Bacon's world is much more dense, nuanced, and social than Fish's.

With Burton's *Anatomy of Melancholy*, Fish would seem to be on firmer—that is, truly absent—ground. *The Anatomy of Melancholy* does often seem close to nihilism, and Burton is given to sudden and surprising inclusions that sweep away apparent distinctions. In Burton, Fish would seem to have found a writer whose "delight in giddiness" and hyperbole match his own. Yet Fish's treatment of *The Anatomy of Melancholy* in *Self-Consuming Artifacts* is at least as misleading as his treatment of Bacon's *Essays*. Fish wants Burton always to be self-canceling, never taking or implying a firm position, but Burton simply is not always so.

Burton's treatment of the figure of Democritus (the namesake of Burton's persona in the astonishing prologue to the *Anatomy*, "Democritus Jr. to the Reader") is probably as tricky as Fish says it is. Where Fish begins to skew the picture is in analyzing a sentence in which Burton seems to be making a moral distinction. "'Tis an ordinary thing with us," says Burton, "to account honest, devout, orthodox, divine, religious, plain-dealing men idiots, asses, that cannot or will not lie and dissemble, shift, flatter, *accommodare se ad eum locum ubi nati sunt*, make good bargains, supplant, thrive, *patronis inservire*, . . . that cannot temporize as other men do, hand and take bribes, etc., but fear God and make a conscience of their doings." Fish argues that "since the force of the verb phrase ('to account') lessens as the sentence continues, the groups whose confusion Burton is supposedly lamenting become, in the experience of the prose, more and more confused" (320). But the groups do not become confused. It is impossible to miss *the contempt* in Burton's list of corrupt practices, and this tone is certainly part of an actual reader's "experience of the prose," an experience of content and tone as well as of syntax (Fish's reader does not seem to "experience" tone). The sentence does come to focus more on the vicious than on the virtuous, but that is a separate point. The sentence ends, moreover, by returning to the virtuous, another fact that Fish entirely occludes. Burton sees the groups as utterly distinct. It is Fish, not Burton, who brings into this passage the phrase and the idea that "'tis all one." This phrase is Burton's, and it is indeed from "Democritus Jr. to the Reader," but it occurs in a different passage, a passage where, it should be noted, the phrase is used fairly straightforwardly in that the distinctions it negates are not very sharp to begin with.[19] What is lost in Fish's interpretive sleight-of-hand is any feeling for the passion of Burton's prose, for the intensity of his hatred *for particular abuses*, for, in this passage, accommodation, temporizing, and fawning. Needless to say, any sense of specific positive values (making "a conscience of their doings") is also lost.

There must be no positive models in the *Anatomy*, especially not in "Democritus Jr. to the Reader." So Fish must discount Burton's praise of particular "bodies politic" as peaceable, rich, flourishing, and non-melancholic. Burton cites Augustan Italy, contemporary China, and "many other flourishing kingdoms of Europe" (79). Fish discounts the reference to Augustan Italy by noting that it was "conveniently in the past" for Burton and was marred by Catiline's rebellion (which Burton mentions later). Fish also notes that China is said (also later) to be "infested" with wandering Tartars. How these later passages affect the "experience" of the passages one reads earlier is unclear and stands as another case of Fish not doing affective stylistics. As to the "many other flourishing kingdoms of Europe," Fish simply dismisses this and pretends to be at a loss as to what kingdoms Burton could possibly have in mind (*SCA*, 324–25). But Burton obviously does not see (as there is no reason to see) Catiline's abortive rebellion, which took place under the republic, as destabilizing Augustan Rome, and Burton consistently refers to contemporary China as a social and legislative norm (*Anatomy*, 91, 93, 103). Most importantly, Burton specifies at length exactly what "flourishing kingdoms of Europe" he has in mind, namely, the Low Countries, "those rich United Provinces of Holland, Zealand, etc." (86). Burton's praise of the Low Countries is sustained and straightforward (88–89); he explicitly contrasts the "flourishing" of these con-

---

19. The passage is about different senses of "melancholy": "So that, take melancholy in what sense you will, properly or improperly, in disposition or habit, for pleasure or for pain, dotage, discontent, fear, sorrow, madness, for part or all, truly or metaphorically, 'tis all one." Robert Burton, *The Anatomy of Melancholy*, ed. with an introduction by Holbrook Jackson (New York: Random House, Vintage, 1977), 40. All citations of Burton are from this edition. Page references will be included in the text.

temporary bodies politic with the relatively wretched condition of contemporary England. In meditating on this contrast, Burton offers both an analysis (81–95) of the social and political causes of social wretchedness and some general guidelines for reform. Burton consistently asserts that "the most frequent maladies" of bodies politic "are such as proceed from ourselves" rather than from nature (e.g., 80) and are therefore subject to reform.

Fish must deny all of this. He cannot allow Burton to assert the possibility of "flourishing" through ordinary means. Fish passes over in silence the entire section I have indicated. He has something much more important to discount. In order to assert Burton's nihilism, what Fish has to discount most of all is the idea that, as J. Max Patrick put it, "there is a Utopia in Burton's preface" to the *Anatomy*.[20] The attack on this thesis is a job that Fish relishes. He hastens over the problem of the "flourishing kingdoms" to get to what is for him the crucial moment, the knockdown argument, a passage Fish likes so much that he quotes it twice (325 and 339). It is a passage that occurs when, after fifteen pages of analysis and recommendation, Burton stops and seems to undercut (as Fish would have it) the whole idea of social reform. Burton makes fun of millenarian fantasies of total reform (96) and asserts that "these are vain, absurd, and ridiculous wishes not to be hoped." Most important of all for Fish, Burton then makes the complementary assertions that "all must be as it is" and (Fish's very favorite), "there is no remedy" (97). Fish would seem to be unassailable here. The undercutting of Utopianism would seem to be complete. Yet again, Fish will not stay for an answer. He does not take into account what follows "there is no remedy." Where Fish's analysis stops, Burton's continues. The beginning of the next paragraph draws a further conclusion about reform. Insisting strongly on continuity with what has just been said, Burton writes, "Because, therefore, it is a thing so difficult, impossible, and far beyond Hercules' labours to be performed, let them [people in general] be rude, stupid, ignorant . . . let them tyrannize, epicurize, oppress," etc. (97). The object, in short, of Burton's satire here is the idea of giving up all attempts at reform. He is satirizing the idea that "all must be as it is" if things cannot be perfect.

It is in this context, in the context of praise of Holland and criticism of millenarianism, that Burton offers his Utopia. Fish entirely misses the

20. See J. Max Patrick, "Robert Burton's Utopianism," *Philological Quarterly* 27 (1948): 345–58; SCA, 329.

nature of this Utopia, treating Burton's project as if its premise were, as Fish puts it, "the banishing of human nature" (326). Fish passes over another five pages of specific proposals—common granaries, public schools, good roads, long leases, etc.—to get to what he sees as another devastatingly anti-Utopian passage. "If it were possible" (already thereby, for Fish, giving up the game), Burton states that he would have perfect versions of all the professions and states of life ("such priests as should imitate Christ, charitable lawyers," etc.), but, he concludes, "this is impossible, I must get such as I may" (102). Fish is triumphant. Burton here "admits defeat," not only—and here we get the familiar move from the specific to the universal—"on the particulars" but "on Utopia itself" (328). With this acknowledgment of human nature, for Fish, the Utopian idea fails. But Burton's project was always to conceive of a "Utopia" within the bounds of the easily conceivable, a "Utopia," in fact, rather like Holland or China. To use J. C. Davis's immensely helpful distinction, Fish confuses the idea of a Utopia with that of a perfect moral commonwealth.[21] In the text, the assertion that "I must get such as I may" is not a moment of "weary" conclusion, as Fish says (328), but of renewed energy. Burton immediately returns to his specific, non-millenarian reforming proposals. Right after "I must get such as I may," Burton continues: "I will therefore have of lawyers, judges . . . etc. a set number" (102). His nonrevolutionary Utopia continues with unabated energy for five more pages after he has (according to Fish) supposedly given up in weariness and disillusion. And Burton knows exactly what he is doing. His treatment of the place of usury in his Utopia (106) exemplifies perfectly the *kind* of ideal that he is imagining—that he is, in fact, proposing.

Fish's "all or nothing" framework makes him especially unable to acknowledge moments of nondisillusioned realism. "I must get such as I may" is one such moment; Burton's treatment of war is another. Fish is certainly justified in finding the latter discussion unsatisfactory. I would argue, however, that the reasons for this are historical and specific, having to do with the nature of this particular topic, not with the Utopian project in general. Burton tended, as did Erasmus before him, toward an extreme revulsion toward war. Burton's revulsion was so powerful that he felt it necessary explicitly to deny that he was a total pacifist like

---

21. For the distinction, see J. C. Davis, *Utopia and the Ideal Society: A Study of English Utopian Writing, 1516–1700* (Cambridge: Cambridge University Press, 1981), chap. 1. For Davis's fine treatment of Burton, see chap. 4.

"those phantastical anabaptists" (59). In his treatment of war, Burton
was stymied, I think, precisely by his commitment to a nonrevolutionary,
nonheretical Utopia. Whether or not this is the correct explanation for
Burton's problems with the topic of war in his Utopia (a topic with which
More also had notable problems), I am convinced that it is the right *kind*
of explanation.[22]

We can see another example of Fish's difficulty with nondisillusioned
realism if we return briefly to his treatment of friendship. Bacon asserts
that "if a man have a true friend, he may rest almost secure that the care
of those things [the person's long-range projects] will continue after
him." Fish can only read "almost secure" here as devastatingly ironic:
"a more uncomfortable state can scarcely be imagined" (148). Yet
Bacon wants to be reassuring—without being unrealistic. The tone of
his phrase is difficult to capture, but to see it as a crudely jocular sarcasm
is surely to miss the balance that Bacon is attempting. If the most that
can be hoped for is not everything, surely that doesn't make it nothing.
This is an important point. The assumption that the failure of a postulated absolute means that nothing can be positively asserted is familiar
as the central premise of the metaphysics and epistemology of deconstruction ("We will never know *for sure* what Nietzsche wanted to
say. . . .").[23] But surely—again—this is to set the ante too high.

The experience of the texts that Fish discusses is simply not as he
describes it. The texts are more nuanced, less wildly and frantically
paradoxical than Fish asserts. Most of all, the texts espouse values. They
are not endlessly ironic. They have positions. They have moments of
passion and earnestness. They do not leave the reader nowhere, even if
they do not leave him or her in a world of simplicities and perfection.
There is an intelligible place to stand in these works between total

22. For Erasmus and More, see the superb treatment in Robert P. Adams, *The Better
Part of Valor: More, Erasmus, Colet and Vives, on Humanism, War, and Peace, 1496–1535*
(Seattle: University of Washington Press, 1962); for Erasmus's role in the history of
pacifism, see Peter Brock, *Pacifism in Europe to 1914* (Princeton: Princeton University
Press, 1972), 61, 90.

23. See Jacques Derrida, *Spurs: Nietzsche's Styles*, trans. Barbara Harlow (Chicago:
University of Chicago Press, 1979), 123. Italics in the original. For a brilliant account, with
regard to a crucial text, of the problems with Derrida's way of reading (which is very close
to Fish's), see Foucault's critique of Derrida's reading of Descartes's *Meditations* in Michel
Foucault, "My Body, This Paper, This Fire," trans. Geoff Bennington, *Oxford Literary
Review* 4 (1979): 9–28. Derrida's "*Cogito* and the History of Madness" appears in Jacques
Derrida, *Writing and Difference*, trans. Alan Bass (Chicago: University of Chicago Press,
1978), 31–63.

ignorance of the world and total capitulation to it. Politics, ordinary politics, is possible. Particulars matter. All distinctions do not, a priori, break down. Attending to content gives us variety. I am afraid that the model of "self-consuming artifacts" is precisely the sort of bewitchingly attractive and oversimplifying schema that Fish rightly presents Bacon as eager to combat. Like not only Bacon but Wittgenstein, we must struggle against such bewitchment.[24]

24. See Ludwig Wittgenstein, *Philosophical Investigations,* trans. G. E. M. Anscombe (New York: Macmillan, 1953), 47e. The German is "*Verhexung*" (47).

ESSAY 3

"Theory"

When René Wellek and Austin Warren published *Theory of Literature* in 1942, they included chapters on virtually every topic in literary study that they thought could be theoretically—meaning generally, or philosophically—treated. Throughout most of the 1980s, "theory" in North American literary studies had come to have a very limited and specific meaning. It had come to mean primarily literary criticism showing the influence of the Yale version of deconstruction.[1] I will henceforth refer to this version of literary theory, the Yale version of deconstruction, as Theory, to indicate the special status that it then had. The two volumes on Shakespeare that I will consider were published at the height (or perhaps I should say crest) of the Theory boom. One, *Shakespeare and the Question of Theory*, is a large collection of essays by various hands, mostly American or American-affiliated academics; the other, *William Shakespeare* by Terry Eagleton, a tiny monograph by an engagé British academic.[2] Taken together, these volumes complement each other interestingly and provide an occasion to think through the value of Theory and of some other theories for practical and historical literary studies.

1. See the helpful collection edited by Jonathan Arac, Wlad Godzich, and Wallace Martin, *The Yale Critics: Deconstruction in America* (Minneapolis: University of Minnesota Press, 1983).

2. Patricia Parker and Geoffrey Hartman, eds., *Shakespeare and the Question of Theory* (New York and London: Methuen, 1985); Terry Eagleton, *William Shakespeare* (New York and Oxford: Blackwell, 1986).

I will begin by analyzing two explicitly deconstructive essays in the Parker-Hartman volume. I will argue that these essays are led into distortion and bad faith by their problems in dealing with the literal and the social. The social and the political turn out to bulk unexpectedly large in *Shakespeare and the Question of Theory*. A number of other essays in the volume—some, but not all, connected to Theory—explicitly wish to focus on political, social, or economic matters yet have great difficulty in keeping (or in intelligibly keeping) the political, social, or economic focus they purportedly wish to have. I will argue this in relation to essays by Jonathan Goldberg, Thomas Greene, Stanley Cavell, and Terence Hawkes. The final section of the Parker-Hartman volume considers essays that explicitly reject Theory (though not necessarily other theories) in the name of social and political realities, essays by Elaine Showalter, Stephen Greenblatt, and Robert Weimann. I then turn to an essay in the volume (by Joel Fineman) that I see as suggesting a way of making Theory productive by reducing its generality and abstractness and making it historically specific.[3] The discussion of Fineman's essay leads directly into consideration of Terry Eagleton's book. I will argue that Eagleton has two distinct critical modes and that the more successful of these also suggests a way in which Theory can be made critically productive through being focused on social and political issues rather than on Language in general.

I

The piece that opens the Parker-Hartman volume announces its commitment to "Theory" in its subtitle, "The Deconstruction of Presence in *The Winter's Tale*," and the methods and assumptions of this essay by Howard Felperin can be taken as paradigmatic of applied Theory. Felperin begins with a good question about the initial action of the play: "Why do we take it for granted" that Hermione has not had an affair with Polixenes, that Leontes is deluded about this? Instead, however, of exploring the ways in which Shakespeare makes us

3. Those familiar with the Parker-Hartman volume will note (and those unfamiliar with the volume should be alerted) that this chapter by no means constitutes an inclusive review of the volume. For those seeking such a review, see my "Shakespeare and the Question of Theory," *Modern Philology* 86 (Summer 1988): 56–76.

feel certain of Hermione's innocence and of the pathological nature of Leontes' jealousy, Felperin insists (unsurprisingly) that there is a major epistemological problem here: "neither Leontes nor we can know for sure, short of divine revelation." This is a trick sentence. We have met "for sure" before.[4] It works to make us hesitate, upping the epistemological ante to the level of the "hyperbolic" and "ridiculous" doubt that Descartes both mocked and made familiar (the adjectives for this doubt are Descartes's own).[5] The mention of divine revelation sets up the rest of Felperin's essay. Felperin makes it sound as if the word of the oracle is our only reason for not sharing Leontes' doubts. The straw man is now fully in place. Having rigged the epistemological situation in this way, Felperin's task is clear: to attack the oracle, and thereby undermine our (unearned) certainty.

Felperin's strategy, a paradigmatic deconstructive one, fails in two ways. First, the basic premise, that our assurance rests only on the oracle, is false; second, the attack on the oracle, made falsely crucial, fails in itself. To take the latter point first, Felperin is constantly in a position of discounting facts within the play—always, I would argue, a sign of bad criticism. Critical sentences beginning with "although," like those discounting "surface rhetoric," are often a bad sign, a syntactical badge of special pleading.[6] With regard to Leontes' refusal to believe the oracle, Felperin writes, "Although this is the only point in the play where such a conventional mistrust [of oracles] is ever hinted at, it would seem that such mistrust is well grounded." Why "it would seem" this way has nothing to do with *The Winter's Tale*. Again we get the technique of importation. We get something like "tradition" as Tuve deploys it: there are riddling oracles elsewhere in Shakespeare; there is a long classical and Renaissance tradition (documented in a footnote) of distrusting oracles. This is all well and good, but no contextual reason is offered for distrusting what Felperin to his credit recognizes as the distressingly "plain-spoken and un-Delphic" oracle in the play. We are close here to the kind of historical criticism that tells us what, given the prevailing beliefs, etc.,

4. See Essay 2, p. 40 above.

5. See the end of the Sixth Meditation in *The Philosophical Works of Descartes*, trans. Elizabeth S. Haldane and G. R. T. Ross (Cambridge: Cambridge University Press, 1931), 1:198–99. For persuasive accounts of Descartes's project in the *Meditations*, see Harry G. Frankfurt, *Demons, Dreamers, and Madmen: The Defense of Reason in Descartes's "Meditations"* (Indianapolis: Bobbs-Merrill, 1970); E. M. Curley, *Descartes against the Skeptics* (Cambridge: Harvard University Press, 1978); and the essay by Foucault cited in note 23 of Essay 2 above.

6. On "surface rhetoric," see Essay 2, p. 34 above.

a text *must* be saying. Felperin's argument for the rightness of Leontes' distrust draws no evidence from the play; it must discount not only the words of the oracle ("surface rhetoric" again) but also the whole scene in which we hear, as Felperin puts it, Cleomenes' "reported awe" at the oracle. Yet the point of the scene between Cleomenes and Dion seems to be precisely to *defuse* skepticism about the oracle. The language is as replete with religious and mystical solemnity as Shakespeare can make it. Felperin finds here what he rather coyly says "might be termed the problem of linguistic indeterminacy." He finds this problem here because he must find it.

Felperin argues that Leontes' interpretation of Hermione's behavior is not logically impossible. Hermione's behavior *could* mean what Leontes takes it to mean; the words that Leontes puns or seizes on *could* have the meanings Leontes finds in them. But the point of the play is not that to interpret the way Leontes does is logically impossible but that it is crazy. In order to use Leontes as a spokesperson for the essential difficulties of interpretation and for "the defects of language" in general, Felperin must discount the fact that the play presents Leontes as, at least temporarily, mad. Everyone in the play understands exactly what Leontes takes to be evidence for his beliefs. And everyone in the play agrees that it is mad to interpret the data in this way. What is striking in the play is not how plausible Leontes' interpretations are—how difficult it is to interpret human behavior—but how isolating and mistaken Leontes' interpretations are, how thoroughly they cut him off from the interpretive and political and familial community of which he ought to be a part. The problem with which the play is concerned is not that of linguistic indeterminacy but that of the role of faith in the constitution of human community. The problem, to use Stanley Cavell's favorite distinction, is not one of knowledge but one of acknowledgment.[7] The programmatic nature of Felperin's reading leads him away from the play's central concerns.

A similar process occurs in Margaret Ferguson's essay on *Hamlet*, wonderfully entitled "Letters and Spirits." Ferguson purports to accept de Man's deconstruction, following Derrida, of the idea of the literal.[8] She uses Hamlet as Felperin uses Leontes. Hamlet leads us "to question

7. See "Knowing and Acknowledging" in Stanley Cavell, *Must We Mean What We Say?* (New York: Scribner's, 1969), 238–66.

8. See Paul de Man, "The Epistemology of Metaphor," *Critical Inquiry* 5 (1978): 13–30; Jacques Derrida, "White Mythology: Metaphor in the Text of Philosophy," *New Literary History* 6 (1974): 5–74.

the distinction between literal and figurative meanings," to confront "the problem of distinguishing between multiple—and perhaps equally figurative—meanings." These formulations are produced by Theory. Inaccurate as descriptions of Hamlet's verbal behavior, they are used to license a kind of criticism that gives greater weight to metaphors and semantic possibilities than to narrative and stylistic facts. This bears careful watching.

Ferguson approvingly quotes a comment by Lawrence Danson on the puns in Hamlet's opening speeches, but she misreads this comment in a characteristic and significant way. Where Danson states that Hamlet's puns demand "that words be given their full freight of meaning," Ferguson takes this to imply that words be given multiple meanings, more meanings rather than more meaning. Moreover, Ferguson sees puns as "driving a wedge between words and their ordinary meanings," a tendentious description of what puns do, since they often rely on multiple "ordinary meanings." The key move for Ferguson is to link the (supposed) violence of this linguistic behavior—"*driving a wedge* between words and their ordinary meanings"—to the physical violence that we see Hamlet perform. The violent metaphor, it should be noted, is entirely the critic's invention, and this turns out to be a crucial strategy. We are told that Hamlet performs a "rapier attack" on the word "matter" in his early conversation with Polonius. So described, this behavior "foreshadows the closet scene in which [Hamlet] both *speaks* daggers to his mother and literally stabs Polonius." But this is mere critical sleight-of-hand. The critic's metaphor (Hamlet's "rapier attack" on a word) is used to establish a connection that is then ascribed to Shakespeare. The critic must ignore the fact that when Hamlet vows to "speak daggers" to his mother, his emphasis is on the distinction between this activity and using daggers. What Hamlet distinguishes, the critic conflates. Yet there is a characteristic sort of bad faith at work here. It can be seen in Ferguson's use of "literally." She uses the term perfectly normally and properly. What this implies is that the "foreshadowing" that Ferguson strives so hard to establish is not something in which she herself strongly believes. Her argument about Hamlet's movement in the play from verbal to nonverbal action relies precisely on the distinction between speaking daggers and using them. The essay cannot hold to its premise about the nonexistence of the literal.

If the only result of a commitment to Theory were to produce a halfheartedness disguising itself as wit, this would not be a serious matter. What is serious is the way in which this commitment prevents Ferguson from distinguishing her cogent points from her forced ones, and therefore from developing her cogent points in productive ways that, unencumbered by Theory, she could have. The last quarter of Ferguson's essay is devoted to a passage in Claudius's discussion with Laertes about the duel with Hamlet in which Claudius speaks in a (for him) unusually glowing and poetical way about the horsemanship of "a gentleman from Normandy." Ferguson beautifully characterizes Claudius's speech as, in some sense, "a digression from the world of tragedy itself," and she tellingly connects this "digression" both to Ophelia's description of Hamlet as a perfect courtier and to certain characteristic moments of description in Shakespeare's romances. But instead of exploring these connections, Ferguson insists that the key to this passage is the name that, in the the Second Quarto only, is given to the Norman, "Lamord" (he is "Lamound" in the Folio). For Ferguson, Lamord quickly becomes La Mort and L'Amour, so that the passage is secretly about death and love, a secret "letter" from Shakespeare to his audience. In this way of reading, a noncontextual pun becomes more important than the straightforward stylistic and thematic connections that Ferguson has also noted. Allegorizing distracts Ferguson from hard thinking. She ends up seeing the passage as suggesting that *Hamlet* could have been a romance if its plot had not been arbitrarily darkened. Something like this is true of some of the tragedies, most notably of *Lear*, but it is not true of *Hamlet*. Serious thought about the plot of *Hamlet* (like that of Helen Gardner in an essay that Ferguson cites) would have made this clear.[9] But Ferguson's method does not really allow her, as Empson puts it, to "attend to the story."[10]

We have already discussed the role of hyperbolic skepticism in Theory. Ferguson attempts to deny that Hamlet can draw "a clear epistemological distinction" between his father and Claudius. This attempt is based on the general view that there simply cannot be "a clear epistemological distinction," and it is halfhearted and tendentious in ways that we have seen. On the other hand, Ferguson's argument for some similarities between Hamlet and Claudius is a very different matter. This claim is based on the overt content of some of their speeches and on aspects of the (literal) plot. When Ferguson argues that, with the killing of Polonius, Hamlet takes a crucial step toward occupying "the place of the king as the play defines it: not in terms of an individual, but in terms of a *role* associated both with the power to kill and with the tendency

9. See Helen Gardner, "The Historical Approach: *Hamlet*," in *The Business of Criticism* (Oxford: Oxford University Press, 1959), 35–51.

10. See Essay 1, p. 22 above.

to justify killing with lines of argument unavailable to lesser men," we are in a different, and I think better, critical world. Ferguson tries to relate this point to Language by making it a hermeneutical one about "the desire to interpret literally," but the power of the point is ethical and structural, not linguistic. Moreover, on the linguistic level, the claim is false. Metaphors are often quite useful in establishing "lines of argument" that justify killing. There is a point to be made here about particular uses of language, not about Language in general. And it is potentially a historical point. It sends us to the actual, literal world of Renaissance politics and Renaissance political thinking, with and without its metaphors.

II

The literal is the ghost that haunts *Shakespeare and the Question of Theory* with its nagging "Remember me." That a major section of the volume is entitled "Politics, Economy, History" is interesting in itself, suggesting that even in the heyday of Theory, "politics" and "history" were becoming, as they certainly are now, privileged terms in literary studies. Yet even more interesting and revealing is the way that such terms are used in many of the essays. Such terms are often used in thin and metaphorical ways, ways that are actually at variance with the literal meanings of the terms. Despite significant gestures to the contrary, gestures that indicate an uneasy awareness of the problem, many essays in the volume are unable to maintain a focus on (literal) politics, economy, or history.

Jonathan Goldberg's "Shakespearean Inscriptions: The Voicing of Power" is a good example, even in its bifurcated title, of the difficulties of treating political issues in a deconstructive mode. Goldberg has notably solved this problem in his recent work on sodomy in English Renaissance texts, since the slippages of that key term are historically and politically revelatory, but in this essay on "the voicing of power" the deconstructive destroys the political.[11] The essay is extremely cryptic. Insofar as I am able to reconstruct it, the argument seems to be that although the plays present power as a matter of occupying certain

---

11. See Jonathan Goldberg, *Sodometries: Renaissance Texts, Modern Sexualities* (Stanford: Stanford University Press, 1992).

culturally defined speech positions, this does not mean that silence, in the cultural system of the plays, can be taken to imply powerlessness. Not unexpectedly, the positive argument is convincing. The apparently—and truly—contradictory argument for silence is not. Like any speech act, falling silent needs to be contextualized. To equate the entrapped Shylock, reduced to silence by manipulation and coercion, with the exultant Bassanio, reduced to silence by joy, seems merely ingenious, not to say disingenuous. The argument that the Roman Portia of *Julius Caesar* participates in political power through her suicide seems equally disingenuous. To compound the problem, the one moment that Goldberg cites in which powerful female speech is actually represented, Emilia's assertion, near the end of *Othello*, that she feels "bound" to break out of the silence to which wifely duty would consign her, is converted by Goldberg, through a misleading historical analogy (regarding witnesses being legally bound to speak), into an act of constraint rather than of freedom. To counteract the effect of the silence of Hermia and Helena in act 5 of *A Midsummer Night's Dream*, Goldberg appeals to two queens, Hyppolyta and Elizabeth, as if their examples contravened rather than confirmed the general rule of female silence. In short, that queens could speak out and that men were sometimes silent are not facts that, in themselves, alter the cultural status of speech as empowered and male and of silence as unempowered and female. What we can see in this essay is the way in which dialectical ingenuity, the rejection of simple binaries, can produce political obtuseness. The metaphorical treatment of "voicing" in the essay blurs and confuses its political focus. I cannot see that Goldberg ever attended to Constance Jordan's point, to which he alludes, about the specific, political meaning of "having a voice."

In Thomas M. Greene's essay on "failed husbandry" in the Sonnets, it is the economic rather than political that disappears into metaphor. Although Greene's essay appears under the "Politics, Economy, History" rubric of the volume, the essay is much closer to Hubler's "economy of the closed heart" than to Empson's attempt to make the class issue central in the Sonnets.[12] The essay does not perform an Empsonian or (Kenneth) Burkean class analysis. The real connections of the essay are not with any sort of social or economic analysis but with New

---

12. Edward Hubler, *The Sense of Shakespeare's Sonnets* (Princeton: Princeton University Press, 1952), chap. 5; William Empson, *Some Versions of Pastoral* (1935; pap. rpt. New York: New Directions, 1960), chap. 4. For reasons that escape me, neither of these critics, indeed no critics other than the editors of the editions Greene uses, are mentioned or referred to in Greene's essay.

Criticism and deconstruction, and this essay helps us see the connections between these movements. Greene approaches Empson in describing an argument in which "the bourgeois poet accuses the aristocratic friend of a dereliction of those responsibilities incumbent on the land-owning class," but in general Greene uses class terms in a metaphorical and arbitrary way. He never makes clear why the claim that "in black inck my love may still shine bright" is a "desperate *bourgeois* maneuver," just as he never makes clear why the desire for intelligibility in human relations is "bourgeois"—surely many peasants and aristocrats have wanted this! The essay is concerned with the *language* of economics and (to use a fashionably chiastic but, I am inclined to think, empty construction) with the completely metaphorical "economics" of language.

Greene rightly points to the prominence in the Sonnets of economic terms and of terms that have economic as well as other (especially sexual) meanings in their semantic range. The fundamental effort of the essay is to show: (1) that the "economic" systems in the Sonnets are unstable; (2) that the Sonnets are aware of this instability; and (3) that the Sonnets are therefore profoundly poignant. The discovery of poignance is Greene's theme (here as elsewhere), but it is also his scheme.[13] A theme merely has to be significantly present; a scheme requires the critic to show its presence everywhere. Schemes produce forced readings and hyperbole.[14] For instance, the fact that the elements aligned against poetry are "cosmic" does not necessarily leave the poet and his poetry "in a confusing limbo"; affirmations of linguistic power do not occur only in the couplets of the Sonnets, nor do the affirmative couplets invariably "lack the energy of the negative vision of the 12 lines that precede them."[15] Greene's major effort, however, does not lie in these particular assertions but in his more general analysis of the "rhetorical economics" of the poems. His central argument is that, in the linguistic world of the Sonnets, riches make Shakespeare poor: "the enriching of metaphor . . . is indistinguishable from a mutability of metaphor [in the Sonnets], a fragmentation which might be said to demonstrate instability." At one

13. See, for instance, the treatment of Petrarch in *The Light in Troy* (New Haven: Yale University Press, 1982), esp. chaps. 6 and 7.

14. A theme, in my usage, need not be totalized. One can trace "the theme of such and such" in a work without claiming more than that the theme in question exists there. It need not be dominant, central, or "the" theme. A scheme, in my usage, is a view that insists on its own ubiquity and necessity.

15. For sonnets that, I would claim, escape this generalization, see numbers 18, 63, and 65.

point, in a Derridean moment, Greene extends this view to all Language, but the *"inopem me copia fecit"* scheme is most cogent with regard to Shakespeare's poetic practices.[16] It structures Greene's readings.

One result of Greene's commitment to this scheme is that he has to see the Sonnets as written entirely in the high style—"every rift is loaded with ore." Greene must therefore downplay the stylistic variety of the Sonnets and give short shrift to the plain-style ones.[17] He is committed to a way of reading that sees all semantic possibilities as actual in every context, without regard for what Empson called "situations." This way of reading is fundamental to both New Critical and deconstructive poetics.[18] It is interesting to compare Greene's readings with those of Stephen Booth, whose practice is close to that of the New Critics and who is definitely no eschewer of multiplicities. Booth turns out to be more judicious. In two major and rather surprising cases, Booth issues warnings that Greene ignores. Regarding Sonnet 80 ("O, how I faint when I of you do write"), Booth states that this poem "contains many words used elsewhere in sexual senses" but notes that "none of them is fully activated here." Greene, on the other hand, is tempted "to interpret the sonnet primarily in erotic terms." Sonnet 125 ("Were 't aught to me I bore the canopy") is central to Greene's argument; it is the poem toward which and from which his essay moves. Greene must reveal irony and pathos in the poem. The presence of a Eucharistic reference in the tenth line, "And take thou my oblation, poor but free," is crucial to this endeavor. Booth, on the other hand, again notes that while there are potential Eucharistic references in the sonnet, the analogy is "never applied or activated while the poem is in process."[19] Greene's "economic" thesis does not allow for any distinction between potential and actual (or "activated") meanings in poetic contexts. Moreover, these multiple meanings must conflict with one another to generate the requisite pathos. Oddly and significantly, Greene has no comment what-

---

16. The assertion *"inopem me copia fecit"* (abundance makes me poor) occurs in Ovid, *Metamorphosis*, 3.466. It is spoken by Narcissus.

17. For a great plain-style poem in the Sonnets, see for instance number 120.

18. For the continuities between New Criticism and deconstruction along these lines, see, inter alia, Frank Lentricchia, *After the New Criticism* (Chicago: University of Chicago Press, 1980), 169. For some caveats, see Shuli Barzilai and Morton W. Bloomfield, "New Criticism and Deconstructive Criticism, Or What's New?" *New Literary History* 18 (1986): 151–69.

19. *Shakespeare's Sonnets*, ed. Stephen Booth (New Haven: Yale University Press, 1977), 273, 430. I will cite the Sonnets from this edition.

ever on the couplet of his central sonnet ("Hence, thou suborned informer! A true soul / When most impeached stands least in thy control"). He is not interested in Shakespeare's conception of the "true soul" (nor in the status of "suborned informers" in Shakespeare's world). The proud Stoic voice of this couplet, like the voice of the entire previous sonnet ("If my dear love were but the child of state")—which Greene virtually ignores—hardly seems a pathetic one. Greene's way of reading may not wholly derive from Theory, but it certainly relies on and is reinforced by a fashionable sense of language as based on or somehow permeated with loss, as if, in Robert Hass' wonderful paraphrase, "a word is elegy to what it signifies."[20]

Just as "economics" in Greene's essay turns out to be rhetorical, "politics" in Stanley Cavell's essay turns out to be nonexistent. Although Cavell's essay mentions politics in its subtitle ("*Coriolanus* and the Interpretations of Politics") and occurs with Greene's in the "Politics, Economy, History" section of the collection, the torque of Cavell's essay is strongly away from political readings. He attempts to defuse this by presenting his reading as being about "the formation of the political" (whatever this means) if not about politics, and also by including a Kenneth Burkean "Postscript," but the main effort of the essay is not toward concern with politics or even "the political" in the play. One would think that the orientation of the essay would be psychoanalytical, since (despite his professed admiration for Burke) Cavell sees the psychoanalytic perspective as having produced "more interesting" readings of the play than the political, but this turns out not to be the case either. Cavell has already asked the question, "Politics as opposed to what?"[21] It may be foolhardy, but in this context I am prepared to offer an answer, and that is: religion. The main effort of the body of Cavell's essay is to read *Coriolanus* in relation to Christianity.

This effort seems to me to be unsuccessful, and it seems to me to derive from the least productive strand in Cavell's previous work on Shakespeare. The work on Shakespeare, like the essays on other literary texts and on films, is part of Cavell's lifelong project, his attempt to provide a fully textured account and critique of post-Cartesian philosophical skepticism. Cavell's work on Shakespeare seems to me most incandescent when it is clearly part of this project, as in the treatment

---

20. Robert Hass, "Meditation at Lagunitas," in *Praise* (New York: The Ecco Press, 1979), 4.

21. See the essay by that title in *Critical Inquiry* 9 (1982): 157–78.

of shame in the essay on *Lear* and in the superb essay on *Othello* that forms the coda of *The Claim of Reason*.[22] There is a philosophical moment like this in the essay on *Coriolanus* when Cavell offers as a reason why Coriolanus "spits out" words the fact "that they *are* words, that they exist only in a language," and that "a language is something metaphysically shared." This is not, however, the mode of the essay as a whole. Like Cavell's *Lear* essay, his *Coriolanus* essay is not content with reading that hews to the literal, even though both essays pay significant and even memorable lip service to such reading.[23] Cavell applauds Brecht's discussion of *Coriolanus* for "*getting us not to interpret*, not, above all, to interpret food." Nonetheless, the essay proceeds to a resounding "Yet" (248). This signals the moment when a scheme kicks in. Suddenly the literal, the obvious, the surface is rejected. With this reversal, Cavell devotes himself to exactly what he praised Brecht for getting us not to do: interpreting food in the play (against which Kenneth Burke also cautioned).[24] Cavell's discussion of interpretations of food in the play culminates in his approving quotation of Janet Adelman's reading of the strange lines in act 1, scene 3, in which Volumnia equates Hector's forehead wounded in battle with Hecuba's breasts when she suckled Hector. This too is followed by a crucial "But." Even Adelman's psychoanalytic reading is too literal. For Cavell in this mode, what is most important in the equation of blood and milk, the image of a male provider of blood that is food, is to get to the point where Coriolanus can be seen in relation to the sacrificial Christ—and "not so much imitating Christ as competing with him." The "proof" of this claim is the juxtaposition of bits and pieces of action and lan-

---

22. See "The Avoidance of Love: A Reading of *King Lear*," in *Must We Mean What We Say?* and *The Claim of Reason* (New York: Oxford University Press, 1979). Both of these essays appear in *Disowning Knowledge in Six Plays of Shakespeare* (Cambridge: Cambridge University Press, 1987).

23. Cavell orients the first part of his *Lear* essay against an essay by Paul Alpers on "*King Lear* and the Theory of the Sight Pattern," which appeared originally in Reuben A. Brower and Richard Poirier, eds., *In Defense of Reading* (New York: Dutton, 1963), 133–52). Alpers's essay is both an attack on the symbolic reading of "the sight pattern" in *King Lear* and an attempt to suggest the power, importance, and ethical sanity of a literal reading of the material from which the "sight pattern" is constructed. Cavell seeks to defend and reinstate the "sight pattern." The phrase initially (or at least most prominently) appeared in Robert B. Heilman, *This Great Stage: Image and Structure in "King Lear"* (Baton Rouge: Louisiana State University Press, 1948), chap. 2, "'I Stumbled When I Saw': The Sight Pattern."

24. See Burke's "*Coriolanus* and the Delights of Faction," in *Language as Symbolic Action* (Berkeley and Los Angeles: University of California Press, 1966), 95.

guage in the play with bits and pieces of action and language from the New Testament.

Cavell is nervous about this. He acknowledges that "some good readers" may find these connections strained, but he nevertheless insists that "good reading may be guided, or inspired, by the over-excitement such conjunctions can cause." I am not sure of this. I suppose good reading can be inspired by almost anything, but these excitements seem to me more likely to produce bad reading, reading that is constantly discounting rather than acknowledging the obvious meanings of the words in the texts. Cavell here dismisses, through patronizing, more literal readings than his own (they "cannot be wrong, but . . ."). The important paradox is that Cavell's own best reading, in this essay as elsewhere, works to respect the literal, to focus on the "ordinariness" of the given words in their contexts rather than to find secret patterns in them, to understand what has been said *as* what has been meant.[25]

Although Terence Hawkes's *"Telmah"* (*Hamlet* spelled backward) does not appear in the "Politics, Economy, History" section of *Shakespeare and the Question of Theory*, Hawkes's essay has a very peculiar relation to politics: his essay relates criticism to politics by conflating them. It is a very peculiar piece. Its first part is an essay on *Hamlet*, focusing, as Ferguson does not, on the structure of the plot; its second part is an elaborate argument about the cultural and ideological meanings of John Dover Wilson's account of the plot in *What Happens in "Hamlet"* (1935). The two parts of the essay are linked by both being oriented against the same straw man; the first part attacks it literarily, the second ideologically. The straw man in Hawkes's essay is "our inherited notion of *Hamlet* as a structure that runs a satisfactorily linear, sequential course." This "sense of straight, purposive, linear motion forward through the play" is, we are told, "required by most interpretations of it" and is, apparently, the same as "the orthodox Hamlet-centered interpretation of the play." Given this description of the inherited orthodoxy, any observations that show the play or the character not to proceed with "a sense of straight, purposive, linear motion" are therefore subversive—politically as well as literarily.

But this version of the "orthodox" reading is absurd. Both the play and the title character are notorious for not developing a proper plot, and Hawkes's notion of "linearity" is so simplistic that any narratives of past events or patterns of repetition are taken to disturb it. They are all

25. See "The Avoidance of Love," 269–70; *Disowning Knowledge*, 40.

part of *Telmah*, the "recursive," backward-moving elements in the play. The central element of *Telmah*, for Hawkes, is the stature of Claudius. The orthodox, linear reading of the play apparently requires that Claudius be "the simple stage-villain described by the Ghost." It is perhaps worth saying that the figure of uncannily seductive eloquence described by the Ghost is not at all a "simple stage-villain," but the important point is that Hawkes writes as if the recognition of Claudius as a powerful figure, truly Hamlet's "mighty opposite," were a new and startling discovery, one that deeply unsettles our sense of the plot of the play, revealing the alien and unexpected shape of *Telmah*.

One cannot miss the presence of a scheme at work here. For Hawkes, recognition of the stature of Claudius must be subversive so that Hawkes can make the connection that he wants to posit between readings of *Hamlet* and political ideologies. The key fact for the second part of the essay is John Dover Wilson's extraordinary response to an article by W. W. Greg on *Hamlet* that appeared and Dover Wilson read in the fall of 1917. Greg's article apparently gave Dover Wilson a more than Hamlet-like sense of mission; he felt he "had been born to answer" this article. And Greg's article, in Hawkes's words, "promoted" Claudius, and was therefore highly "subversive." Hawkes's effort is to show this (supposed) literary subversiveness to be truly in tune with its moment (1917)—to be, in other words, genuinely Bolshevik. This is done by connecting Dover Wilson's career as a writer and lecturer on Russia and an opponent of revolutionary trade-unionism at home, with his major work of literary criticism.

One (or, at least, I) can only feel indebted to Hawkes for the fascinating material about Dover Wilson, and I very much applaud Hawkes's attempt to link Dover Wilson's political life to his literary criticism (to see it all as part of his political life), but I think that Hawkes draws the circle too tightly. Only a very importunate scheme would lead one to see W. W. Greg as a Bolshevik. And Dover Wilson's book cannot in turn intelligibly be seen as pseudo-Fascist. Ascribed political "meanings" are here being substituted (or taken) for facts. This is especially disturbing because there are, pardon the expression, some real facts here. Where Hawkes is on firm ground is in his demonstration of the cultural meaning and avowed political function of English studies in England after 1917. Hawkes does not have to do "interpretation" to show this. In the words of the remarkably outspoken "Newbolt Report" of 1921, English studies would serve to establish "a bond of union between classes" and thereby defuse the possibility of working-class revolution (326–27). I think that, contrary to his intentions, Hawkes's position is dangerously antipolitical in this essay. To think that we can be genuinely revolutionary either by subscribing to a particular literary interpretation (*"Telmah"*) or by asserting that there is no such thing as a definitive interpretation seems to me disturbingly self-promoting and delusive. It is certainly good to have studies of the ideological determinations and functions of English studies in general and of Shakespeare studies in particular, but there are, I would maintain, less arbitrary ways of saving the study of Shakespeare from the ideals of a ruling elite than through the arbitrary political ascriptions of *"Telmah."*

III

The essays that I will now consider, those by Elaine Showalter, Stephen Greenblatt, Robert Weimann, and Joel Fineman, intend to be literal in their relation to "politics, economy, history" (though only one of them, that by Greenblatt, appears under that rubric in the Parker-Hartman volume). Although these essays are all, in some sense, against Theory, they show different ways in which the relation between the literal and the theoretical remains a problem. Only the essay by Joel Fineman suggests a way in which Theory and history can be brought productively together. I will argue that Eagleton's book at times succeeds in a similar way.

Showalter's work on "Representing Ophelia" is determinedly literal and social. Recoiling from the obsessive textuality and abstractness of Theory, Showalter calls for a wide-angled but specific feminist cultural history. As an example of such an endeavor, she presents some fascinating material on the representation of Ophelia in the theater, in the visual arts, and—most suggestively—in the actual discourse of nineteenth-century psychiatrists. Yet, from a methodological point of view, what can be seen in Showalter's essay is that the retreat from theory and from "critical hubris" can be too complete. An essay need not be "theoretical" to be reflective. One leaves Showalter's essay wishing that she had offered some speculations on, for instance, the theatricality of madness (which Ellen Terry apparently thought was excessive) and on the ways in which life imitates art. It seems that a critic's materials can be too raw as well as too cooked. If one has to choose between Theory and "stuff," I would certainly choose the latter, but need one make this choice?

Stephen Greenblatt, in "Shakespeare and the Exorcists," meditates on the relations between life, art, and theatricality in a sharply defined cultural context. He means to cook his cultural materials—though not to overcook them—and also to do some literary analysis.[26] The topic of his essay is not so much the relation between its texts, Samuel Harsnett's *Declaration of Egregious Popish Impostures* and Shakespeare's *King Lear*, as what the relation between these texts tells us about the culture that produced them both (within, probably, two or three years of each other). Greenblatt acknowledges the usefulness of deconstruction in calling into question the boundaries between the literary and the nonliterary and in depriviledging and demystifying the literary (which I am not sure it does), but he backs away from Theory insofar as it leads, as he puts it, "too readily and predictably to the void." However uncomfortable he might be in saying so (since "sophistication" seems to require hyperbolic skepticism), Greenblatt is committed to the view that there is something *there* in cultures to be studied, and that what is there is not to be found merely by thinking about Language.

While Greenblatt rejects Theory, he does, of course, have a theory: "new historicism," or "cultural poetics." I will consider this theory in some detail in the next chapter (see Essay 4 below). What I want to do here is to begin to suggest the way in which even a theory that is against Theory can generate the pressure of a critical scheme and can lead away from an acceptance of the literal. Much of what Greenblatt asserts in "Shakespeare and the Exorcists" seems to me indisputable. He establishes the presence of theatrical metaphors in Harsnett's text and, more importantly, he establishes the function of these metaphors in the text, the ideological and political function of them. He shows Harsnett's need for "an analytical tool" that would account for both the fraudulence and the power of the Catholic exorcisms that Harsnett was attacking, and he shows that Harsnett found this "tool" in the metaphor of theater. The major connection to *King Lear* comes through consideration of the mock-miracle that Edgar provides to reassure Gloucester of the benignity of the gods. Greenblatt argues that this scene is precisely parallel to the mock-exorcisms in Harsnett's account. The play thus provides "theatrical confirmation of the official position" that exorcism is a fraud. Up to this point, the essay is straightforward and convincing. Shakespeare's play and

26. This essay is included (though without the discussion of deconstruction and theory) in Greenblatt's *Shakespearean Negotiations: The Circulation of Social Energy in Renaissance England* (Berkeley and Los Angeles: University of California Press, 1988), 94–128.

Harsnett's treatise are shown to inhabit the same ideological as well as literal world, and Greenblatt assures us that he finds Shakespeare's "theatrical confirmation of the official position" (Harsnett's) to be "neither superficial nor unstable." But Greenblatt proceeds, as Cavell does at a similar moment, to a significant "And yet." The whole essay takes a turn here; Greenblatt now aims to show that *King Lear* serves not to reinforce but to undermine the intended effect of Harsnett's *Declaration*.

The idea, put crudely, is that Shakespeare uses theater to resacralize what Harsnett used theater to desacralize. Greenblatt wants to argue that the representation, in the actual theater, of the desacralizing power of theater serves, paradoxically, to undermine itself and to reinstate what it seems to be attacking. But why must the cultural transactions in question be paradoxical and circular in this way? It is here that we can detect the presence of a scheme. Suddenly the critic finds himself clutching at straws. He refers portentously to a performance of *Lear* in the home of a Yorkshire Catholic in 1610, and oddly but significantly flirts with allegorizing. The Edgar-Edmund story suggests the persecution of Catholicism by its "skeptical bastard brother." Both the text and history disappear. Protestantism becomes merely a form of skepticism. Greenblatt sees Harsnett wanting his readers to delight in the silence of the supernatural, while Shakespeare, on the other hand, makes us experience this silence as negative, as a loss rather than a liberation.

Yet Greenblatt knows that Harsnett is not in fact arguing for "the silence of the supernatural," but rather for its presence only in the Bible and properly authorized rites. Nonetheless, Greenblatt sees the force of Harsnett's argument only as negative. There is no possibility that Shakespeare's play is more skeptical and more secular than Harsnett's pamphlet. But why not see it in this way? If the dramaturgy of *Lear* awakens in us "the forlorn hope of an impossible redemption," why shouldn't the play be seen as criticizing this hope (so often voiced by Albany and Edgar) rather than, however complexly, encouraging and indulging it? Why can it *not* be liberating, if sobering, to know that the evil is not supernatural? Why should the play be seen as preferring evacuated rituals to none at all? The answer seems to be that, for Greenblatt if not for Shakespeare, there are no such things as "evacuated rituals." Rituals, even when performed as frauds, seem to function *ex opere operato*—as long as they are, in any sense, performed.[27] We are in the

---

27. In "Resonance and Wonder," Greenblatt repeats the claim that "when Catholic ritual is made into theatrical representation," the transposition at once "naturalizes,

presence of a scheme here. We know that something has gone seriously awry when Greenblatt is led to conclude that "the force of *King Lear* is to make us love the theater." Surely "the force of *King Lear*" is something deeper and more humanly central than that. One need not hold an idealized, noncontextualized view of Shakespeare to doubt that the ultimate aim of his art was to be self-promoting. Greenblatt has rejected Theory in the name of history, but nonetheless there are pressures on his analyses that skew his treatment of the texts and events with which he engages.

Robert Weimann's essay on "Mimesis in *Hamlet*" is a direct meditation on Shakespeare and Theory. He does not argue against deconstruction in general but specifically against its application to Shakespeare. The essay presents a series of theses about the particular nature of Shakespearean drama, or rather, of Shakespearean theater. Weimann sees text and theater as in many ways at odds in Shakespeare, and he takes this tension to be constitutive. He does not grant a privileged position to the textual.[28] Weimann sees Shakespearean drama as questioning this (and all other) privilege. Deconstruction is rejected as irrelevantly text-centered and irrelevantly targeted against closure and authority. Weimann wants to see both aesthetic and political authority as constantly put into question in the plays. He relates the mimetic multiplicity of the Shakespearean play to the specific social and cultural situation of the Elizabethan theater. The essay is a program piece calling for a specific type of historical criticism.[29]

---

denaturalizes, mocks, and celebrates." The first three of these terms are relatively clear in themselves and in Greenblatt's analyses, but the final term—the one that makes the "circulation" fully circular—is presented in a completely mystificatory way: the stage "celebrates such practice by reinvesting it with the charismatic magic of the theater." The technical anthropological edge of "charismatic" is not, I think, enough to make "magic of the theater" into a meaningful analytical category. See *Learning to Curse: Essays in Early Modern Culture* (New York: Routledge, 1990), 163.

28. Not to grant privileged status to the textual distinguishes Weimann's from Harry Berger's essay in the volume ("Psychoanalyzing the Shakespearean Text: The First Three Scenes of the *Henriad*," *Shakespeare and the Question of Theory*, 210–29). Berger claims that only a text-centered, "anti-theatrical" reading can capture the hidden resonances of scenes like the opening of *Richard II*. Berger sees the Shakespearean text as the Lacanian Other to Shakespearean theater. The argument seems to me to rely on a programmatically impoverished sense of what theater can do.

29. Unlike Greenblatt's, Weimann's essay is not a full-fledged example of the criticism for which it is calling. For what such criticism would look like, Weimann directs the reader to his essay on "'Appropriation' and Modern History in Renaissance Prose Narrative," *New Literary History* 14 (1983): 459–95, as well as to his earlier *Shakespeare and the*

Yet there is perhaps something too flat in Weimann's as in Showalter's rejection. Isn't there some way in which Theory, or some version of it, can be put in the service of history and help with Shakespeare? Fineman's "The Turn of the Shrew" is the only essay in *Shakespeare and the Question of Theory* that demonstrates how theoretical awareness, in the deconstructive sense, can inform textually and historically specific practical criticism and—this is important—vice versa (how historical can inform "theoretical" awareness). Fineman does not use his Shakespearean text merely as an example. He sees *The Taming of the Shrew* as embodying a discursive system—indeed, he would say, *the* discursive system—in which contemporary Theory fully and massively participates. Fineman's essay is fundamentally antideconstructive, but not, as Yeats would say, without vacillation. It sides with Lacan and the "not so freely floating signifier" rather than with Derrida. Writing from within the Freudian tradition, Fineman is interested not in the indeterminacy of language but in the determinedness of it, in the ways in which patriarchal structures seem to reassert themselves even in the face of and within their own subversion. Fineman builds on a textual crux: Grumio saying that Petruchio will rail at Kate "in his rope-tricks." Fineman's point about this crux is very delicately and carefully put. The meaning of the crux "is not altogether indeterminate or, rather, if it is indeterminate, this indeterminacy is itself very strictly determined."[30] Fineman sees the gendered violence in Petruchio's "rope-tricks"/rhetoric as fully and determinately meaningful. Fineman is able to show in detail that Petruchio exploits the subversive "language of woman" in order to silence Kate (this is something like the opposite of Goldberg's thesis). Through a clearly motivated if overly elaborate detour through Robert Fludd's cosmology, Fineman shows that the traditional patriarchal cosmology includes and is in no way disturbed by a *mise en abyme* and various kinds of (female) indeterminacy. In Fludd as in Shakespeare, indeterminacy determines a specific story. This essay seems to show Theory fully and historically applied.

Popular Tradition in the Theater, ed. Robert Schwartz (Baltimore: Johns Hopkins University Press, 1978). I would call attention to Weimann's "History and the Issue of Authority in Representation: The Elizabethan Theater and the Reformation," *New Literary History* 17 (1986): 449–76.

30. Patricia Parker implies something like this about another textual crux, "dilations" in the Folio *Othello*, but she does not explicitly develop the point (see "Shakespeare and Rhetoric: 'Dilation' and 'Delation' in *Othello*," *Shakespeare and the Question of Theory*, 54–74.

IV

_____

Terry Eagleton's monograph is, as one would expect, deeply aware of both politics and Theory. In one of its modes, the monograph attempts, in a pragmatic and deceptively modest way, an "articulation" of Marxism and deconstruction.[31] In this mode, I think that it manages some striking successes at such articulation. The interesting question is how. The answer seems to be that Eagleton sees deconstruction as raising a general structural problem: the tension within any psychological or signifying system between the need for and power of distinctions and the need for and power of overriding distinctions. Conceiving the issue in this way allows Eagleton to tap into some of Shakespeare's deepest and most fully expressed concerns while at the same time making analytical use of deconstructive theory. The key conceptual breakthrough is that Eagleton does not see deconstruction as only a theory about Language. He can acknowledge the content of Shakespeare's actual concerns; he does not have to show these concerns to be all, ultimately, about Language. He can, following Lacan, use Language as a paradigm without making it his subject. Like Fineman, Eagleton does not have to "translate" Shakespeare's concerns into those of Theory. In this mode, Marx comes into Eagleton's book as one of the great theorists of the tension between differentiation and undifferentiation, between the world of differentiated objects and the abstracting and undifferentiating force of money. Eagleton is thus able to use some of the most haunting passages in Marx as part of his general analytical framework. Eagleton does not seem to know the adage, but his book brings new cogency to Wallace Stevens's remark that money is also a form of poetry.[32] Perhaps paradoxically, Marxism enters Eagleton's book most powerfully as a form of Theory, not as a theory in itself. Unfortunately, as we will see, there are other moments in which Marxism appears in the book as the crudest sort of a priori theory. Eagleton's structural model, based on Marx on money, is much more powerful and sophisticated than his historical one.

"Language," Eagleton's first chapter, establishes the productive paradigm. The chapter begins with a stunning reading of *Macbeth*. With

31. Compare Michael Ryan, *Marxism and Deconstruction: A Critical Articulation* (Baltimore: Johns Hopkins University Press, 1982).

32. See Wallace Stevens, *Opus Posthumous*, ed. Samuel French Morse (New York: Knopf, 1957), 165.

wonderful insouciance, Eagleton remarks that "it is surely clear that positive value in *Macbeth* lies with the three witches." He is not merely being a critical bad boy here. He has a serious and persuasive case to make, even if he somewhat overidealizes the witches. Eagleton's major point is that order in *Macbeth* is "based on routine oppression and incessant warfare." The witches "are exiles from that violent order, inhabiting their own sisterly community on the shadowy borderlands, refusing all truck with its tribal bickerings and military honour." The sexual, material, and linguistic ambiguity of the witches is seen as subversively and precisely deconstructive, striking at "the stable social, sexual and linguistic forms which the society of the play needs to survive." This all seems powerfully and surprisingly right; it gives the witches a thematic force consonant with the power of their theatrical presence. And even if the witches are much more involved with "linear" history than Eagleton acknowledges (he does not mention their visions of the future royal house) this is an illuminating and thoroughly contextualized use of Theory. On the other hand, in his other critical mode, when Eagleton describes Lady Macbeth as "in short . . . a bourgeois individualist," we are in a critical world that is both literarily and theoretically cruder and less convincing.

Only a major critic can take on the challenge of saying something interesting about a topic that is explicitly central to a work. Law in *The Merchant of Venice* is obviously such a topic, and Eagleton's treatment of this topic is one of his triumphs (in his chapter on "Law"). He begins with a showstopping parallel to his opening assertion about the witches in *Macbeth*: "In *The Merchant of Venice*, it is Shylock who has respect for the spirit of the law and Portia who does not." As in the earlier case, Eagleton can back up his claim. Shylock respects the spirit of the law through knowing that a legal document cannot possibly specify "all conceivable aspects of the situation to which it refers." There are problems with this view—it ignores Shylock's insistence on what is "nominated" in his bond and his refusal to accept anything but what is so "nominated"—but it usefully problematizes the play at a point where we might too easily rest in apparent clarity. A similar moment of perhaps perverse illumination occurs in a wonderful discussion of Shylock's relation to the meaning of human embodiedness. Eagleton hauntingly links Shylock's famous speech on "organs, dimensions, senses" to the "merry bond" regarding Antonio's body. Eagleton argues that "Shylock's ferocious insistence on having Antonio's flesh must be read in the light of his sufferings at the hands of anti-semites; not just as revenge for them—though this is no doubt one of his motives—but as a scandalous exposure of that which Antonio owes him—his body" in fellowship or communion. This has a Cavellian quality of profound "ordinariness," of reminding us what communion as incorporation, having (or being) "one body," means. Eagleton is idealizing Shylock as he did the witches (Shylock's desire for revenge is passed over in a concessive clause) but Eagleton's reading again draws attention to something powerfully present in the play. The same is true of Eagleton's treatment of Shylock's motivelessness, his extraordinary refusal to give a reason for his behavior toward Antonio. Eagleton sees this refusal as a perverse mirror image of *agape* ("motiveless" love), the value for which Portia is always taken to speak.[33] This is a stunning insight, and one that follows from Eagleton's structural analysis.

Troilus and Cressida is a play that seems temptingly open to appropriation by Theory.[34] The play is deeply cynical, and it is easy to make it seem deeply skeptical as well. But here, surely, some wariness is called for. In his treatment of this play, and in his treatment of the issue of selfhood in general, Eagleton falls into very standard and programmatic deconstruction. Perhaps the problem is that the attack on selfhood is part of the program, so Eagleton's application of Theory to the topic seems predictable rather than fresh. The argument proceeds along familiar lines. Eagleton recognizes that Shakespeare "stands with Hector," who holds that "Value dwells not in the particular will," against the nihilism of Troilus's "What's aught but as 'tis valued?" So Hector's position must be deconstructed. It is worth looking at this argument because it is so standard. The key to the argument, the coup de grâce, is the supposedly devastating observation that "all that can be appealed to against the subjectivism of Troilus is simply a wider intersubjectivity" (60). But this "simply" is entirely unearned. A wider intersubjectivity need not "be anchored in anything beyond itself." Cavell is very good on this point in his (overtly) philosophical work, as is, for instance, Donald Davidson, who uses one of the key passages of *Troilus*, Ulysses' speech on "com-

33. On "motivelessness" as constitutive of *agape*, the New Testament conception of love, see Anders Nygren, *Agape and Eros*, trans. Philip S. Watson (New York: Harper and Row, 1969), 61–104. For an argument that Shakespeare, like Luther and George Herbert, recognized this feature of *agape*, see Richard Strier, *Love Known: Theology and Experience in George Herbert's Poetry* (Chicago: University of Chicago Press, 1983), 22; see also 78–81.

34. See, for instance, Elizabeth Freund's extremely programmatic essay in *Shakespeare and The Question of Theory*, "'Ariachne's Broken Woof': The Rhetoric of Citation in *Troilus and Cressida*," 19–36.

munication," as part of his attack on subjectivism.[35] Davidson shows, for instance, that "radical interpretation" among persons, leading to successful communication, is, as he puts it, both "commonplace" and of enormous metaphysical significance.[36] The deconstructive strategy is, as always, to take the failure of an impossible absolute—here, something beyond intersubjectivity—to discredit every other kind of success.

To assert that selves are inconceivable without language and that language is a social product is not to imply that stable selves do not exist (though it may imply that totally "private" selves do not exist—a different matter). The nonexistence of the stable self is a premise rather than a conclusion of Eagleton's analyses. His extended treatment of selfhood focuses, naturally enough, on *Hamlet* and occurs in a chapter entitled "Nothing," an extremely witty and provocative rubric but also, in its content, quite predictable. Eagleton begins the chapter with a discussion of *Othello,* so he has to make a reverse-chronological transition to *Hamlet,* which he does by very cleverly employing his rubric: "If *Othello* tells the story of a man in hot pursuit of nothing, *Hamlet* tells the story from the standpoint of that nothing itself." In *Othello,* "the mysterious opacity" is, as Eagleton puts it, "none other than woman and desire," whereas in *Hamlet,* he says, "that opacity, while closely related to female sexuality, is quite evidently the hero himself." This is beautifully said; it is also, I think, accurate. It is not, however, fully compatible with Theory; an opacity is not the same as a void. Eagleton's major effort in his discussion of *Hamlet* is to obscure this distinction. It is useful to compare this treatment of *Hamlet* with Eagleton's treatment of the play in his first book on Shakespeare, *Shakespeare and Society,* written almost twenty years earlier, long before his commitment to Theory. In the earlier treatment, as in the more recent one, Eagleton focuses on Hamlet's unwillingness "to take up a determinate position within the 'symbolic order' of his society."[37] This is a powerful insight, now as then. In the earlier discussion, though, Eagleton's emphasis was on this situation *as*

35. For Cavell, see "Knowing and Acknowledging" (note 7 above) and *The Claim of Reason,* parts 1 and 4 (note 22 above). For Donald Davidson, see *Inquiries into Truth and Interpretation* (Oxford: Clarendon Press, 1984). Davidson uses the quotation at the end of "Thought and Talk," p. 170.

36. For radical interpretation as commonplace, see "Communication and Convention," *Inquiries into Truth and Interpretation,* 279. For the claim that "successful communication proves the existence of a shared, and largely true, view of the world," see "The Method of Truth in Metaphysics," *Inquiries into Truth and Interpretation,* 201.

37. Terry Eagleton, *Shakespeare,* 71; Terence Eagleton, *Shakespeare and Society* (New York: Schocken, 1967), 61–62.

tragic; here the emphasis is on the claim that Hamlet's "'self' consists simply in the range of gestures with which he resists available definitions." This is another unearned "simply." A "range of gestures" can, after all, be powerfully expressive. The idea of authenticity, of "truth to self," was central to Eagleton's earlier book on Shakespeare, and it was clearly the advent of Theory that shifted Eagleton from his earlier view. Terence Eagleton's conceptions of spontaneity and authenticity may have been somewhat naive and Romantic, but they provided him, I would argue, with a more accurate sense of Shakespeare's view of selfhood than Terry Eagleton's acceptance of Theory does.

Eagleton's commitment to the programmatic version of Theory skews a powerful insight into Hamlet; his commitment to an unnecessarily simplistic version of Marxist historiography skews his treatment of Coriolanus yet further. This is Eagleton in his other mode, his more "classical" Marxist mode, the mode of British Marxist criticism of the thirties, of a critic like Christopher Caudwell.[38] The signs of special pleading are everywhere apparent: "Coriolanus, *though literally a patrician*, is perhaps Shakespeare's most developed study of a bourgeois individualist." The literal and the obvious are being discounted through the application of the theory. As the discussion proceeds, Eagleton seems to dig himself further into the hole of a crudely a priori historicism. Coriolanus is seen not only as "a bourgeois individualist," but also as the prophet of successful capitalism. Hamlet becomes "even more proleptic than Coriolanus." Something has gone very wrong with the whole framework here.

When Eagleton writes as a "classical" Marxist, he writes, as Blake would say, "in fetters." He is best when he is working most boldly and speculatively. It is a measure of Eagleton's refreshing boldness (or chutzpah) as a critic that he attempts to specify Shakespeare's sense of the fundamental tensions in the human condition and to explore Shakespeare's "solution" to these tensions. The tensions have to do with the relation between freedom and community. This would seem to be a rich context in which to discuss *Lear*, a play with which Marxists have often been successful, but Eagleton's discussion of *Lear* is weakened by Theory in a way that should by now be familiar—it is linguistic and metaphysical rather than social. The "linguistic animal" is (necessarily) the same as the social one, but the formulations point in different directions. The irony

---

38. See Christopher Caudwell, *Illusion and Reality: A Study of the Sources of Poetry* (New York: International Publishers, 1937).

of this treatment is that its key term, "excess" (sometimes "surplus"), could, in fact, do much of the work that Eagleton wants it to, but it will not do so when thought of, à la Greene, primarily in terms of Language.

What, then, can we conclude about Shakespeare and the question of Theory? It seems that the moments of greatest fruitfulness in the Shakespearean criticism influenced by Theory are not those focused on Language (or even language), but those focused on patterns in the Shakespearean texts that are structured *like* a language. When Language as such is the focus, the result tends to be a reduction of the Shakespearean texts to mere examples of the truths of Theory or tendentious attempts to show the Shakespearean texts to manifest sufficiently hyperbolic epistemological skepticism. The richer approaches either reject Theory or attempt to bring it in line with particular, nonepistemological content. The revelation of general indeterminacy seems sterile; the study of particular, historically conditioned indeterminacies seems fruitful, as does the study of the ways in which representational systems in Shakespeare and elsewhere are (and came to be) quite determinate, however richly plural.

ESSAY 4

"New Historicism"

The phrase, "the new historicism," is fundamentally ambiguous. It takes its force from the contrast it establishes with something
else, "the old ———," but this is precisely where the ambiguity comes
in.[1] What is the contrasting term? If the stress is on the noun in the
phrase, then the stress is on the new *historicism* as opposed to the old
formalism. This is a perfectly understandable interpretation of the
phrase, and it probably accounts for much of the phrase's success as a
slogan. The opposition between formalism and historicism is immediately intelligible, and almost no one now willingly confesses to being a
formalist—which, as John Hollander, among others, would remind us,
is too bad (who will care about such things as meter?).[2] The New
Historicism thus nicely fits into a dialectical sequence with, and becomes
the successor of, the New Criticism. The sequence becomes purely
American, and deconstruction, with its complex and ambiguous political
and philosophical entanglements, fades from the scene almost entirely.

As initially formulated by Stephen Greenblatt, however, the point of
the phrase was not the new *historicism* but the *new* historicism.[3] The

1. See my remarks in Claude J. Summers and Ted-Larry Pebworth, eds., *"The Muses
Common-weale": Poetry and Politics in the Seventeenth Century,* (Columbia: University of
Missouri Press, 1988), 212–15.

2. In *The Happier Eden: The Politics of Marriage in the Stuart Epithalamium* (Ithaca:
Cornell University Press, 1990), 269, Heather Dubrow has called for a "new formalism."
It is a call, with full, ironic self-awareness, with which I am deeply sympathetic.

3. See Greenblatt's foreword to "The Forms of Power and the Power of Forms in the
Renaissance," special issue of *Genre* 15 (1982): 3–6.

contrast was not with formalism but with an older kind of historical scholarship, the new as opposed to the old historicism.[4] It is this version of the contrast that captures the intended polemic of the phrase, and it is this polemic that I wish here to explore and, to some extent, to deplore. New Historicism seems to me best as a certain kind of critical praxis, a praxis that does not need to be theorized to be effective, and that does not need to indulge in polemics of any kind.[5] One of the reasons Greenblatt prefers "cultural poetics" to "new historicism" is that it is not only wittier, more obscure, and more descriptive than the latter but also less polemical.[6] The profession, however, has fixed on "New Historicism" as the name of the "movement" with which Greenblatt is associated because in the current atmosphere polemics are strongly encouraged. Both the agonistic mode and what is taken to be theoretical self-consciousness are de rigueur.

Both these demands seem to me unfortunate. Polemics are certainly necessary at times, but they are only justified by being necessary; otherwise they produce more heat than light. More importantly, I do not believe that the demand that all praxes be fully and systematically theorized, especially by those who are performing the praxes, is a legitimate demand, or even a sensible one. Why should we expect a good literary or cultural critic—or even an outstanding one like Stephen Greenblatt—to be a competent philosopher as well? There is no evidence that this is a common conjunction. The demand for the conjunction is, I think, a legacy of Theory. I certainly believe that scholars, critics, and historians should perform their praxes as intelligently and reflectively as possible, but intelligent and even reflective performance of a praxis is not the same as having the ability to give an abstract and systematic account of the principles that actually or supposedly underlie that praxis. The demand for such an account seems to me both to mistake the kind of praxis that historically informed literary or cultural scholarship is— namely, a mixed bag of other praxes—and to imply a false belief about

4. For a useful and historically well-informed but somewhat inconclusive meditation on the propriety of the notion of a "new" historicism, see Brook Thomas, "The New Historicism and Other Old-fashioned Topics," in H. Aram Veeser, ed., *The New Historicism* (New York: Routledge, 1989), 182–203.

5. On the lack of necessity of new historical practice to attempt to theorize itself, and on some of the problems it falls into when its practitioners attempt to do so, see Stanley Fish, "The Young and the Restless," in Veeser, *New Historicism*, 306–8.

6. For "cultural poetics," see *Renaissance Self-Fashioning from More to Shakespeare* (Chicago: University of Chicago Press, 1980), 4–5 (hereafter *RSF*), and "Towards a Poetics of Culture," in Veeser, *New Historicism,* 1–14.

the general relation of praxes to philosophical accounts thereof. For quite a while (and to his credit), Greenblatt tried to resist the demand to "theorize" his practice, but his attempts at finally doing so ("The Circulation of Social Energy" and "Resonance and Wonder") do not seem to me to have produced work on a level with his praxis.[7] This is not surprising, and it is hard for me to imagine rationally wishing for more general essays of this sort from him rather than for more essays on particular cultural and literary phenomena.

There are real differences, I believe, between the newer and the older modes of historical interpretation, and I do not wish to stand with Fish in denying these differences. I will try to describe some of them, but I will also try to show that the practitioners of the new need not be, and indeed cannot coherently be, supercilious to the old, and that current practitioners of the older modes need not feel defensive and entrenched against the new. The modes need each other and answer different questions. I would argue that a strict pluralism is in order here: different questions demand different answers.

One of the striking features of the Introduction to *Renaissance Self-Fashioning,* the book that initiated the new historicism in literary studies, is how halfhearted its polemical moves are (*RSF,* 4–6). Greenblatt warns against three possibilities. The first is a kind of interpretation that "limits itself to the behavior of the author" and thereby risks losing "a sense of the larger networks of meaning in which both the author and his works participate." That this is a risk is obvious, but that a study that focuses on an author necessarily falls into it is not. And these "larger networks of meaning" are left spectacularly unexplicated. It is only through knowing the special place that Greenblatt gives to intercultural violence that the phrase becomes at all intelligible. As we shall see, Greenblatt's approach to historical figures is not strikingly different from "literary biography (in either a conventionally historical or a psychoanalytic mode)" (*RSF,* 4), and where it is so, it buys its difference at a very high price, the price, in fact, of falling into the second, opposite fault that Greenblatt diagnoses. This fault occurs when literature is viewed "exclusively as the expression of social rules and instructions" and there-

---

7. "The Circulation of Social Energy" appears as the first chapter of *Shakespearean Negotiations* (Berkeley and Los Angeles: University of California Press, 1988); "Resonance and Wonder" appears as the final chapter of *Learning to Curse: Essays in Early Modern Culture* (New York: Routledge, 1990). For a discussion of a key passage in "Resonance and Wonder," see pp. 77–78 below. For Greenblatt's reluctance to theorize his practice, see "Towards a Poetics of a Culture," 1.

fore risks "being absorbed entirely into an ideological superstructure." This absorption is seen as negative, but no counsel is given as to how to avoid it, especially if "the behavior of the author" is not given a privileged position (we will see later the importance of the oddly behavioristic phrasing here).

Greenblatt's third caveat is closer to the first. It is against a conception that sees literature as too detached from social codes and that therefore loses its grasp of "art's concrete functions in relation to individuals and to institutions, both of which shrink into an obligatory 'historical background' that adds little to our understanding." Again, it is not clear why such "shrinkage" is necessary. Art can be seen as having a certain distance from prevailing codes without being seen as totally detached from them. And why must "historical background" add little to our understanding? The potential problem surely lies in the metaphor of "background." We all know books and articles in which "Part I: Background" has little or no effect on "Part II: Interpretation," but it is not clear why "background" or contextualization needs to be done in this inert way. In the best works of older historical interpretation, the "background" is anything but inert (to take a work directly related to Greenblatt's "Shakespeare and the Exorcists," William Elton's *"King Lear" and the Gods* comes to mind).[8] The rejected critical modes seem to remain standing; only bad versions of them seem to be rejected. This is, I think, where things should be, but Greenblatt seems to want to establish more distance from these other modes than his own formulations actually allow.

The references to "art's concrete functions" and to "larger networks of meaning" are the phrases that are meant to do the work of suggesting a positive version of Greenblatt's own practice. Putting aside my conviction that the word "concrete" as an adjective always functions in a canting and mystificatory way, the phrase about art's functions points to an important premise of the new type of historical interpretation: art does certain "cultural work"; it participates in the cultural formations that it reflects, reflects on, and helps to create. The central idea is the Geertzian one of a "cultural system." Geertz's essay on "Art as a Cultural System" is perhaps the most important single text behind Greenblatt's new historicism in literary studies.[9] To do a "cultural poetics" is

8. William R. Elton, *"King Lear" and the Gods* (San Marino: The Huntington Library, 1966). For "Shakespeare and the Exorcists," see Essay 3, pp. 57–59 above.

9. See Clifford Geertz, *Local Knowledge: Further Essays in Interpretive Anthropology* (New York: Basic Books, 1983), 94–120.

to "read" a culture in something like the way in which the New Critics read a poem, as a thematically unified whole in which all of what are taken to be the salient parts are "organically" or functionally related.[10] Geertz thinks that there are central themes or modes for particular societies, themes that can be seen to pervade every social formation from high art and religion to the forms of market behavior (he sees his motivating questions as "What is *the general form* of a [particular culture's] life?" and "What exactly are the vehicles in which *that form* is embodied?").[11] Greenblatt accepts this view; he sees the dominant mode of Renaissance (and modern) culture as the theatricalization of the self, and the dominant imaginative and practical activity of that (our) culture as the demonization (and destruction) of the other.

In order to suggest the powers and limits of this kind of historicism, I will look in some detail at the opening chapters of *Renaissance Self-Fashioning*, the chapters on the giant and literally opposed figures of More and Tyndale. What makes Greenblatt's chapter on More so impressive is that it attempts to deal with More's whole corpus and career, from the early epigrams through the controversial and devotional works, with More the hunter of heretics as well as with More the humanist and More the martyr. Greenblatt's treatment of More looks, as I have already suggested, very much like "literary biography (in either a conventionally historical or psychoanalytic mode)." It follows the course of More's life and it presents this life in the context of a familiar historical and causal mode: "as intellectuals emerged from the Church into an independent lay status, they had to reconceive their relations to power and particularly to the increasing power of the royal courts" (36). Greenblatt even— quite correctly, I believe—faults Louis Marin for underestimating the degree of authorial control in *Utopia* (23–24).

What makes Greenblatt's presentation of More distinctive and puts it in touch with "larger networks of meaning" is the idea that More's "project" was a "life lived as histrionic improvisation." "Histrionic improvisation" becomes the key to More's life and works. Greenblatt presents a picture of More as a man who saw all his roles as roles, and who saw selfhood *as* role playing. This sounds awfully Wittgensteinian

10. For some useful background on the notion of "expressive causality" in Taine and in Romantic (Hegelian) historicism generally, see Frank Lentricchia, "Foucault's Legacy—A New Historicism?" in Veeser, *New Historicism*, 231–42.

11. "From the Native's Point of View: On the Nature of Anthropological Understanding," in *Local Knowledge*, 70 (emphasis mine).

and modern, and Greenblatt intends this. He sees More as an inventor and early practitioner of "that complex, self-conscious, theatrical accommodation to the world which we recognize as a characteristic mode of modern individuality" (37). This is a brilliant and rich scheme, but it is a scheme nonetheless. The problem, as always, lies in denial and hyperbole. The scheme beautifully captures More's commitment to role playing, but it is committed to denying two things: (1) More's sense of interiority, and (2) More's sense of role playing as a specific and important *skill* rather than an inevitable condition. This second point indicates where hyperbole and metaphysical inflation set in. Greenblatt twice takes a passage in which More emphasizes the importance of playing one's part correctly *if* one is going to take on a role as being about the necessity of role playing. The idea of role playing *as an option* drops away. Geertzian totalizing produces a whole set of misreadings.

For Greenblatt, *Utopia* is like Marx's *Economic and Philosophical Manuscripts* in propounding communism "less as a coherent economic program than as a weapon against certain tendencies in human nature" (37). This may be true—though I think More goes to some lengths to suggest that Utopian communism *is* "a coherent economic program"— but Greenblatt states this thesis only as a matter of degree ("less . . . than as"). The signs of special pleading—the discounting of the obvious and the "surface"—occur more clearly when Greenblatt specifies the "tendencies in human nature" that *Utopia* is attacking. He has to bypass the tendencies that More explicitly targets ("selfishness and pride, to be sure") in favor of the elimination of the histrionically conceived self, the focus of Greenblatt's scheme. Utopia has to be seen as a project for the elimination of selfhood, not for the elimination of economic acquisitiveness and need. So the reading of *Utopia* becomes familiarly dystopian. It must be the case that there is no real interiority in Utopia—no real freedom, no real pleasure, no real toleration of different beliefs. Both the nonasceticism of Utopia and its genuine allowance of diversity of beliefs and intellectual tastes have to be downplayed by Greenblatt. The author—here, More—has been "absorbed entirely into an ideological superstructure."

A moment in Greenblatt's reading of *Utopia* simultaneously demonstrates the power and the limits of his approach. The characterization of Utopia (the imagined society) as a shame-culture is a fresh and major insight generated by Greenblatt's anthropological awareness. Like all important literary insights, it makes many details of the text fall into place (especially about Utopian beliefs about the dead). But this insight itself becomes a limitation when it is totalized, and when the shame/guilt contrast is invoked in a schematic way. Utopia is seen not as an idealized classical society—the view that the best intellectual-historical treatment of the text suggests[12]—but rather as a vision of freedom from guilt (*RSF,* 52). Guilt becomes the absent center of the text, and the theme of relief from guilt provides an entirely adventitious connection to Luther (for whom freedom from guilt was indeed central).[13] Anthropological awareness here produces a scheme, shame *versus* guilt, that leads to a false historicization of a genuine and genuinely historicizable insight.

Both the connection to Luther and the question of interiority point us to Greenblatt's treatment of Tyndale and, therefore, of the Reformation. With regard to Tyndale, we can directly compare an "old historical" and a new historical approach, since much of the same material that Greenblatt treats in the second chapter of *Renaissance Self-Fashioning* is treated by C. S. Lewis in *English Literature in the Sixteenth Century*.[14] Religion in general is something of a problem for New Historicism, which tends—unlike Renaissance English culture—to have a radically secular focus. This is not a problem when the historical materials themselves are strongly secular, as in Frank Whigham's work on courtesy books, but it is a problem when the materials themselves are religious.[15] The tendency of New Historicism is to equate religion with ritual. Since the Reformation posits the centrality of an internal, non-ritual experience, it becomes a special difficulty for New Historicism. Practitioners of the mode tend to see the Reformation only as a process

12. See R. W. Chambers, *Thomas More* (London: Jonathan Cape, 1953).

13. Luther's account of conversion (his own and that of others) stressed freedom from anxiety and guilt. See "Preface to the Latin Writings" (1545) and *The Freedom of a Christian,* both in *Martin Luther: Selections from his Writings,* ed. John Dillenberger (Garden City, N.Y.: Doubleday, 1961), 11–12, 52–85.

14. C. S. Lewis, *English Literature in the Sixteenth Century, Excluding Drama* (Oxford: Clarendon Press, 1954). Hereafter cited as *ELSC*.

15. Frank Whigham, *Ambition and Privilege: The Social Tropes of Renaissance Courtesy Theory* (Berkeley and Los Angeles: University of California Press, 1984). It should be noted, however, that there are some interesting moments of scriptural awareness in, for instance, Castiglione's *Courtier* (see the moment in book 2 of *The Courtier* in which Cesare Gonzaga claims that Federico Fregoso "stole" his point about strategic humility from the gospels; Baldesar Castiglione, *The Book of the Courtier,* trans. Charles S. Singleton [New York: Doubleday, 1959], 113). It should also be noted that the courtesy tradition did interact on a large scale with the religious tradition; see Essay 5 below.

of desacramentalization.[16] They have great difficulty seeing in the Reformation any positive content. We have already noted Greenblatt's disposition to see Protestantism as Catholicism's "skeptical younger brother."[17] Greenblatt knows that the Reformation was not simply a negative movement, but he has a great deal of difficulty conveying any positive sense of it.

Greenblatt's treatment of Tyndale is based upon paradoxes. The first is "the violence of Tyndale's vision of obedience"; the second is Tyndale's (and the general early Protestant) "fetishism of Scripture" (*RSF*, 90, 94). Both of these paradoxes derive from the sixteenth-century materials *as described by the critic*; they are not produced through direct analysis of or quotation from the materials themselves. The function of both these formulations is to depict the early reformers as in a state of major tension and psychological stress. The Protestant rejection of so many of the long-standing institutions of European social life—confession, pilgrimages, prayers for the dead, etc.—seems to require this. Yet there is nothing necessarily paradoxical in Tyndale's rejection of a church that he considered idolatrous, nor in his simultaneous affirmation of a secular order that he believed to be divinely instituted and autonomous. The paradox of "violent obedience" is a way of psychologizing and pathologizing what seems (to Greenblatt) an almost unintelligible cultural radicalism.

The second paradox, the notion of the "fetishism of Scripture," is a partly anthropological and partly Freudian way of seeing Protestantism as continuous with the cultural processes that it attacks, as simply locating popular piety elsewhere—in the Book rather than the church, the relic, or the priest. There is an important truth here, but it is a purely behaviorist truth. It relies, as the early Protestants never did, on treating the Bible as an object in the world rather than as the conveyor of a message. The message was what was important, the content, not the physical existence of the book. A book is not simply an object. But, of course, it is an object, and Greenblatt is excellent on the newness of the object in question, the printed vernacular Bible, in the European world. As he says, "only those who had been brought up to think of the Bible as a Latin work could experience the full shock of the voice of God speaking to them in English from its pages" (96). This is a powerfully

---

16. For this tendency, see Steven Mullaney, *The Place of the Stage: License, Play, and Power in Renaissance England* (Chicago: University of Chicago Press, 1988), chap. 4.
17. See Essay 3 above, p. 58.

historical insight, as is the idea (shared by John Foxe, the martyrologist) that printing was the most essential agent of the Reformation. What is missing from the account is any clear notion of what the voice of God was taken by the first generation of printed vernacular Bible readers to be *saying*. Greenblatt's approach here is like that of a keenly observant anthropologist who does not speak the language of the community he is observing.[18]

Much of Greenblatt's account would have seemed straightforwardly correct to C. S. Lewis, especially the discussion of the influence of humanism on Tyndale (*RSF*, 102). This is a point, in fact, that Lewis made.[19] Yet the one and only mention of Lewis in Greenblatt's chapter is oddly and jarringly hostile. In comparing More's career, at least apparently bifurcated between the tolerant humanist and the hammer of Protestants, with Tyndale's apparently single-minded career, Greenblatt notes, in a rather shocked tone, that Lewis "can even speak of 'the beautiful, cheerful integration' of [Tyndale's] world."[20] Greenblatt goes on to acknowledge that what Lewis means by this phrase, which has nothing to do with Tyndale's biography, is true: "It is quite true," Greenblatt grudgingly concedes, "that Tyndale utterly denies the medieval distinction between religion and the secular life." This is the gesture that we have come to identify with special pleading. Something is being dismissed as merely true. But what Greenblatt concedes, the denial of the distinction between religion and the secular life, was Lewis's entire point. And it is a giant one. The distinction that, as Greenblatt acknowledges, Tyndale "utterly denies" was fundamental to the institutional life of the Middle Ages. It was the foundation of monasticism. The folding of the "religious" into the "secular" was, as Weber and others along with Lewis have seen, a profound intellectual and cultural revolution.[21] So Lewis was right to focus on the importance of the "cheerful integration" of the secular, the physical, and the spiritual in

---

18. Compare James Holstun's trenchant remarks on the way in which, in the vivid opening pages of *Discipline and Punish*, Foucault "stripped Damiens' story [the attempted assassination of Louis XV] down to pure spectacle, *giving no account at all of his reasons* for attacking the king." See "Ehud's Dagger: Patronage, Tyrannicide, and *Killing No Murder*," *Cultural Critique* 22 (Fall 1992): 100–101 (italics mine).

19. See *ELSC*, 31, 164, 186.

20. *RSF*, 112; *ELSC*, 190.

21. For the historical importance of the denial of this distinction, see *ELSC*, 163–64, 189–91; Max Weber, *The Protestant Ethic and the Spirit of Capitalism* (1904–5), trans. Talcott Parsons, foreword by R. H. Tawney (1930; pap. rpt., New York: Scribner's, 1958), especially chap. 3.

Tyndale's (Luther's) world view. Nevertheless, the phrase itself somehow acts, despite the specificity of its original context, as an irritant to
Greenblatt. "Cheerful integration" cannot in any way be associated with
Tyndale. "Nervous alliance" must be substituted for it. The suggestion
of harmony, of lack of tension, is unacceptable. Like New Criticism,
cultural poetics is a poetics of tension. The language of paradox must be
present in or relevant to any serious object of study.[22] Lewis is rejected—
here and in regard to Spenser—for asserting wholeheartedness and
affirmation. Even when Lewis is right he must be wrong.[23]

In a deep sense, Tyndale is unintelligible in Greenblatt's account.
Why would any sane person have wanted to be an early Protestant? After
quoting a number of passages on original sin from Tyndale, Greenblatt
notes, with obvious dutifulness, that "this vision of human loathsomeness is proclaimed, of course, only to be redeemed by the glad tidings"
(94). "Of course." Greenblatt (like Fish) is not interested in "glad
tidings," and he gives us no sense that we should be. The second half
of the dialectic falls away. The vision of loathsomeness matters; the "glad
tidings" do not. Greenblatt does follow Lewis in quoting Tyndale
speaking (in, it should be noted, a characteristic early Protestant way) of
laughing "from the low bottom of his heart," yet Greenblatt's only
comment on this remarkable joy is the dutifully learned one that it echoes
Luther's "famous *sola fide*" (*RSF,* 95).[24] Lewis, on the other hand, using
many of the same passages, provides a psychological and philosophically plausible account of what the conception of total depravity was
actually about—namely selfishness, egoism—and therefore of what the
experience of feeling freed from it might have been like (*ELSC,* 187–90).
It was freedom from niggling and anxious self-concern that produced
this laughter from the bottom of the heart. Lewis evokes "the gigantic

22. For "the language of paradox," see Cleanth Brooks, *The Well Wrought Urn:
Studies in the Structure of Poetry* (New York: Harcourt Brace, 1947), chap. 1.

23. It should be said that in the Spenser chapter of *RSF*, the rejection through partial
acceptance of "Lewis's brilliant account" is more fully argued (170). Nonetheless, the
harshness of his treatment of Lewis stands out sharply against Greenblatt's customary
generosity.

24. See "A Pathway to the Holy Scripture," in *Doctrinal Treatises and Introductions
to Different Portions of the Holy Scriptures by William Tyndale*, ed. Rev. Henry Walter
(Cambridge: Cambridge University Press, 1848), 9. *The Parable of the Wicked Mammon*
is Tyndale's ode to joy; see *Doctrinal Treatises*, 45–126. For other early Protestants,
especially Thomas Bilney, see E. G. Rupp, "The Cambridge Reformers," in *Studies in the
Making of the English Protestant Tradition* (Cambridge: Cambridge University Press,
1947), 15–46.

effort" of Tyndale's theology "to leave room for disinterestedness," and he historicizes this evocation by suggesting "the desperate need for such an effort" that existed in the late medieval context.

This kind of sympathetic recreation of a world view, within a fully historicized context, is indispensable. At the same time, one would not want to forget the importance to the Reformation of the printed book. Anthropological and sociological awareness are important modes of perception and of historicization—new questions are raised and new patterns come into view—but we cannot do without intellectual history, especially when intellectual history is conceived of as involving not just what various ideas mean but also what it meant, and felt like, to hold them. For Lewis, "we want, above all, to know what it felt like to be an early Protestant" (*ELSC*, 32). "We" may not "want" this "above all"—we may want to be more resistant and suspicious readers—but we, as historicizing scholars, cannot do history only from the outside. The new historicism needs the old to give history an existence *in persons;* the old history needs the new to give persons an existence in a complex and often violent social world. The agent's conception of an action is neither irrelevant to it on the one hand nor fully constitutive of it on the other. Unlike Geertz, Greenblatt is not worried about "what happens to *verstehen* when *einfühlen* disappears." What Greenblatt seeks to know about Renaissance people is not Geertz's "what the devil they think they are up to." Geertz is as suspicious of empathy as Greenblatt is, but Geertz allows it a non-sinister, even necessary role, and he is deeply concerned with means of attaining the inside or "experience-near" point of view.[25]

One of the theoretical charges that Greenblatt is most concerned to defend New Historicism against is the charge that, as a "historicism," it implies "the belief that processes are at work in history that man can do little to alter."[26] Greenblatt is as notably unsuccessful in this defense as he is defending against the related charge that his work encourages a sense of political helplessness.[27] In his comment on "processes . . . at work in history that man can do little to alter," Greenblatt objects to the ahistoricity of "man" (and, I suppose, its implicit sexism) by insisting

25. Geertz discusses the problem of empathy in "From the Native's Point of View," *Local Knowledge*, esp. 59 and 70. The quotations from Geertz in the previous sentence are from pp. 56 and 58 respectively of this essay. For Greenblatt's stunning identification of a certain concept of empathy with what "Shakespeare calls 'Iago,'" see *RSF*, 225ff.

26. See "Resonance and Wonder," in *Learning to Curse*, 164.

27. On the imagination of resistance to established power in Greenblatt's work, see Essay 6, n. 1 below.

that New Historicism studies "selves fashioned and acting according to the generative rules and conflicts of a given culture." But this gives us selves without giving us agents. Greenblatt attempts to remedy this and to assert the New Historicism's "insistence on agency" by stating that in the New Historicism "even inaction or extreme marginality *is understood to possess meaning* and therefore to imply intention."[28] But the issue of meaning is not the same as the issue of agency. All sorts of actions and events that are not the products of intention possess meaning. And to say that "to possess meaning" is "therefore to imply intention" short-circuits (in a familiar way borrowed from Stanley Fish and Walter Benn Michaels) the whole issue of intention on whose part.[29] What becomes clear in Greenblatt's defense of "new historicism" against a dictionary definition of "historicism" is that, as would be equally true of a structuralist or a New Critic, it is in fact *meanings rather than intentions* that Greenblatt is interested in. He is not interested in the intentions and experiences of individual persons. He returns to cultural systems, to studying the patterns rather than the experiences of meaning in the past. Greenblatt's culturally fashioned selves are curiously empty, like the behaviorists' black boxes. They are created and recreated from the outside. These selves do not quite seem to be persons, a term that is missing from Greenblatt's "insistence on agency"—though not, it must be said again, from Geertz's anthropology.[30]

Greenblatt's most extended treatment of the concept of a person is in his highly polemical, brief essay on "Psychoanalysis and Renaissance Culture."[31] He there uses a rather spectacular case of imposture as a model for Renaissance selfhood and treats Hobbes's definition of a person as capturing the meaning of personal identity in the period. Yet the case of the false Martin Guerre seems to be one of straightforward fraud; the major ambiguities in the situation center on Bertrande, the wife, rather than on the impostor. If the impostor had claimed that even though he was born Arnauld du Tilh, he had, through the marital and social relations he had established in his assumed identity, a better title to being "Martin Guerre" than did the man given the name at birth, the case would suit Greenblatt's view and might bear the weight that he places

---

28. "Resonance and Wonder," 164; emphasis mine.

29. See W. J. T. Mitchell, ed., *Against Theory* (Chicago: University of Chicago Press, 1985).

30. On the centrality of "the concept of person" to Geertz, see "From the Native's Point of View," 59 and 69.

31. *Learning to Curse*, 131–45.

on it. But Arnauld never took this route. The question at issue in the case, and in Hobbes's treatment, is legal identity.[32] That this question does not bring subjectivity to the fore does not indicate anything about the status of subjectivity and the experience of personal identity in the period. It would not do so today. What this essay reveals, in its almost conscious hyperboles, is the strength of Greenblatt's desire to see Renaissance persons as entirely other than ourselves, as not persons, in our sense, at all.

The new historicism in Stephen Greenblatt, like the old historicism in Rosemond Tuve, is worst when it is at its most polemical. That "empathy" can have a sinister dimension is one of the most remarkable and important things that Greenblatt has taught us. But it does not have only a sinister dimension. We cannot successfully do history (or live in the world) without it. It name is not only Iago.

32. See Natalie Zemon Davis, *The Return of Martin Guerre* (Cambridge: Harvard University Press, 1983). Davis returns to this case, and dissents from Greenblatt's view of it, in "On the Lame," *American Historical Review* 93 (1988): 572–603 (esp. 602).

PART TWO

Against Received Ideas

ESSAY 5

Impossible Worldliness

"Devout Humanism"

François de Sales is officially a saint from the early seventeenth century, and George Herbert is as close to being one (unof-
ficially) as the Church of England will allow. This is all well and good,
but from the point of view of intellectual and cultural history, the
problem with the special status of these writers is that their works tend
to be read with presuppositions about piety in mind, which is to say that
some of their works, especially directly moralistic ones, tend not to be
read in any strong sense at all. The aim of the following essay is to read
carefully two major texts by these writers (and some bits from John
Donne) that have been associated with the movement in early seventeenth-century France and England characterized as "devout humanism." The essay does not mean to uncover anything "hidden" in these
texts. Indeed, as I hope the first section of this book has made clear, I
have serious doubts about the necessity and desirability of seeking for
hidden or "below the surface" meanings. The reading that I intend to
do in this essay is precisely a reading of the surface of these texts, an
attempt to think hard about what these texts actually say—not about
what they might be construed in a general way to mean but what they
are truly saying. I want to take these texts as literally as possible at their
words, and to hold them fully accountable for these words.

My aim is not debunking but clarity. The class implications of the
texts, and of "devout humanism" in general, have been obscured or
downplayed by what commentators the texts have had. Christianity is
not simply a nose of wax. The difficulties, acknowledged or unacknowl-

edged (or in between), that the authors in question had in reconciling their social perspective with the teaching of the gospels are instructive for the way in which a dimension of radical critique can never be completely extinguished from a version of Christianity that is haunted to any degree by the gospels. Aside from determinedly literal reading, the mode of this essay might be called *Ideologiekritik*. The essay is certainly informed by the Marxist tradition, but I am happy to say that (as we shall see) some of the "Marxism" in the essay is actually derived from a seventeenth-century text, since the critic of devout humanism on whom I have most strongly relied is Blaise Pascal.

"Devout humanism" needs to be seen in the context of a larger picture. One of the great problems of late medieval and early modern spirituality in Western Europe was the religious status of ordinary Christians, of persons living in "the world," outside of monastic or religious orders. The *devotio moderna* and the popularization of Rhineland mysticism were responses to this problem—created by the increase in lay wealth and education—as was, in part, the Lollard movement in England.[1] At the beginning of the sixteenth century, Erasmus's exaltation of baptism as the essential Christian "vow" and "the holiest of ceremonies" was a sustained attempt to break down the barrier between the layman and the "religious."[2] Luther's baptismal doctrine of the priesthood of all believers asserted this position more powerfully ("we who have been baptized are all uniformly priests by virtue of that very fact") and provided a theological framework more coherent than Erasmus's for proclaiming the religious value of "worldly" activity.[3] Luther's revolution, according to Weber, was to declare the fulfillment of worldly duties "the highest form which the moral activity of the individual could assume."[4] Luther held, quite spectacularly, that "the common work of

1. See, for instance, Preserved Smith, *The Reformation in Europe* (1920; pap. rpt., New York: Collier, 1962), chap. 1; A. G. Dickens, *The English Reformation* (New York: Schocken, 1964), chaps. 1–2; Albert Hyma, *The "Devotio Moderna" or Christian Renaissance (1380–1520)*, 2d. ed. (Hamden, Conn.: Archon, 1965); and Steven Ozment, *The Age of Reform, 1250–1550* (New Haven: Yale University Press, 1980), chap. 5.

2. See *The Enchiridion of Erasmus*, trans. Raymond Himelick (Bloomington: Indiana University Press, 1963), 40, 116, and passim.

3. *The Babylonian Captivity [Pagan Servitude] of the Church*, in *Martin Luther: Selections from his Writings*, ed. John Dillenberger (Garden City, N.Y.: Doubleday, 1961), 345; see also pp. 311, 349, and, in the same volume, *An Appeal to the Ruling Class*, 407–12. Erasmus's Platonism works against a celebration of the ordinary and mundane (see chap. 14, "The Fifth Rule," of the *Enchiridion*, 101ff.).

4. Max Weber, *The Protestant Ethic and the Spirit of Capitalism* (1904–5), trans. Talcott Parsons, foreword by R. H. Tawney (1930; pap. rpt., New York: Scribner's, 1958),

a serving man or maid is more acceptable [to God] than all the fastings and other works of monks."[5]

The Puritan movement in England and America can be seen as continuing the anti-elitist note of Luther.[6] The Jesuits spearheaded the Roman church's attempt to recapture the laity as "religious." Unlike the Puritans, however, the Jesuits concentrated their efforts almost exclusively on the social elite, and it was out of this emphasis and the anti-ascetic strands within Loyola's teachings that the movement known primarily in France as "devout humanism" took its orientation.[7] Devout humanism might be described as a movement that set out to show Christianity to be fully possible within the bounds of ordinary and recognizable aristocratic life. Its class orientation is essential to it in both its Catholic and its Protestant forms, though this has mostly been obscured by commentators.[8] For the Catholics, "devout humanism" was a way of capturing the part of the laity that mattered, keeping the lay elite from either Protestantism or "libertinage."[9] For the English, it was a way of defusing the democratic and anti-elitist strains in Protestantism (and perhaps in the gospels).

The major text of "devout humanism" is François de Sales's *Introduction to the Devout Life* (first edition, 1609). Pascal's *Provincial Letters*, later in the century (first edition, 1656), is the great attack on both

---

80. Weber sharply distinguishes this position from what he calls "the liberal utilitarian compromise with the world at which the Jesuits arrived" (81).

5. *The Babylonian Captivity*, in *Luther: Selections*, Dillenberger, ed., 311.

6. See Weber, *Protestant Ethic*, chap. 4; R. H. Tawney, *Religion and the Rise of Capitalism* (1926; pap. rpt. New York: Mentor, 1954); and Christopher Hill, "The Industrious Sort of People," *Society and Puritanism in Pre-Revolutionary England* (New York: Schocken, 1967), 124–44. The distinctiveness of "Puritan" economic views has been seriously questioned by Charles H. George and Katherine George, *The Protestant Mind of the English Reformation, 1570–1640* (Princeton: Princeton University Press, 1961). They argue that the sermon literature of English Protestantism in general in the earlier seventeenth century incorporates "the most outgoing and positive view of work which exists in the Christian tradition" (143).

7. The phrase seems to have been coined by Henri Bremond in *Devout Humanism* (1914), trans. K. L. Montgomery, vol. 1 of *A Literary History of Religious Thought in France* (New York: Macmillan, 1928).

8. Bremond's presentation of the movement obfuscates its social elitism. The elitism is noted, in somewhat metaphysical form, in Paul Benichou, *Morales du grand siècle* (Paris: Gallimard, 1948), chap. 3, English translation by Elizabeth Hughes, *Man and Ethics* (New York: Doubleday, 1971); and is noted very clearly in A. W. S. Baird, *Studies in Pascal's Ethics* (The Hague: Martinus Nijhoff, 1975), chaps. 3–4.

9. For "libertinage," see Antoine Adam, *Les Libertins au XVIIe siècle* (Paris: Buchet-Chastel, 1964).

the Jesuit and the Salesian movements. George Herbert has been claimed for "devout humanism" in England, as has John Donne.[10] Donne's "A Litanie," together with some of his sermons, and Herbert's "The Church-porch" can plausibly be related to the aims and ideals of St. François's treatise. One of the things that I want to explore, especially in St. François and Herbert, is the peculiar mixture of ingenuousness and disingenuousness that the texts of this movement, from the seventeenth-century to its contemporary equivalents, seem necessarily to involve.[11] François de Sales's book is the most impressive and elaborate of the texts. It comes closest, at moments, to presenting a version of aristocratic behavior that actually seems to partake of fundamental Christian values. Herbert's poem is the crudest of the texts, and perhaps therefore gives us the most revealing picture of the aristocratic mentality (at least in England) in the early seventeenth century. The crudeness of the values of this early poem of Herbert's also perhaps helps explain some of his later revulsion against the attitudes that he there expressed and against some of the aims of "devout humanism."

In the ninth of the *Provincial Letters*, Pascal's Jesuit interlocutor notes that "men of the world are generally deterred from devotion by the strange ideas they have been led to form of it"; to counter this "strange idea," he especially praises Father Le Moine for drawing a "perfectly charming" picture of devotion in his work entitled *Devotion Made Easy*.[12] I had initially thought that this was parody. But it is not. The book exists, and as Bremond observes, Le Moine's treatise "does little

10. For Herbert, see Louis L. Martz, *The Poetry of Meditation: A Study of English Religious Literature of the Seventeenth Century*, rev. ed. (New Haven; Yale University Press, 1962), 249–59. For Donne, see Helen Gardner, ed., *John Donne: The Divine Poems*, rev. ed. (Oxford: Clarendon Press, 1956), xxvi. Neither Martz nor Gardner claim direct influence, though it seems that Martz would like to. Martz's distinctions between Jesuit and Salesian spirituality (*Poetry of Meditation*, 144–52) are plausible, but Martz overlooks the historical continuity between the two movements.

11. For some interesting reflections on a nineteenth-century version of a very similar problematic, see Haddon Willmer, "'Holy Worldliness' in Nineteenth-Century England," in Derek Baker, ed., *Sanctity and Secularity: The Church and the World* (New York: Harper and Row, 1973), 193–211. A twentieth-century American version of the movement can be recognized in Michael Novak's *Toward a Theology of the Corporation* (Washington, D.C.: American Enterprise Institute, 1981).

12. Blaise Pascal, *The Provincial Letters*, trans. Thomas M'Crie, in *Pensées and The Provincial Letters* (New York: Random House, Modern Library, 1941), 438; *Les Provinciales*, ed. with an introduction by Louis Cognet (Paris: Garnier, 1965), 158 (the plural in "strange ideas" is not in the original). Page references will hereafter be included parenthetically in the text, first to the translation, second to the original.

more than paraphrase some chapters of the *Introduction à la vie dé-vote*."[13] Devotion Made Easy—the fundamental premise of François de Sales' book is that "the way to heaven is not as difficult as the world makes it out to be."[14] The aim, as Pascal's Jesuit (following Le Moine) says, is to produce "genteel saints and well-bred devotees [*saints polis et . . . devots civilisés*]" (438; 159), Christian versions of the *honnête-homme*.[15] The devout life, for St. François, can happily include a re-markable range of normal aristocratic behavior: sports, banquets, parties, and balls (77; 65), as well as hunting and games of skill played for (nonexorbitant) stakes (208; 247). Cleanliness is seen, by virtue of a remarkable use of a passage in Isaiah, as "to a certain extent" (*en quelque façon*) next to godliness (192; 226), and St. François "would have devout people, whether men or women, always the best dressed in a group" (193; 227). The premiere courtly virtue, *sprezzatura*, (the appearance of) unaffectedness, is the key to proper social and Christian behavior: "If beauty is to have good grace, it should be unstudied [*negligée*]" (133; 143). The devout are not only to be the best dressed but also "the least pompous and affected." One can maintain the dignity due one's rank "without damage to humility" if this is done *negligem-ment* (134; 145). Unaffectedness also extends to the spiritual and emo-tional realm. One must speak of one's sufferings only "in a natural, true, and sincere way," and not exaggerate them in order to get sympathy (130; 137). This latter case, in which St. Paul becomes the perfect model of a gentleman, shows the way in which this perspective can offer something more than mere accommodation. The critique of affectation becomes a critique of "very subtle and refined ambition and vanity" (130; 137) in this diagnosis of unbecoming ostentation in suffering.

With similar sensitivity to the manipulation of (virtuous) appearances, the aristocratic ethos is at times subject to moral criticism in the *Intro-*

13. Bremond, *Devout Humanism*, 296. Bremond notes that "Port Royal, too prudent to attack the master, gladly delivered the disciple over to the scourge of Pascal."

14. St. Francis de Sales, *Introduction to the Devout Life*, trans. John K. Ryan (Garden City, N.Y.: Doubleday, Image Books, 1950), 68; *Introduction à la vie devote*, ed. Dom B. Mackey, vol. 3 of *Oeuvres de Saint François de Sales* (Annecy: Niérat, 1893), 53. Page references hereafter included parenthetically in the text, first to the translation, second to the original.

15. For a precise seventeenth-century formulation of the conception of the *honnête-homme*, see Chevalier de Méré, "De la vraïe honneteté," *Oeuvres Complétes* (Paris: Fernand Roches, 1930), 3: 69–84, esp. 70: *"si quelqu'un me demandoit en quoi consiste l'honnêteté, je dirois que ce n'est autre chose que d'exceller en tout ce qui regarde les agréments and les bienséances de la vie."* I am grateful to Philippe Desan for calling my attention to this text.

duction, yet the important point is that the drive toward accommodation keeps the criticism from being sustained. In speaking of the way in which everyone can take and keep his proper rank without damage to humility, St. François notes that his defense of this assertion might seem to pertain "to wisdom rather than [to] humility" (134; 145). He then, however, provides a brilliant critique of the sorts of strategic humility that Castiglione discusses. Castiglione's Federico recommends that the courtier modestly refuse favors and honors that are offered him, but do so "in such a way as to give the donor cause to press them upon him more urgently."[16] St. François speaks of humility as false when "we make a show of flying away and hiding ourselves so that people will run after us and seek us out," when "we pretend to want to be last in the company and to be seated at the foot of the table, but it is with a view toward moving more easily to the upper end" (135–36; 147). True humility is either hidden or, when expressed, sincere. Yet St. François cannot end the discussion at this point. The position that he has been developing is overly rigorous with regard to the ordinary interactions of polite social life. He goes on to add that while the devout person must (perhaps) not play the game himself, "sometimes good manners require us to offer precedence to those who will certainly refuse it," and he insists that "this is neither duplicity nor false humility" (136; 147). The same is true of employing "certain words of honor which do not seem to be strictly true," but which ordinary social decorum requires. It is certainly, says St. François, "not always advisable to say all that is true" (206; 244), and it is neither necessary nor desirable to be a fool for Christ's sake (138; 150). If certain great servants of God have pretended to be fools in order to render themselves more abject in the eyes of the world, "we must admire but not imitate them."

For François de Sales, sociability is the essence of charity. It even covers sins. In discussing games, St. François makes a clear distinction between games of skill and of chance, allowing games of skill and prohibiting those of chance (208–9; 247–48). Yet a few pages later, participation in games

16. Baldesar Castiglione, *The Book of the Courtier*, trans. Charles S. Singleton (New York: Doubleday, 1959), 113. In the dialogue, Cesare Gonzaga jokingly provides gospel ratification for Federico's strategic advice in Luke 14:8–10. These strategies, in Renaissance conduct as well as in the books on which the conduct was modeled (though not the *Introduction to the Devout Life*), have been penetratingly analyzed, by way of Burke, Bourdieu, and Goffman, in Frank Whigham, *Ambition and Privilege: The Social Tropes of Elizabethan Courtesy Theory* (Berkeley and Los Angeles: University of California Press, 1984).

of chance is said to be allowable "when prudence and discretion direct you to be agreeable," since "to be agreeable is part of charity, and makes indifferent things good and dangerous things permissible." Agreeableness even "removes harm from things in some way evil [*aucunement mauvaises*]" (212; 253). We are inevitably reminded of Pascal's discussion of the Jesuit relaxations of the conception of "proximate occasions of sins" (457–58; 181–82). St. François's appeal to the image of Ignatius Loyola at genteel card parties hardly removes the discomfort. For St. François, this image is of the same sort as that of St. Catherine of Siena "turning the spit" in her father's kitchen (214; 255). The difference in the nature and social meaning of the activities is irrelevant. François de Sales does not see Christian values as exerting any pressure on the class orientation of his text. Concern for reputation, one of the great aristocratic obsessions, is upheld because "good name is one of the bases of human society [*l'un des fondemens de la societé humaine*]" (143; 155). There is no conflict between humility and concern for one's honor. At times, St. François does seem to allow biblical testimony to threaten social norms, as when he speaks of St. Paul and David bearing shame in the service of God. "Nevertheless [*J'excepte neanmoins*]," St. François immediately adds, certain reproaches cannot be borne, and certain persons, "on whose reputations the edification of many others depends" need not bear reproaches at all (144; 160). Again, Christ and the biblical exemplars are to be followed, but "with prudence and discretion [*mais sagement et discretement*]" (145; 159).

Charity requires sociability, and sociability in turn requires full participation in and skillful management of the forms, fictions, and practices of polite society. *Eutrapelia*, "which we call pleasant conversation" (196; 231), is redeemed from its Pauline status as a vice and returned to its Aristotelian standing as a virtue.[17] The seemingly dour virtue of mortification is brilliantly adapted to the demands of social life. Building on the Ignatian conception of "indifference" as a form of humility, François de Sales goes further than Ignatius does in exalting "indifference" above renunciation.[18] With regard to food, St. François concedes

17. For Paul's condemnation of *eutrapelia*, see Ephesians 5:4, in George Ricker Berry, *The Interlinear Greek-English New Testament* (Grand Rapids: Zondervan, 1897), 508; for Aristotle's praise of *eutrapeloi*, see *Nicomachean Ethics*, 1128a10, ed. and trans. H. A. Rackham 1968 (Cambridge: Harvard University Press, Loeb Classical Library, 1932), 246.

18. For the conception of "indifference," see Ignatius's discussion of "Three Occasions when a Wise and Good Choice can be Made," in *The Spiritual Exercises of St. Ignatius,* trans. Anthony Mottola (New York: Doubleday, 1964), 85. There is some

that although "always to choose the worst" seems more austere, the truest kind of mortification is to eat without preference whatever is put before you, *even if you like it* (186; 219). In this way, we renounce our choice as well as our taste, since the austere-seeming form of mortification involves continuous assertions of will. The proper exercise of mortification, mortification through adaptability and acquiescence, "doesn't show in public, bothers no one, and is well-adapted to social life [*est uniquement propre pour la vie civile*]." One can be "mortified," in other words, by continually eating one's favorite food—as long as it is spontaneously served to one. At a moment like this, it is difficult to distinguish ingenuousness from disingenuousness in the text.

The conceptions of humility and mortification are sticking points for "devout humanism," requiring a series of delicate distinctions and adjustments. These adjustments are at times, as we have just seen, brilliantly made by François de Sales. But the gospel condemnations of wealth are particularly unsettling. St. François's way around this is to stress Jesus' praise of "the poor in spirit" (Matthew 5:3) and therefore to distinguish, again more sharply than Ignatius did, between spiritual and material poverty.[19] A whole chapter (3.14) is devoted to the claim that poverty *of spirit* can be observed in the midst of riches. You can possess riches without being spiritually hurt by them "if you merely keep them in your home and purse, and not in your heart" (162; 185); moreover, "you may take care to increase your wealth and resources" through just means (163–64; 187). For almsgiving, which is recommended, God will repay us "not only in the next world but even in this" (165; 189). One can be "poor in effect" through *any* experience of inconvenience, as when "our best clothes are in one place and we need them in another" or when (God forbid) "the wines in our cellar ferment and turn sour" (166; 190).

St. François tells us that St. Elizabeth, daughter of the King of Hungary, sometimes for recreation among her ladies "clothed herself like a poor woman, saying . . . 'If I were poor, I would dress in this manner,'" and thereby manifested poverty of spirit (as, presumably, did Marie Antoinette later). The ideal, which François de Sales is sure is fully possible, is to have "the advantages of riches for this world" together with "the merit of poverty" in the world to come (162; 185). It is just

---

ambivalence here. In the meditation on "The Three Classes of Men," the indifferent are the highest (p. 78), while in the discussion of "The Three Modes of Humility," the indifferent are second, behind the actively ascetic (82).

19. For Ignatius's use of this distinction, see *Spiritual Exercises*, 77.

this happy harmony that Pascal sought to disrupt. A. W. S. Baird cogently argues that the reason why casuistical arguments legitimizing
aristocratic pastimes are singled out so frequently in the *Provinciales* is
not merely because these represent the most vulnerable point in the
Jesuit armor but also "for the more basic reason" that, as Baird puts it,
"the aristocratic way of life requires more numerous and more serious
attenuations than any other" in the standard of Christian conduct.[20]

In the introduction to his study, Bremond mentions that if time and
space had allowed he "would fain have shown how among the Anglicans
of the first half of the seventeenth century was produced a temper analogous to French devout humanism."[21] Donne's "A Litanie" may well
have been one of those works which Bremond would have treated. As
I have already noted, Helen Gardner, citing Bremond, links the poem
to the movement.[22] In "A Litanie," Donne professes a heroic willingness
to endure life for God, stating, "Oh to some / Not to be Martyrs, is a
martydome" (lines 89–90). The poem seems to pray for a balanced view
of worldly splendor, to be saved "from thinking that great courts im-
mure / All, or no happinesse." The dramatic enjambment, however,
betrays the balance. "All" is clearly the greater temptation, and the rest
of the stanza is not devoted to finding a mean between two excesses, but
to the problem of *undervaluing* worldly (that is, courtly) delights. The
"or" clauses in the stanza become elaborative rather than antithetical as
Donne prays to be saved from thinking "that this earth / Is only for our
prison fram'd, / Or that thou art covetous / To them whom thou lov'st,
or," worst of all, "that they are maim'd / From reaching this worlds
sweet, who seek thee thus" (lines 129–34). The God of this poem is
emphatically not a "covetous," jealous God. He does not demand absolute honesty—"Good Lord," Donne prays, "teach us when / Wee may
not, and we may blinde unjust men" (lines 170–71)—and He does not
demand antisocial behavior.[23] A moment very close to St. François de
Sales in "A Litanie" is that in which, after stressing "our mutuall duties,"
Donne prays to be delivered "From indiscreet humilitie," which might
scandalize "the world" (lines 149–51). Discretion, not humility, is the

20. Baird, *Studies in Pascal's Ethics,* 42.

21. Bremond, *Devout Humanism,* xiii.

22. *Donne: The Divine Poems,* ed. Gardner, xxvi. I will cite "A Litanie" from this
edition.

23. If Helen Gardner is correct in seeing in the lines on blinding unjust men "a clear
reference to the bitter contemporary debate on 'equivocation,'" (*Divine Poems,* 90), then
these lines are a direct link to Jesuit moral casuistry.

commanding virtue. Donne returns to this perspective in some almost consciously disingenuous lines in "The First Anniversarie" in which the external manner of an action is given virtual priority over the motive of the action, since "Wicked is not much worse than indiscreet."[24]

Needless to say, the God of "A Litanie" also does not demand or privilege poverty. Donne insists that Christians are "to both waies [riches and poverty] free" (line 162). This is again close to Ignatian "indifference."[25] Donne sees the gospels as perfectly balanced on the matter of wealth. In direct colloquy with Christ, Donne concedes that "through thy poore birth . . . thou / Glorifiedst Povertie"; the next line, however, begins "And yet." Donne argues that "soone after" His birth, Jesus "riches didst allow, / By accepting Kings gifts" (lines 158–61). As in the stanza on "this worlds sweet," the balanced treatment falls away. Poverty is punitive or dangerous whereas plenty is seen as both "Gods image" and His "seale" (line 185). Moreover, kings are privileged. It is no accident that Jesus specifically accepted "*Kings* gifts" in the Epiphany. To allow "bold wits" (like the Donne of his own Satires?) to "jeast at Kings excesse" is seen to lead one easily "To'admit the like of majestie divine" (lines 223–24).[26] Arthur Marotti has argued that throughout "A Litanie" Donne "conflates spiritual and monarchical authority," and Marotti remarks that the defense of riches in the poem "looks suspiciously like an apology for the extravagance of James's court."[27]

Although Gardner approvingly associates "A Litanie" with "devout humanism," she nonetheless remains a bit troubled by what she calls its "rather exaggerated stress" on "the compatibility of the service of God with 'this worlds sweet.' "[28] Gardner offers some plausible biographical reasons why Donne may have fallen into such exaggeration in 1608, but John Carey has shown that Donne's position stays the same in his sermons (after his ordination in 1615).[29] In a characteristic moment, Donne assures his auditors in 1621 that "Salvation it selfe being so often presented to us in the names of Glory, and of Joy, we cannot thinke that

24. "The First Anniversarie," lines 329–38 (on "proportion") in *The Complete Poetry of John Donne*, ed. John T. Shawcross (New York: Doubleday, 1967).

25. See note 18 above.

26. For the radicalism of the Satires (written in the 1590s), see Essay 6 below. "A Litanie" was probably written in 1608; see *Divine Poems*, ed. Gardner, 81.

27. Arthur F. Marotti, *John Donne, Coterie Poet* (Madison: University of Wisconsin Press, 1986), 250.

28. *Divine Poems*, xxv.

29. John Carey, *John Donne: Life, Mind and Art* (New York: Oxford University Press, 1981), 113–14.

the way to that glory is a sordid life affected here, an obscure, a beggarly, a negligent abandoning of all wayes of preferment, or riches, or estimation in this World." A "sordid" beggarly life is seen as a life of affectation. "The glory of Heaven," Donne explains, "shines downe in these beames" of preferment, riches, estimation. Like St. François de Sales and Father Le Moine, Donne is concerned lest "men thinke, that the way to the joyes of Heaven, is a joylesse severenesse, a rigid austerity." Receiving is as holy as giving: "as God loves a cheerefull giver, so he loves a cheerefull taker."[30] In another sermon, Donne uses the conception of poverty in spirit just as St. François does. "This poverty," Donne explains, "is humility; it is not beggary," and so the key point emerges: "a rich man may have it" (6:303). Donne then develops the hint in "A Litanie" that poverty is more spiritually dangerous than wealth. Elsewhere Donne explains that the biblical injunction to seek God with a whole heart does not require material renunciation or, indeed, any sort of material ad-justment: "To seeke him with a whole heart, is not by honest industry, to seeke nothing else." God, Donne explains, "weares good cloathes, silk, and soft raiment, in his religious servants in Courts, as well as Cammels haire, in *John Baptist* in the Wildernesse"; God manifests Himself to man "as well in the splendor of Princes in Courts, as in the austerity of *John Baptist* in the Wildernesse" (9:328). Again, the glory of God shines down in the beams of silk, wealth, and preferment.

If Donne's version of "the devout life" is splendid and that of Fran-çois de Sales polished, what is striking about Herbert's "The Church-porch" is that it is hard to see it as offering any version of the "devout life." It is not concerned with the love or service of God at all, although it is concerned with Christian behavior (almsgiving, tithing, and church attendance) and with proper behavior in church (not flirting and, es-pecially, not making fun of the preacher, on which topic there are four stanzas).[31] There is no equivalent in "The Church-porch" to Donne's conception of "splendour" or to St. François's sustained attempt to transform sociability into a version of charity. Unlike St. François's *Introduction*, "The Church-porch" does not attempt either a critique or a transformation of the courtesy-book tradition. It merely places a

30. *The Sermons of John Donne*, ed. George R. Potter and Evelyn M. Simpson, 10 vols. (Berkeley and Los Angeles: University of California Press, 1957), 3:270 (further references cited in text).

31. Stanzas 72–75. All citations of "The Church-porch" and other writings of Herbert are from *The Works of George Herbert*, ed. F. E. Hutchinson, rev. ed. (Oxford: Clarendon Press, 1945). Hereafter cited as "Hutchinson."

distinct version of that tradition, unalloyed, in an overtly Christian framework.[32] The version of the courtesy tradition on which "The Church-porch" draws is that which, to borrow John Lievsay's distinction, addressed the *gentiluomo* rather than the *cortegiano*.[33] It is important to take note of Frank Whigham's reminder that both these figures were members of the privileged class of gentry, but the distinction nonetheless remains useful.[34] It helps us see that Herbert's poem is no more concerned with service of a prince than with service of God; its focus is not political but purely social. Like Bacon's *Essays*, the most popular "courtesy book" in Renaissance England, "The Church-porch" is a collection of "counsels, civil and moral."[35] Bacon makes clear in *The Advancement of Learning* that "civil" counsels are quite distinct from moral ones; they are entirely pragmatic.[36] Jacob Zeitlin has argued that Bacon goes beyond Machiavelli in his pragmatism, for where Machiavelli allowed the criterion of efficacy only to princes or states, Bacon, as Zeitlin says, "applies it to private persons in their quest for worldly success."[37] Herbert follows Bacon in this. In "The Church-porch," as in Bacon's *Essays*, "civil" rather than moral counsels are dominant, and since Herbert's perspective is more relentlessly on "private persons" than is Bacon's, it is no surprise that Herbert's poem is especially admiring of and

32. For a similar perspective on "The Church-porch," see Michael C. Schoenfeldt, *Prayer and Power: George Herbert and Renaissance Courtiership* (Chicago: University of Chicago Press, 1991), 5–6. While Schoenfeldt and I share a view of "The Church-porch," we differ in our senses of the relation of the bulk of the lyrics to this poem. For a discussion of these disagreements, and some reflections on their theoretical significance, see the appendix to this chapter, "Impossible Transcendence."

33. John Lievsay, *Stefano Guazzo and the English Renaissance, 1575–1675* (Chapel Hill: University of North Carolina Press, 1961). For Lievsay's view as requiring some modification to fit the English rather than the Italian sixteenth-century situation, see Daniel Javitch, "Rival Arts of Conduct in Elizabethan England: Guazzo's *Civile Conversation* and Castiglione's *Courtier*," *Yearbook of Italian Studies* 1 (1971): 178–98.

34. For his dismissal of the relevance of this distinction to Elizabethan and early Jacobean England (and his caveats about both Lievsay's and Javitch's reading of Guazzo), see Whigham, *Ambition and Privilege,* chap. 3, n. 12 and n. 29 (p. 214).

35. For the popularity of the Bacon's *Essays or Counsels, Civill and Morall,* see Whigham, *Ambition and Privilege,* 28, and the table of editions in chap. 1, n. 99 (p. 199).

36. For "Civil Knowledge" as distinct from moral, see the lengthy discussion in book 2 of *The Advancement of Learning,* in *Selected Writings of Francis Bacon,* ed. with an introduction by Hugh G. Dick (New York: Random House, Modern Library, 1955), 345–77. On the distinction between the civil and the moral counsels in the *Essays,* see Douglas Bush, *English Literature in the Earlier Seventeenth Century* (Oxford: Clarendon, 1962), 196–97, and, especially, Jacob Zeitlin, "The Development of Bacon's *Essays* and Montaigne," *Journal of English and Germanic Philology* 27 (1928): 496–512.

37. Zeitlin, "The Development of Bacon's *Essays* and Montaigne," 502.

concerned with what Bacon called the "small wares and petty points of cunning."[38]

The normal view of "The Church-porch" is that it is both moral and boring. Both of these claims are wrong (I do not, by the way, mean to suggest that if the poem were moral, it would be boring; my point is about the nature of the counsels in the poem, not about the quality of the writing). Attempts to read "The Church-porch" as moral have been notably unsuccessful. This points to a real weakness in much of the "old" historicism. Louis Martz connected Herbert with François de Sales and "*l'humanisme dévot*," but the social dimension of the movement is as invisible in Martz's treatment as it is in Bremond's. Martz has little to say about "The Church-porch," and what he does have to say about it is inaccurate in ways that are instructive. Naturally, he sees the poem as purely moral. It falls, he says, into three general divisions, reprehending in turn sins "related to individual conduct" (stanzas 1–34); "sins related to social behavior" (stanzas 35–62); and "sins related to specifically religious duties" (stanzas 63–77).[39] The central section of the poem, however, that on social behavior, is concerned not with sins but with strategies. And this section takes up five-sixths, not merely one-third, of the poem. By the fifth stanza, Herbert is already dealing with the perils of sociability. The opening of this stanza constitutes a striking and (in this poem) typical descent in level of discourse: from the high moral ground of stanzas two through four ("O what were man, might he himself displace") to "Drink not the third glasse." Despite Martz's neat scheme of sins, the high moral ground is virtually abandoned after stanzas two through four of the poem. The scheme of sins that Joseph Summers offers is more nuanced but equally inaccurate. Summers sees the poem as moving through the seven deadly sins, from lechery, "the least important," to "the greatest spiritual sins" of anger, envy, and pride.[40] This is, again, perfectly plausible, but the moral scale that Summers employs is nowhere endorsed or utilized by the poem. The

38. Bacon, "Of Cunning," in *Selected Writings*, 63. On Herbert and Bacon, see Joseph H. Summers, *George Herbert, His Religion and Art* (Cambridge: Harvard University Press, 1954), 195–97; Hutchinson, xl, n. 1; William A. Sessions, "Bacon, Herbert, and an Image of Chalk," in Claude J. Summers and Ted-Larry Pebworth, eds., *"Too Rich to Clothe the Sunne": Essays on George Herbert* (Pittsburgh: University of Pittsburgh Press, 1980), 165–78; and some suggestive comments throughout Arnold Stein, *George Herbert's Lyrics* (Baltimore: Johns Hopkins University Press, 1968), esp. 23 and 120.

39. *The Poetry of Meditation*, 291.

40. Joseph H. Summers, *The Heirs of Donne and Jonson* (New York: Oxford University Press, 1970), 90.

poem does not consider lust and drunkenness "least important." The attack on these sins is abrupt and passionate; in an earlier version stanza two began "Beware of Lust (startle not)."[41] The stanzas on drunkenness provide the most savage moment in the poem: "He that is drunken may his mother kill."[42] These opening stanzas are, in fact, the high points of the poem's moral counsels. The critiques of anger and envy in the poem are, as we shall see, anything but traditional (or boring). And the poem defends pride.

The trouble with envy, in "The Church-porch," is not that envy is a "spiritual sin" but that it implies self-deprecation. Toward "great persons"—persons, that is, holding positions of power—Herbert recommends using "respective [i.e., respectful] boldnesse," since "That temper gives them theirs, and yet *doth take / Nothing from thine*" (lines 253–56; emphasis supplied). Envying "great" persons is counterproductive: "thou mak'st thereby / Thy self the worse, and so the distance greater" (lines 259–60). Envy only increases "the distance" that one seeks to lessen. "Be not thine own worm," the next line begins. Canon Hutchinson rightly glosses this as "Do not disparage yourself and your qualities," and he rightly connects this to the advice Herbert gave to his younger brother Henry in a letter, a connection that helps date the original composition of "The Church-porch."[43] Amy Charles has convincingly redated this letter to 1614, making George Herbert a twenty-one-year-old who had just proceeded B.A. when he wrote it.[44] "Be proud," Herbert advised, "not with a foolish vaunting of yourself . . . but by setting a just price on your qualities." "It is the part of a poor spirit," Herbert continues, "to undervalue himself and blush." One would certainly not want to be poor in spirit and to "undervalue himself" and show shame. Aristotle would have agreed.[45] "The Church-porch" shares this view. Its ideal is Aristotelian rather than Pauline, proper pride rather than humility. One should "get substantiall worth" and then boldly show it forth. "Boldnesse guilds finely." "Solid braverie" is the

41. Hutchinson, 6. This version of stanza 2 is preserved in the "Williams manuscript" (see Hutchinson, lii-lvi).

42. The passion of these stanzas is evident in this startlingly Neronian example, a completely arbitrary instance of drunken behavior that the young George Herbert would have found especially appalling and perhaps, in some Freudian depth, appealing.

43. Hutchinson, 480. For the letter, see 365–66.

44. Amy M. Charles, *A Life of George Herbert* (Ithaca: Cornell University Press, 1977), 78, 82–84. Hutchinson had ascribed this letter to 1618.

45. For Aristotle on proper pride (magnanimity, *megalopsychia*) and inappropriate humility, see *Nicomachean Ethics*, 1123b-1125a, ed. Rackham, 212–27.

ideal (stanza 35), and it is important to read "braverie" here as meaning something like "fine stuff to be displayed."[46] The contrast is not with cowardice but with insubstantial "braverie," with "empty boldnesse." The use of boldness is again the topic (compare Bacon's bemused remarks on the virtually magical effects of boldness in "civil business").[47]

The world of "The Church-porch" is overwhelmingly the world of the *beau monde*, of what Guazzo called "civil conversation" among the gentry. Summers is on much firmer ground when he recognizes the elitism of the poem, its exclusive concern for the gentry rather than for either "simple parishioners" or universalized catechumens.[48] He correctly identifies the intended reader as "a worldly young man of the contemporary ruling class." The poem sees such persons as especially valuable: "Thou, whose sweet youth and early hopes *inhance / Thy rate and price, and mark thee for a treasure*" (lines 1–2). There is no irony here. The argument is that "Kneeling ne'er spoil'd silk stocking" (line 407). That silk stockings—a specific class privilege—might hurt devotion is not an issue that ever arises.[49] "Stay not for *th' other* pin" is the poem's "compromise" position (line 411; emphasis mine), a position very close to that of François de Sales.

The message of the poem to the gentry is, be proud and have ambition. The stanza on envying greatness changes course midway; it ends by commending envy (since it can serve as a spur to ambition [lines 261–3]). In the most impassioned moment in the poem, Herbert assumes a prophetic stance to rebuke the English gentry for lack of ambition. It is interesting to watch "sloth" in this stanza slip from its traditional standing as a deadly sin to its more relevant standing as a national disgrace; "sloth" seems to be a specification of generalized "sinne" in the first line,

46. See OED meaning 3: a ("splendour"); c ("an adornment, an embellishment"); and especially d ("a thing of beauty or interest, a thing to exhibit") and e ("a fine thing, a matter to boast or be proud of").

47. See "Of Boldness," in Bacon, *Selected Writings*, 32–34.

48. *The Heirs of Donne and Jonson*, 89. For the intended audience as "simple parishioners," see, *inter alia* , Valerie Carnes, "The Unity of George Herbert's *Temple*," *ELH* 35 (1968): 512. In *The Living Temple: George Herbert and Catechizing* (Berkeley and Los Angeles: University of California Press, 1978), Stanley Fish's insistence on the catechistical character of "The Church-porch" leads him to deny the class bias of the poem (p. 126) and to obfuscate the specific social dimension of many of its precepts. Again a scheme eliminates particular content, though here Fish's scheme, with its apparent historical basis, is closer to Tuve's "tradition" than to the purely abstract scheme of self-consumption. See Essays 1 and 3 above.

49. On who was entitled to wear silk stockings, see the chart in Whigham, *Ambition and Privilege*, 164–65.

but turns out to be (as the grammar perhaps more strongly suggests),
a different and more serious problem:

> O England! full of sinne, but most of sloth;
> Spit out thy flegme, and fill thy brest with glorie:
> Thy Gentrie bleats, as if thy native cloth
> Transfus'd a sheepishnesse into thy storie. (lines 91–94)[50]

The antidote to aristocratic "sheepishnesse" (brought on, it seems, by
the economic situation of the country) is education conceived as a spur
to ambition.[51] To reconcile Pauline with Aristotelian values, one stanza
offers the following advice: "Pitch thy behaviour low, thy projects
high; / So shalt thou *humble and magnanimous* be" (lines 331–32;
emphasis mine). It is clear, however, that "Sinke not in spirit" (line 333)
is a more important message than "Pitch thy behaviour low." Moreover,
"Pitch thy behaviour low, thy projects high" sounds like a formula for
hypocrisy, or more precisely, for a purely strategic humility, a humility
of "behaviour" familiar, as we have seen, in the courtesy tradition.[52] The
next stanza asserts that only "active and stirring spirits" can truly be said
to "live" (lines 341–42). "Humblenesse" is associated by both rhyme
and argument with "lethargicknesse" (lines 335–36). Glory is the goal.

The stress on glory is one of the poem's strategies: to present its moral
counsels as adventurous. "Dare to be true" (line 77); "Dare to" be
introspective and to spend some time alone (line 147).[53] The final stanza
begins, "In brief, acquit thee bravely; play the man" (line 457). The
stanzas on "respective boldnesse" suggest the poem's other and more
major strategy: to present morality as prudential. Swearing "gets thee
nothing" and can lose you everything (stanza 10); gambling is "a civil
gunpowder" (line 203). The prudential focus provides the link between

---

50. In line 91 here, "sloth" is either in apposition with "sinne," specifying a particular
kind of sin, or in opposition to it (sloth *versus* sin). Taking the line in isolation, the former
is almost certainly the proper (and traditional) reading, but in the stanza as a whole, the
second possibility emerges, since the issue of sin disappears and is replaced with that of
"sheepishnesse." It is no accident, I think, that being lamblike is strongly derided in this
poem.

51. Herbert apparently did not observe the "zeal for education" with which J. H.
Hexter has credited the English aristocracy; see "The Education of the Aristocracy in the
Renaissance," *Reappraisals in History*, pap. rpt. (New York: Harper and Row, 1963),
45–70, esp. 58, n. 1).

52. See p. 88 above on Castiglione and François de Sales.

53. On the relative rarity of voluntary solitude in the period, see for instance Anne
Ferry, *The 'Inward' Language: Sonnets of Wyatt, Sidney, Shakespeare, Donne* (Chicago:
University of Chicago Press, 1983), 47–55.

the moral and the civil counsels of the poem. A line like "Who keeps no guard upon himself, is slack" unites the types of counsel (line 139). Summers recognizes the prominence of prudential argument in the poem, rightly sees this prominence as determined by the intended audience, but then goes on to praise this prominence as demonstrating Herbert's knowledge of "the fact that moral persuasion is likely to be most effective when a speaker addresses an audience in its own language."[54] To say this is to ignore the equally pertinent "fact," insisted on by Pascal (among others), that moral teaching can aim to transform the values of its audience rather than merely to rely on them. Pascal denies that it is "part of a rule to bend in conformity to the subject which it was meant to regulate" (376; 78).[55] Despite its opening mention of turning delight "into a sacrifice" (line 6), "The Church-porch" does not aim to transform its audience morally. It is not clear, moreover, that the speaker of the poem, fully identical with the young George Herbert, believes that his audience needs to be morally transformed.[56] There is no indication in the poem that the values of its speaker are different from those of his audience—except, that is, insofar as he wants them to work harder and be more disciplined. The poem is certainly part of "the civilizing process" defined by Norbert Elias, but this is a modernizing process, not a Christianizing one.[57]

Self-interest is the only motive to which "The Church-porch" appeals. The George Herbert of 1614, already on the fast track at Cambridge, does not expect religious considerations to move his peers, and he does not attempt to give such considerations weight. His exhortation to the slothful gentry to educate their children concludes, "And if Gods image move thee not, let thine" (line 102). He is perfectly at ease with

54. *The Heirs of Donne and Jonson*, 99.

55. See also the opening of *Factum pour les Curés de Paris* on those who *"au lieu d'accomoder la vie des hommes aux préceptes et les règles de Jésus-Christ, ont enterpris d'accomoder les préceptes at les règles de Jésus-Christ aux intérêts, aux passions et aux plaisirs des hommes," Provinciales*, ed. Cognet, 406.

56. To "assume always that the speaker [of a poem] is someone other than the poet himself" (Lawrence Perrine, *Sound and Sense: An Introduction to Poetry*, 4th ed, [New York: Harcourt Brace, 1973], 22) seems to me the merest dogma. It also seems to me exactly wrong as a working assumption. I would assume that in general the speaker of the poem is identical with the historical author unless there is some good reason (as there certainly is in some cases) not to make this assumption. I have argued for this view in "John Donne Awry and Squint: The 'Holy Sonnets,' 1608–1610," *Modern Philology* 86 (1989): 357–84, and I employ the view again in Essay 6 below.

57. See Norbert Elias, *The Civilizing Process* (1939), trans. Edmund Jephcott (New York: Pantheon, 1978), 2 vols.

the priority of the second consideration over the first. Whatever weight religious concerns have in the poem is entirely derived from their analogy to earthly ones. In urging his reader (specifically male as well as aristocratic) to "Doe all things like a man, not sneakingly," Herbert instructs him to "Think the king sees thee still; for his King does" (line 122). In this line, the entire fearfulness of God derives from the connection that is asserted between the king's King and ours. "Think the king sees thee still" is the real message. God is merely a surrogate for imagining the king's omnipresence. In picturing conscience (or self-consciousness) as an extension or version of the kingly gaze, which is, in turn, modeled on a vision of God conceived as a king, Herbert is participating in the conflation of inner and outer theatricality, kingly and divine vision, that Jonathan Goldberg has identified in his remarks on the ideology of the royal gaze in this period.[58] A similar attempt to lend God something of the *mana* and magnetism of the king occurs toward the end of Herbert's poem. In urging church attendance on Sundays, Herbert asserts that "God then deals blessings." This, however, is not presented as a consideration that in itself will carry much weight. To give the point force, Herbert asks: "If a king did so, / Who would not haste, nay give, to see the show?" (lines 389–90). This speaker cannot imagine a person who would not "haste, nay give" to be where a king deals blessings. He has nothing to say to those who take no care for the morrow: "Who say, I care not, those I give for lost; / And to instruct them will not quit the cost" (lines 347–48). Summers assures us that Herbert is here merely acknowledging that those who "say, I care not" would, as Summers rather nervously puts it, "at any rate, be unavailable to prudential argument."[59] This does not, however, account for Herbert's obvious scorn for such "unavailable" persons—"those I give for lost; / And to instruct them will not quit the cost."

As the vision of God dealing blessings suggests, the religion in "The Church-porch" is a matter of straightforward spiritual commercialism. One goes to church and behaves in a Christian manner in order to get something. The conception of perceiving "God's image" in persons as a possible factor in motivating one's behavior toward them recurs in the context of almsgiving—"man is Gods image; but a poore man is / Christs stamp to boot" (lines 379–80)—but the true motive for almsgiv-

---

58. See *James I and the Politics of Literature* (Baltimore: Hopkins University Press, 1983), 147–63, esp. 149.
59. *The Heirs of Donne and Jonson*, 90.

ing is prudential: "Think heav'n a better bargain than to give / Onely thy single market-money for it" (lines 374–75). Summers, as an apologist for the poem (surely it cannot be so crude), finds these lines especially troubling. He finds the appeal to self-interest so naked in them that "a reader may misunderstand." Summers hastens to assure us that Herbert "does not mean to imply that *he* thinks salvation is something we can purchase."[60] But the poem is quite insistent. Why must the critic defend it from itself? Even less in "The Church-porch" than in *Introduction to the Devout Life* is almsgiving an act of spontaneous charity.[61] Almsgiving is a matter of calculation in the short term—"In Almes regard thy means, and others merit"—and prudence in the long—"Let thy almes go before, and keep heav'ns gate / Open for thee; or both may come too late" (lines 373; 383–84).[62]

Alms open heaven's gate. The reader can hardly misunderstand. It is only the critic who is reluctant. There is no subtlety or irony to be missed. What the poem means is what it says. The accounting mentality is the key to success—in both the spiritual and the material realms. In the spiritual realm, "since we shall be / Most surely judg'd, make thy accounts agree" (lines 455–6); in the worldly realm,

Slight not the smallest losse, whether it be
In love or honour: take account of all;
Shine like the sunne in every corner; see
Whether thy stock of credit swell, or fall. (lines 343–346)

To "Shine like the sunne" does not mean to be sublimely undifferentiating in one's outpourings (as in Matthew 5:45 and various Neoplatonic traditions) but to be, as is always necessary with regard to points of honor, constantly and unremittingly watchful.[63] To "care not" about

---

60. *The Heirs of Donne and Jonson*, 92 (emphasis in original).

61. For François de Sales on almsgiving in the *Introduction*, see p. 90 above.

62. I find it hard to believe that young Herbert seriously intended the advice that one ought to impoverish oneself in giving to a "good poore man" (lines 378–79), but it is interesting that he felt the pressure toward such a gesture of traditional saintliness, however hedged about with considerations of worthiness.

63. On watchfulness and honor, see Pierre Bourdieu's "The Sentiment of Honour in Kabyle Society," in J. G. Peristiany, ed., *Honour and Shame: The Values of Mediterranean Society* (Chicago: University of Chicago Press, 1966), 208–11. On "outpouring" in Neoplatonic tradition, see Arthur O. Lovejoy, *The Great Chain of Being: A Study of the History of an Idea* (1936; rpt., New York: Harper and Row, 1960), 61–66; for the New Testament conception, see Anders Nygren, *Agape and Eros*, trans. Philip S. Watson (1953; rpt., New York: Harper and Row, 1969), 77–78.

one's "stock" is as inadvisable in the spiritual as in the material realm. "See / Whether thy stock of credit swell, or fall" applies equally well in both realms. This language of stock and accounting might seem more mercantile than aristocratic, but as Derek Hirst has reminded us, we must, with regard to England especially, resist "any simplistic distinction between 'feudal' and 'capitalist,'" since in England the nobility was not barred from engaging in trade and aristocrats were among the kingdom's greatest capitalists.[64]

As Herbert's economic metaphors suggest—"Think heav'n a better bargain"; "make thy accounts agree"—the ideal in social behavior is to get maximal returns from minimal outlays. Two of the three stanzas on friendship in "The Church-porch" are concerned (regarding suretyship) with placing proper limits on what one ought to do for a friend.[65] Prudence and calculation are at the heart of the poem. This is, inter-estingly, more true of its social than its strictly economic thinking. About wealth and monetary accumulation, the poem is ambivalent. In stanzas 18 and 19, it uses a Stoic critique of wealth in a way similar to that in which Donne and François de Sales make use of the gospels: poverty and wealth are both redefined; contentment becomes true wealth. This would seem to lead to a rejection of material wealth, but Stoic "contentment" produces a state of freedom from need, which allows actual wealth to be treated as abundance rather than excess ("If thy sonne can make ten pound his measure, / Then all thou addest may be call'd his treasure [lines 113–14]). The praise of the quiet mind is divorced from that of the mean estate. The stanzas on thrift and accumulation (26–29) are very nervous about the evils of hoarding. "Surely use alone / Makes money not a

64. Derek Hirst, *Authority and Conflict: England, 1603–1658* (Cambridge: Harvard University Press, 1986), 12.

65. As in Bacon's *Essays*, the treatment of friendship in Herbert's poem is both idealistic—"Thy friend put in thy bosome"—and cynical: "the way of friendship's gone" (lines 271–75). On Bacon's essay on friendship, see Essay 2, pp. 33–36 above. In *The Merchant of Venice*, standing surety for a friend is seen, as in "The Church-porch," as dangerous, though it is (arguably) less warily treated. In discussing the virtue of "hu-manity" (observing "the common courtesies of life in our dealings with our fellow men") in *Christian Doctrine* (2.11), Milton warns that "humanity" can be "of a rash and ill-advised kind," and his example of this excess (citing Proverbs 6:1–2) is being "too eager to stand surety for someone"; *The Complete Prose Works of John Milton*, vol 6, ed. Maurice Kelley (New Haven: Yale University Press, 1973), 745. Lacey Baldwin Smith has argued for the importance of the biblical "wisdom literature," especially Proverbs and Ecclesiastes, in shaping the Tudor mentality of suspicion; see *Treason in Tudor England: Politics and Paranoia* (Princeton: Princeton University Press, 1986), 102–5. A full study of suretyship in the period is strongly to be desired.

contemptible stone" (lines 154–55), so that the "scraping dame" is seen, paradoxically, as "wasteful" (line 173). Here Herbert seems to want to distinguish aristocratic from bourgeois behavior, but early capitalism would certainly have shared this emphasis on the *use* of money.[66]

With regard to social rather than strictly economic life, hoarding, calculation, and thrift are entirely approved in "The Church-porch." Individual survival and gain are the only concerns. The poem contains no vision of community. "At Court," one of Herbert's *Outlandish Proverbs* asserts or observes, "every one for himselfe."[67] This seems to be true of social life in general. The Herbert of "The Church-porch" very much shared the view that Smith has argued was normative in the Tudor period: social interactions are fraught with danger.[68] In a scene of drunkenness, one is to remember that "All in a shipwrack shift their severall [i.e. individual] way" (line 44). One must look out for oneself. "Who keeps no guard upon himself, is slack"; "lose not thy self"—these are the watchwords. As Herbert says elsewhere, "Life is a businesse, not good cheer; / Ever in warres."[69] Overmuch laughter is dangerous; there is as great a fear in the poem of laughing as of being an object of laughter. Wit is distrusted as "an unruly engine, wildly striking / Sometimes a friend, sometimes the engineer" (lines 241–42). In recommending solemnity, the image of social life as war is made explicit:

A sad wise valour is the brave complexion,
That leads the van, and swallows up the cities.

66. Marx notes that "capital becomes capital only through circulation" in *Grundrisse: Foundations of the Critique of Political Economy*, trans. Martin Nicolaus (Harmondsworth, Eng.: Penguin, 1973), 520. For Foucault, "exchange" is central to the "episteme" of the "Classical age" in early modern Europe; see Michel Foucault, *The Order of Things: An Archeology of the Human Sciences*, trans. Alan Sheridan (New York: Random House, 1970), chap. 6, esp. part 3, "Mercantilism".

67. Number 795, Hutchinson, 347. See also number 874: "So many men in Court and so many strangers." On the authorship and provenance of the *Outlandish Proverbs*, see Hutchinson, 568–73.

68. Smith, *Treason in Tudor England*, chap. 2. Smith probably overstates his case in calling this view of social life "paranoid," but Whigham's picture of court life is similar; see *Ambition and Privilege*, esp. 137–47. For a judicious review of Smith's book, see Christopher Hill, "Under the Tudor Bed," *New York Review of Books* 34 (May 7, 1987): 36–38.

69. "Employment" (II), lines 16–17, Hutchinson, 79. The rest of this stanza, contrasting the vulgarly undiscriminating nature of the sun with the elegant calculation of the stars, which "Watch an advantage to appeare," are also reminiscent of "The Church-porch." On this imagistic context, see n. 63 above. Since "Employment" (II) appears in the "Williams manuscript" (see n. 41 above), there is a chance that it is early.

> The gigler is a milk-maid, whom infection
> Or a fir'd beacon frighteth from his ditties. (lines 247–50)

Seriousness is manly and leads to total victory; to be a "gigler" is to be weak-minded, cowardly, lower-class, countrified, and effeminate.[70]

The long section on conversation (stanzas 49–54) is particularly revealing. The rhetoric is that of courtesy (being considerate; avoiding boorishness), but the imagery is pure capitalist strategy. In conversation,

> Entice all neatly to what they know best,
> . . . .
>   Steal from his treasure
> What to ask further. Doubts well rais'd do lock
> The speaker to thee, and preserve thy stock. (lines 295; 299–300)

The piece of advice that begins next stanza combines the military with the capitalist imagery: "If thou be Master-gunner" in a conversation, "spend not all / That thou canst say at once; but husband it." One must never be "lavish" (line 304), and one must never lose control. As another master of civil counsel suggests, "Give every man thine ear, but few thy voice; / Take each man's censure, but reserve thy judgment."[71] Above all, always be calm. The stanzas on calmness bear careful examination. In a discussion of autonomy as a mode of social power, Richard Sennett has noted that "keeping calm in the face of someone else's anger is always a way to stay in control of a conflict."[72] Herbert certainly knew this. The first stanza on calmness in "The Church-porch" begins with an other-directed consideration ("fiercenesse makes / Errour a fault, and truth discourtesie") but immediately shifts from "Don't offend others" to "Don't be offended by others": "Why should I feel another mans mistakes / More then his sicknesses or povertie?" (lines 309–10).

These are remarkable lines. They open a window into the world of "The Church-porch." They accept quite casually a world in which persons do not take to heart the sickness or poverty of others. The

---

70. I am not certain of the meaning of "infection" in these lines. Could it be the rumor of plague?

71. The still widespread critical perception of Polonius as a fool and windbag fails to come to terms with the content of his precepts. It also fails to come to terms with their social dimension. Polonius's precepts are *a courtier's* advice to his son, a very successful courtier's advice. For relevant comparisons, see the texts gathered in Louis B. Wright, *Advice to a Son: Precepts of Lord Burghley, Sir Walter Raleigh and Frances Osborne* (Ithaca: Cornell University Press, 1962).

72. Richard Sennett, *Authority* (New York: Random House, 1981), 102.

argument of the lines depends on the premise that we do not "feel" these things. To be moved by another's *mistakes* would be inconsistent. This is truly "the economy of the closed heart," in which the ideal is to be unmoved by any other: "moving others," but oneself "as stone, / Unmoved, cold, and to temptation slow."[73] Herbert's counsel in these lines, however, is so directly contradictory of the social ethic of the gospels that Herbert is constrained to note that "In love I should" (feel other men's "sicknesses or povertie"). He immediately, however, dismisses the relevance of love to the issue ("but anger is not love") and substitutes another criterion—"Nor wisdome neither" (we recall François de Sales's problem with the relation between "wisdom" and humility). "Wisdom," not love, is the guiding ideal. The second stanza on calmness clarifies the nature of this wisdom. It argues entirely in terms of "advantage":

> Calmnesse is great advantage: he that lets
> Another chafe, may warm him at his fire,
> Mark all his wandrings, and enjoy his frets;
> As cunning fencers suffer heat to tire. (lines 313–16)

The angry person is viewed from an immense (emotional) distance. He is a kind of freak, a spectacle, foolishly expending rather than preserving his energy. Fencing was apparently the standard Renaissance model of an activity in which, as Donne says, "Passion layes a man as open as unskilfulnesse."[74] "Lord, what fools," is Herbert's perspective on the angry person. But, as is the case with Puck's exclamation, the context here is not genial. The last line of the quatrain recalls us to the issue of "advantage." Manipulation as well as sardonic enjoyment is at work here. The viewpoint is practical, not aesthetic (if "enjoy his frets" has a musical secondary meaning, the aesthetic and the practical viewpoints merge). Coolness is part of "cunning," and cunning in social relations is the ideal. Passion is a form of unskillfulness.

"Cunning" is always positive in "The Church-porch." The term recurs after two stanzas in which Herbert recommends constant calculation: of gains ("Let thy minde still be bent, still plotting where, / And

73. Shakespeare, Sonnet 94. On the complex and bitter ironies of this sonnet in praise of coldness, capitalistic ownership, and aristocratic *hauteur*, see William Empson, *Some Versions of Pastoral* (1952; pap. rpt., New York: New Directions, 1960), chap. 3; and Edward Hubler, "The Economy of the Closed Heart," *The Sense of Shakespeare's Sonnets* (1952; pap. rpt., New York: Hill and Wang, 1962), 95–109.

74. John Donne, *Biathanatos* (New York: The Facsimile Text Society, 1930), 179.

when, and how the businesse may be done" [lines 337–38], and of losses ("Slight not the smallest losse. . . ." [line 343]). In this context of continual "plotting," carefulness, and scorn for those who "care not," Herbert issues a final precept on social interaction. It is suprisingly democratic, seeming to work against rather than with his audience's prejudices: "Scorn no mans love, though of a mean degree" (line 349).[75] The explanation for not exercising one's normal scorn for those "of mean degree" seems to be that love has an extraordinary social viability; it climbs the social scale: "Love is a present for a mightie king." The next lines continue the topic of how one, as a person of some status, is to relate to those "of a mean degree," but the emphasis now shifts from not scorning love to not causing hatred. This is Machiavelli's emphasis (in chapter 17 of *The Prince*, Machiavelli argues that while it is not crucial for the prince to be loved, it is crucial that he not be hated).[76] The argument becomes straightforwardly prudential: "Much lesse make any one thy enemie./ As gunnes destroy, so may a little sling" (lines 351– 52). This, however, is too purely monitory, and it entirely forgets the issue of love from—never for—those of mean degree. The final couplet perfectly integrates the recognition of love into the framework of pru-dential calculation: "The cunning workman never doth refuse / The meanest tool, that he may chance to use." Love makes men serviceable.[77] The ideal is the cool, flexible, and socially uninhibited opportunist; excessive snobbery would limit one's potential "tools." These lines have been used to illustrate Herbert's attitude toward the materials of his art, and their very successful use as such is a striking instance of the tendency of formalist criticism to idealize and depoliticize literary works.[78] Crafts-manship here, however, is the vehicle, not the tenor. When we restore the lines to their original and primary social context, we can see them as truly meriting a share in Blake's general comment on Bacon's *Essays*:

75. It is semantically and syntactically possible to read "though of a mean degree" as modifying "love" rather than man, but I believe that this reading is contextually unsup-ported. The rest of the stanza clearly refers to *persons* "of mean degree."

76. Machiavelli, *The Prince: A Bilingual Edition*, trans. and ed. Mark Musa (New York: St. Martin's, 1964), 136–43. See p. 94 above for "The Church-porch" following Bacon in extending the scope of Machiavelli's perspective.

77. George Ryley's gloss is accurate (though interestingly substituting "respect" for love): "Value ye respect of ye meanest. for you know not whom you may have occasion to use." "Mr. Herbert's Temple & Church Militant Explained & Improved . . . by George Ryley: A Critical Edition," ed. John Martin Heissler (Ph.D. diss., 1960), 27.

78. See, *inter alia*, Stein, *Herbert's Lyrics*, 21.

"Good Advice for Satans Kingdom."[79] The cunning social craftsman will make apt use of any human tool. One never knows when a willing peasant will come in handy.

I have already endorsed the view that "The Church-porch" is an early poem of Herbert's. It seems likely that the extreme sensitivity to and revulsion from prudential and self-enhancing considerations that, as I have argued elsewhere, many of the lyrics demonstrate can be related to the prominence of such considerations in this poem and in the life that this poem reflects and manifests.[80] That the young George Herbert was a man on the make both socially and politically is no secret. At the time around 1614 when "The Church-porch" was probably initially composed, and for at least a number of years thereafter, Herbert continued to believe, as he said in a letter of 1619, that worldly and spiritual ambition "may very well be joined."[81] From this perspective, we can perhaps see why, despite the architectural metaphor, there is no easy transition from the porch to "The Church," why, as Stanley Fish has argued, the poem that directly precedes "The Church" makes the transition from porch to main structure a mysterious and very much less than straightforward matter.[82] Herbert can be seen to have transcended the spiritual com-

---

79. Blake set this comment on Bacon's title page; *The Poetry and Prose of William Blake*, ed. David V. Erdman (New York: Doubleday, 1965), 609.

80. For the argument about Herbert's sensitivity to such considerations in the major lyrics, see Richard Strier, *Love Known: Theology and Experience in George Herbert's Poetry* (Chicago: University of Chicago Press, 1983), esp. chaps. 3 and 4.

81. The quotation comes from Herbert's letter to his stepfather, Sir John Danvers, in October 1619, in which Herbert defends his vigorous pursuit of the Cambridge Oratorship, a position with many perquisites and "Gaynesses, which will please a young man well" (previous letter), against Danvers's suggestion that the Oratorship "being civil may divert [Herbert] too much from Divinity" (Hutchinson, 369–70). Hutchinson certainly seems justified in calling this reply "too facile" (xxviii). Herbert does manifest some nervousness in adding, after the assertion that the Oratorship "hath no such earthiness in it, but it may very well be joined with Heaven," the afterthought, "or *if it had to others*, yet to me it should not" (emphasis mine). This exemption of the self from a recognized spiritual danger is hardly reassuring.

82. See Fish, *The Living Temple*, 128–31. Although I strongly agree with Fish about the mysteriousness and sense of peril in "Superliminare," I do not agree with Fish's view that the crucial qualifying phrase, "at his peril," refers indiscriminately to all three moral types mentioned in the poem (the profane, the pure, and those who groan "to be so," i.e. pure). The profane, I would argue, are simply forbidden to enter ("come not here"); the address to them is finished in the first line, which ends with a full stop. The other two categories, the "holy, pure, and clear" and those who groan "to be so," are allowed to enter the perilous ground. The poem, in other words, *does* distinguish between the profane and the others. Fish, as always, wishes to deny distinctions (see Essay 2 above). Yet the

mercialism of "The Church-porch" through a thorough apprehension of Reformation theology, which was precisely targeted at such an attitude. The "freedom of a Christian" that Luther proclaimed was precisely freedom from this attitude. "I fear," said Luther at the moment of the Reformation, "that in all [our works] we seek only our profit, thinking that through them our sins are purged away." He warned his readers that good works are not to be done *"in order to obtain some benefit, whether temporal or eternal."*[83]

For the claim that Herbert also transcended the disingenuousness with regard to wealth and worldly position that seems intrinsic to "devout humanism," something like documentary evidence can be presented. How much weight one will give to such evidence will depend on one's view on a number of very general matters. Since my general approach allows me to use anything that comes to hand and to consider taking seriously explicit authorial statements (though not to be obliged by these), I have no compunctions. Seeing no good reason not to do so, and good reasons for doing so, I am inclined to give this evidence weight, to take it seriously as evidence.

In writing to his mother "in her sickness" and low spirits in 1622, Herbert classifies "afflictions" as being either of Estate, Body, or Mind. He immediately then dismisses afflictions of Estate with reference to the biblical injunctions against wealth. After doing this, however, he stops to consider the normal devout (and not so devout) humanist response to these injunctions: "But perhaps being above the Common people, our Credit and estimation calls on us to live in a more splendid fashion?"[84] This is the normal justification for ecclesiastical (and princely) splendor.[85] It comes, I think, as a great breath of moral and religious clarity, of true

---

poem does indeed insist on the perilousness of entering even for the two groups who are invited. Fish's reading of the grammar is dubious and typically tendentious. His point, however, about the way the poem problematizes the movement from "The Church-porch" to "The Church" is well taken. The presence of "Superliminare" perhaps helps resolve a problem that arises if my view of the relation of "The Church-porch" to the major lyrics is correct: why did Herbert retain "The Church-porch," in somewhat revised form, in *The Temple?* The more the discontinuity, the better for my view.

83. *The Freedom of a Christian,* in *Luther: Selections,* Dillenberger, ed., 79; emphasis added. The depth of Herbert's commitment to and grasp of Reformation theology, especially as Luther formulated and understood it, is the major argument of Strier, *Love Known.*

84. Hutchinson, 373.

85. See, for instance, Richard Hooker, *Of the Laws of Ecclesiastical Polity, Bks. VI-VIII,* ed. P. G. Stanwood (Cambridge: Harvard University Press, 1981), 7:xix-xxi.

ingenuousness, when Herbert continues, "but, Oh God, how easily is that answered, when we consider that the Blessings in the holy Scripture, are never given to the rich, but to the poor." Unlike Donne, who, as we have seen, often found "the glory of Heaven" shining down in the beams of preferment, and riches, and estimation, Herbert says that he never finds in the gospel, "Blessed be the Rich, or Blessed be the Noble." With regard to wealth and "great place," Herbert became one of those "who say, I care not." In "Submission," he cut through another disingenuous knot when he quietly notes, after echoing the normal claim for the special utility of "place and power" in serving God, "Perhaps great places and thy praise / Do not so well agree."[86]

Appendix: Impossible Transcendence

When "sophistication" or "tough-mindedness" are at is-sue, there is always a danger that cynicism will be taken for wisdom. We have already encountered this problem in dealing with the nihilism of "self-consumption."[87] The New Historicism too can be seen as encouraging, perhaps relying on, this tendency. Especially in its more Foucault-ian or Puttenhamian forms, the New Historicism can be seen as encouraging a rather easy cynicism about motives.[88] Love is never love.[89] From my point of view, this view is another a priori. It would undercut the whole thrust of this book for me to deny the possibility of saintliness. I am as strongly, in other words, against the a priori denial as I am against the a priori assertion of this. Again, as always, I think that one must look. George Herbert, after 1622, seems to me to have effected—by means, as I have already suggested, of a deepening apprehension of Reformation theology—a remarkable transformation in his attitudes.

---

86. For a fuller discussion of this poem and its relation to Herbert's life and writings as a whole, see the appendix to this chapter, "Impossible Transcendence."

87. See Essay 2 above.

88. George Puttenham's *The Arte of English Poesie* (1589) sees poetry in terms of rhetoric and rhetoric in terms of courtly strategies. It is a key text for the current understanding of both rhetoric and courtliness in the English Renaissance. Puttenham's treatise is reprinted in G. Gregory Smith, ed., *Elizabethan Critical Essays* (London: Oxford University Press, 1904), 2:1–193.

89. For the classic essay reading Elizabethan love poetry as fundamentally having political rather than erotic goals, see Arthur Marotti, "'Love is not Love': Elizabethan Sonnet Sequences and the Social Order," *ELH* 49 (1982): 396–428.

A new historicist view would deny this. Michael Schoenfeldt has provided such a view. He has given us sex, violence, and politics in *The Temple*. Schoenfeldt's discovery of sex in a great many of Herbert's lyrics is not especially characteristic of New Historicism, and New Historicism is not, therefore, especially implicated in this practice (which demonstrates, I would argue, the need for contextualization that we have already discussed with regard to Thomas Greene's similar reading of Shakespeare's Sonnets).[90] Schoenfeldt's treatments of torture and of courtliness, on the other hand, are characteristic. The issue of courtliness is especially relevant to New Historicism, since the figure of the courtier, understood as Frank Whigham understands this figure, represents, together with the figure of the conquistador, the fundamental model for human behavior in new historicist studies of the Renaissance.

But first a word on torture. Despite much earlier work on this topic, we owe our intense awareness of this practice in the past (and perhaps the present) to the work of Foucault and the New Historicists.[91] This is certainly a gain, ethically and historically. Yet we must still tread carefully. On the representation of torture in Herbert's poems, Schoenfeldt falls into a systematic confusion of the vehicle with the tenor of metaphors, a confusion that is a constant temptation for New Historicism. Schoenfeldt refuses to acknowledge the metaphorical status of the language of torture in Herbert's poetry. Yet the language of torture exists in the poetry exactly as the language of space does, and Herbert's transformation of spatial into psychological terms has been analyzed at length.[92] Like the language of space, in other words, the language of torture in the poetry is profoundly and systematically psychological. When Herbert speaks of himself in "Affliction" (IV) as "a wonder tortur'd in the space / Betwixt this world and that of grace," he is no more speaking of being physically stretched or shattered than he is speaking of a geographical or cosmological place. Herbert is talking about something that is happening to or within his inner life ("*My thoughts* are all a case of knives"). I am not at all sure that we get closer

90. On Greene's reading of Shakespeare's sonnets, see pp. 49–52 above.

91. The key text here is, of course, Michel Foucault, *Discipline and Punish: The Birth of the Prison*, trans. Alan Sheridan (New York: Random House, 1979), 3–69, though even here there are problems with Foucault's analysis (see Essay 4, n. 18 above). For earlier scholarship, see the useful bibiliographical essay in Edward Peters, *Torture* (New York: Blackwell, 1985), 188–99.

92. See especially Helen Vendler's analysis of "The Temper" (I) in *The Poetry of George Herbert* (Cambridge: Harvard University Press, 1975), 39–41, and Strier, *Love Known*, 227–38.

to the spiritual experience Herbert is describing by taking it to be physical. Again, we need more than a behavioral context.[93] It is certainly good to be reminded that the rack and the "Scavenger's Daughter" were Elizabethan realities, and it is certainly good to be reminded of the actual tortures to which captured priests like Robert Southwell were subjected, yet when we are told that torture is "an unbearably *real metaphor*" in Herbert's poetry, something has gone deeply awry.[94] As we saw before in deconstruction, now in the name of "realism" and historicism, the difference between literal and metaphorical has been fudged or lost.[95] What is the role of "unbearably" in Schoenfeldt's assertion, and, more urgently, what is the meaning of "real"? The rhetorical ante has been upped, but has there been any gain in comprehension of the poetry?

To take a particular instance, I cannot see that our understanding of "Confession" is enhanced by seeing the "open breast" in the poem—an extremely positive and abstract image (contrasted with cleverly and intricately constructed closed spaces)—as suggesting "the grisly spectre of the disemboweled traitor" (129).[96] The critic's sensational image leads us away from the poem. It may perhaps lead us to something that we are in fact more interested in, but that is not the point. The grisly specter conjured by the critic does not help us understand what Herbert is saying in this poem about his topic (confession to God). This tendency toward sensationalism can lead to misreadings of tone (as in regard to "Bittersweet," which is read without any sweetness), and it can lead away from rather than toward history. Perhaps the real trick in reading Herbert's poetry of affliction would be to try to understand how this language could be used of nonphysical suffering. Perhaps the model for suffering need not be physical. Perhaps Lear meant it when he said that the tempest in his mind was worse than the physical one. Schoenfeldt is certainly right that we must attend carefully and knowledgeably to the vehicles of the metaphors that Renaissance writers use, but we must also, I would argue, go on to try to think hard about what the metaphors are metaphors of.

As I have already suggested, however, the key issue is not sex or even torture, but strategic, self-seeking courtliness. Of Herbert's keen and constant awareness of this, there can be no doubt. The question is not

93. See Essay 4 above.

94. Schoenfeldt, *Prayer and Power*, 125 (emphasis mine); further page references will appear in the text.

95. See Essay 3, pp. 45–49 above. The mistakes, however, flow in opposite directions. Where deconstruction metaphorizes the literal, New Historicism tends to literalize the metaphorical.

96. For a passage where such a context is directly relevant, see pp. 218–19 below.

whether but how Herbert's awareness of manipulative courtliness is present in the lyrics of "The Church." Ultimately, the issue concerns authorial control. On my view, Herbert is fully aware of the compromised, strategic nature of courtly supplication and makes ironic, critical use of this awareness; on Schoenfeldt's view, the compromised and strategic nature of courtly language filters into Herbert's poetry unawares. Schoenfeldt (to his credit) waffles on this a bit, but his fundamental commitment is to see Herbert as not fully in control of the manipulative and aggressive resonances of his language. In a typical formulation, Schoenfeldt speaks of how manipulative tactics continually "invade" the "allegedly submissive utterances" that Herbert directs to the "divine" (127). Language of infiltration and insurgence is crucial to Schoenfeldt's view (and qualifiers like "allegedly" must always appear before terms like "submissive" and "humble"). Schoenfeldt is committed to taking "straight" many self-presentations that I would see as ironic and self-mocking. Herbert knows, on my view, that the joke is on him—and therefore it is not. Self-seeking and manipulation seem to me to be *the overt topics* of many of the poems. My view relies on a strong sense of Herbert's authorial control, of him writing the language and not the language him. I would not generalize this. Donne's relation to the materials of his religious poems, for instance, seems to me to be quite different.[97] Like so much else, degree of authorial control seems to me an empirically not a theoretically determinable matter. Some authors in some works are quite fully in control of their materials, and some aren't. Herbert, I would argue, in most of the lyrics of "The Church," is.

In terms of Herbert's career, what this means is that Schoenfeldt is committed to a view that minimizes the difference between "The Church-porch" and "The Church," between the Oratorship at Cambridge and the parsonage at Bemerton. With a belief that is implicit in much new historicist practice, Schoenfeldt sometimes relies on images to do the work of argument. He takes as obviously symbolic the fact that Bemerton is "walking distance" to Wilton (37, 99), although no actual data about Herbert at Wilton is supplied (since none, I believe, exists). Schoenfeldt acknowledges the "immense adjustments" that Herbert's move from Cambridge to Bemerton involved, but his sentence acknowledging this is followed by a resounding and crucial "But" ("But I do not want to let emphasis on the conspicuous changes preclude attention to the considerable continuities" [8]). It may be relevant that Herbert's

97. See Strier, "John Donne Awry and Squint," (n. 56 above).

contemporaries were much more struck by the distance rather than the similarities between Herbert's two lives, but that cannot, obviously, be taken as definitive.[98] The question is not straightforwardly one of fact. Is it possible to settle such a question—or, if that is unrealistic, to establish plausibility? Judgments of tone will be crucial, but such judgments are notoriously difficult and disputable. Such judgments will tend to follow from rather than to determine one's overall view. Theology seems to me to offer a more promising route. If a person truly believed, as Milton puts it (in his most Herbertian poem) that God "doth not need / Either mans work or his own gifts," then it is hard to know how one would seriously attempt to coerce or subtly manipulate Him, especially if one also believed that such attempts were the surest signs of fallen nature. Schoenfeldt waffles on the matter of theology. He seems to want both a strongly Reformation Herbert and a Herbert who seriously attempts to manipulate God. It is not clear that this is coherent.

Perhaps the best way to address this matter is to consider two crucial lyrics. The first, "Submission," is directly relevant, as we have seen, to the matter of Herbert and "devout humanism"; the second, "Love" (III), is central to every critic's sense of Herbert. "Submission" comments directly on the kind of ambition that the young Herbert who sought to "work the heads" to his purpose at Cambridge manifested in his letters to his stepfather, the ambition to combine Divinity with civil dignity.[99] After giving voice to this ambition in the second stanza, Herbert (or his "speaker") rebukes himself in the third stanza, and then asks:

> How know I, if thou shouldst me raise,
>   That I should then raise thee?
> Perhaps great places and thy praise
>   Do not so well agree.

Schoenfeldt places a good deal of weight on "Perhaps." He takes it straight, as expressing dubiety, and he sees "Do not so well agree" as an "exceedingly roundabout" phrase; again there is an "infiltration,"

98. See especially Charles Cotton's prefatory poem to the 1675 edition of Walton's *Lives* (Izaak Walton, *The Lives of John Donne, Sir Henry Wotton, Richard Hooker, George Herbert, and Robert Sanderson* [London: Oxford University Press, 1927], 11–12); and Barnabas Oley's remark in the preface to his edition of Herbert's *Remains* (London, 1652), sig. a 11v–a 12r, that Herbert was widely censured by "sober men" for not having managed "his brave parts to his best advantage and preferment" through having "lost himself in a humble way."

99. See n. 81 above.

this time by "the rhythms of reluctance" (90). I would read the sentence beginning "Perhaps" as devastatingly ironic and self-mocking, as extreme understatement. I would see the doubt raised in "How know I" as making the issue of seeking "great places" from which or in which to "raise" God completely moot. The ironic reading, I would argue, is more coherent and, if I may use the word with all due self-consciousness, more natural. The stanza follows directly from the previous one (barely mentioned by Schoenfeldt) in which speaker directly rebuked himself for raising the issue of "place and power" ("when I thus dispute and grieve / I do resume my sight"). The final stanza of the poem, after what I would see as another bit of fully conscious self-mockery ("Wherefore unto my gift I stand"), ends on a diminuendo: "Onely do thou lend me a hand, / Since thou hast both mine eyes." Schoenfeldt sees this ending as grudging ("the least you can do is 'lend me a hand'") and as different in tone but "not structurally different" from the opening "imprecation" of God for making the speaker miss his "designe" ("But that thou art my wisdome, Lord. / And both mine eyes are thine / My minde would be extreamely stirr'd / For missing my designe"). I would see the wry, self-mocking petition of the ending as quite different, in every way, from the opening assertion of discontent thinly framed as a hypothetical. I would not take the title of the poem as announcing a psychosocial activity that is impossible to attain, even for a moment, and I would not mock the final gesture, however wittily, as "blind obedience" (91).

The other lyric that I will consider, "Love" (III), is the eye of the hurricane in Herbert studies, the calm and maddeningly sublime center around which all the controversies swirl. Schoenfeldt sees this poem as perfectly revealing the contestatory and competitive aspects of courtesy. I see the poem as (again) alluding to that world but purposely establishing a sharp contrast with it. The first line of the poem reads, "Love bade me welcome: yet my soul drew back." We have already seen, through François de Sales and Castiglione, that the initial refusal of an invitation was a standard move in the repertoire of strategic courtliness, and Schoenfeldt develops this point at length and with wonderful examples (202–8). He applies the point to the poem gingerly, but his normal language for describing the place of courtliness in the lyrics surfaces: "the political pressures of courtesy *invade* the socially determined recoil" (204; emphasis mine). But does it make sense to see (or to stipulate) the human character's initial response as *socially* determined? I would argue that this figure's initial response is not a deferral or a refusal or anything of the sort. I would argue that this response is not, in fact, a verbal act at all, and that it is not even a physical one: "*my soul* drew back." Schoenfeldt again allows the vehicle to overwhelm the tenor—even when, as here, the tenor is named. The tiny motion of the soul described is visible only to Love (who is thereby proved, in a wonderful pun, "quick-ey'd" by "observing" it).[100] The human character has not said anything yet. His response is presented as puzzlingly instinctive, not as socially determined or constructed. Herbert explains the phenomenon ontologically: "Guiltie of dust and sinne." "Guiltie of *dust*" is purposely odd. Moreover, when the human figure does finally say something, at the beginning of the second stanza, what he says is not particularly polite. His response to Love's courteously idiomatic query ("sweetly questioning, / If I lack'd any thing") is, as Arnold Stein has said, "a verbal clench": "A guest, I answer'd, worthy to be here."[101] Love's response to this is even odder. Instead of reassuring the guest that he is indeed "worthy to be here"—the normal polite response—or even, more didactically, reminding the guest that worthiness is not the issue, Love unequivocally predicts (or declares), "You shall be he." This is astonishing. And it is socially unintelligible. We are not in the world of normal social interaction here, much as we feel its presence. We are in a much stranger world, a world where the figure we are encountering is clearly divine and says things that no human host, however gracious, could possibly say, things like "You shall be he" and "Who made the eyes but I?"[102]

Schoenfeldt does not deal with this strangeness. He has to see the poem on a competitive model. For him, the interlocutors "maneuver for political power" (228). He is therefore in a position of having to see the human speaker as paradoxically, through professions of unworthiness, seeking "to avoid a recognition of his own complete unworthiness" and "to hold out the possibility that he could be worthy" (209). Professions of unworthiness cannot be taken at face value. The courtesy books are seen as establishing an unavoidable norm. They are seen as defining the language of humility, not as debasing it. This is not an easy position to maintain in the face of "Love" (III). In treating the final stanza of the poem, Schoenfeldt must skip over the speaker's desire for punishment ("let my shame / Go where it doth deserve") and focus only on the very attenuated and theoretical "aggressiveness" of "My deare, then I will serve." This final resolution by the human speaker is answered in such an astonishing way that dialogue ends and action supervenes. For Schoenfeldt, the human speaker's final, wordless action can only be seen as

---

100. "Quick-ey'd" here means, I take it, both "highly observant" and seeing to "the quick."

101. Stein, *Herbert's Lyrics*, 193.

102. On the theology of "You shall be he," see *Love Known*, 78–79.

a great social coup. If the poem is about "the astounding difficulty of responding properly even to the most courteous of divine figures" (224), then the human figure must be given credit for performing this difficult feat. This would fit perfectly with the fifteenth-century Italian paintings of the Annunciation that Schoenfeldt sees as analogous to Herbert's poem, since, as Schoenfeldt accepts from Baxandall's analysis, these paintings are based on a theology of the Annunciation that sees Mary as moving from *Conturbatio* to *Meritatio*.[103]

Yet Schoenfeldt wants to accept the view that "Love" (III) is about "faith alone," which he rightly characterizes as "the Reformation notion of grace" (218–19). This is where confusion sets in. Schoenfeldt cannot actually accept the Reformation reading of the poem. To do so would undermine his entire framework. He seems to think that he can accept part of the Reformation reading. He can accept the "givenness" of grace, but not its irresistibility. But I am afraid that there is a bit of theological naiveté here. In rejecting the idea that the achievement of "Love" (III) is to give a fully humanly acceptable account of the doctrine of the irresistibility of grace, Schoenfeldt cites nothing in the poem.[104] He appeals to a general fact ("people do turn down invitations") and to a quotation from a section of *The Country Parson* about dealing with despairing parishioners (214). He seems to think that to grant human beings "the negative power to shun the welcoming arm of God" is a small concession ("at least the negative Power"). But, as Luther, Calvin, John Cotton, and others would have been quick to point out, this makes salvation ultimately depend not on grace but on the act of accepting it, on "responding properly"—that is, on a form of merit.[105] Theology, or at least Reformation theology, turns out not to be so easily assimilated to the world of ordinary social life.

Herbert certainly had intimate knowledge of the social world of his time. "The Church-porch" shows this. We must certainly have the scholarly equivalent of such knowledge if we are to read Herbert's poems

---

103. *Prayer and Power*, 316, n. 91, citing Michael Baxandall, *Painting and Experience in Fifteenth-Century Italy* (Oxford: Oxford University Press, 1982).

104. *Prayer and Power*, 214, citing *Love Known*, 83.

105. See *Love Known*, chaps. 3 and 4. It may be worth noting in this context that even Aquinas is uncomfortable with asserting that "to impede or not to impede the reception of divine grace is within the scope of free choice." In book 3, part 2 of the *Summa contra Gentiles*, he makes this assertion in chapter 159 but then explains in chapter 160 that it applies only "to those persons in whom natural potency is integrally present" (that is, only to the unfallen). Saint Thomas Aquinas, *Summa contra Gentiles*, trans. Vernon J. Bourke (New York: Hanover House, 1956), 261.

with full understanding. But we must also have theological awareness. Most importantly, we must not assume that all other discourses are necessarily at the mercy of the aggressive and the prudential. To do this—that is, *not* to make this assumption—might help with a historical question with which, as we have already seen, New Historicism has vainly struggled: the question of the appeal of Reformation theology.[106] Assuming a continuity has obscured a dialectic. It may well be that part of the reason for the success of Reformation theology—and part of the reason why it so appealed to figures like George Herbert, Fulke Greville, and Philip Sidney—was precisely that this theology provided a critique of and refuge from the world of competitive and self-serving strategizing of which the new historicists have given us so convincing a portrait.[107]

106. See Essay 4, p. 76 above.

107. In *Habits of Thought in the English Renaissance: Religion, Politics, and the Dominant Culture* (Berkeley and Los Angeles: University of California Press, 1990), chap. 3, Debora Kuller Shuger has suggested something like this dialectic. She argues for the cultural significance of the discontinuity between "The Church-porch" and "The Church" (92–93, 104–5). She goes on, however, to see both the lyrics and Reformation theology as only fitfully capable of presenting or imagining a noncompetitive world. She relegates the Reformation critique of self-interest to a footnote on "another strain of Reformation Christianity" that she sees as rather eccentric (116 n. 75). Shuger gives us a dialectic, in other words, and then essentially eliminates one pole of it. At least with regard to earthly experience, she ends up with a continuity rather than a dialectic. Her view of the lyrics turns out to be close to Schoenfeldt's (she quotes with approval one of his descriptions of how the lyrics are "contaminated by" competitiveness [115]). She too (see Essay 4, p. 74 above) sees the Reformation primarily in terms of loss (the sacred being pushed further and further inward, and the inward being hollowed out [118]). Shuger does not give any sense that love and comfort are experienced realities in the lyrics or in Protestant experience. Her remarks on poems that express and thematize comfort are therefore quite misleading (see 113–14, on "The Dawning" and "The Glance"). Shuger does draw a sharp line between the "pneumatic" and the autonomous self in Renaissance persons (98), but this distinction, as Shuger deploys it, does not allow for preheavenly comfort in the "pneumatic" world, nor does it allow for humor, irony, or critical self-assessment, since the "pneumatic" world is, for Shuger, only a world of longing.

Impossible Radicalism I

Donne and Freedom of Conscience

I

This essay aims to restore a nineteenth and early twentieth-century sense of the young John Donne, a view of him as a bold and radical freethinker, a genuinely independent intellectual. Interestingly, to propound this view of "Jack" Donne sets me against both the older and the newer historicisms, since both of them work to obscure or deny the possibility of true intellectual radicalism in the early modern period.[1] Again I mean to stand with Empson. The sense of Jack Donne that I wish to restore might truly be called an Empsonian one. From the early 1950s

1. Donne seems to have coined the Jack Donne / Doctor Donne antithesis in a letter to Sir Robert Carr probably written in 1619. See *Letters to Severall Persons of Honour by John Donne*, ed. Charles Edmund Merrill Jr. (New York: Sturgis and Walton, 1910), 19; dated by the editor (p. 275). With regard to New Historicism, Frank Lentricchia is correct, I think, in taking Marlowe, among figures that Greenblatt has treated, as the best candidate for an English Renaissance author who either was or at least conceived the "rebellious, oppositional subject." I think that Lentricchia is also correct in seeing the effort of Greenblatt's treatment as being to deny the reality of such opposition; see "Foucault's Legacy—A New Historicism?" in H. Aram Veeser, ed., *The New Historicism* (New York: Routledge, 1989), 239- 40. Greenblatt has attempted to deny that his work implies the impossibility of genuine resistance or oppositionality in "Resonance and Wonder," *Learning to Curse: Essays in Early Modern Culture* (New York: Routledge, 1990), 165–66. With regard to Shakespeare, he states that "one can readily think of plays where the forces of ideological containment break down," but he (oddly and, I think, revealingly) never goes on to specify which plays so readily leap to mind. And even in the course of defending his belief in the possibility of dissent, his emphasis remains on the difficulty of it (166).

on, one of the great projects of Empson's life was the attempt, as he put it, at "Rescuing Donne" from the hands of conservative or cynical scholars who had truly "kidnapped" him (in the early 1930s, Merritt Hughes, in the name of scholarship, had accused the modernists of "Kidnapping Donne").[2] Building on the position that he developed in his controversy with Tuve, Empson continued to inveigh against the conservatism and smoothing out effect of historical scholarship oriented toward "tradition."[3] He warned, in a memorable phrase, against re-covering only "subservient or boot-licking morals" from the past.[4] In our own context, it is important to see that any scholarship obsessed with avoiding "that most dangerous of historical ailments, anachronism,"[5] or, similarly, with establishing the limits of what was "thinkable" in a period will tend to have this effect. "New" and "old" come strikingly together here, since it makes no difference whether the homogeneous framework that defines the supposed limits of what was thinkable is called a "world picture" or an "episteme."[6] The result is the same: what is "thinkable" will be presented as quite finite and predictable—and quite conservative.

2. For Merritt Y. Hughes, "Kidnapping Donne," see *University of California Publications in English* 4 (1934): 61–89. Most of Empson's essays on Donne from 1949 on have been usefully collected in William Empson, *Essays on Renaissance Literature*, vol. 1, *Donne and the New Philosophy*, ed. John Haffenden (Cambridge: Cambridge University Press, 1993).

3. See Essay 1 above. Tuve clearly saw Empson as kidnapping Herbert, though she does not use this particular metaphor (my colleague Douglas Bruster has suggested to me that Hughes's use of it might have been conditioned by the Lindbergh case, so the charge against the modernists is, implicitly, even harsher than it might appear).

4. William Empson, "'Mine Eyes Dazzle,'" review of Clifford Leech, *Webster: The Duchess of Malfi* (1963), reprinted in G. K. Hunter and S. K. Hunter, eds., *John Webster* (Baltimore: Penguin, 1969), 295–301; the quotation appears on p. 300.

5. Kevin Sharpe, *Criticism and Compliment: The Politics of Literature in the England of Charles I* (Cambridge: Cambridge University Press, 1987), 52.

6. On the conception of the "episteme" as "the set of constraints and limitations which, at a given moment, are imposed on discourse," see Michel Foucault, *The Archeology of Knowledge*, trans. A. M. Sheridan Smith (New York: Pantheon, 1972), 192. For Foucault's account of the Renaissance (sixteenth-century) episteme, see *The Order of Things: An Archeology of the Human Sciences*, trans. Alan Sheridan (New York: Random House, 1970), chap. 2. This account is strikingly similar to that of E. M. W. Tillyard, *The Elizabethan World Picture: A Study of the Idea of Order in the Age of Shakespeare, Donne, and Milton* (New York: Random House, 1944). For an examination of the evidence (or exemplary material) that Foucault adduces for his "Renaissance episteme," see George Huppert, "*Divinatio* and *Eruditio*: Thoughts on Foucault," *History and Theory* 13 (1974): 191–207. For the view that Foucault has aptly described one epistemic formation in the Renaissance (namely that of Renaissance magic) rather than the entire Renaissance episteme, see Gary Tomlinson, *Music in Renaissance Magic: Toward a Historiography of Others* (Chicago: University of Chicago Press, 1992).

Obviously, concern about anachronism is useful in a monitory way. I am not sure, however, about the notion of "the limits of what was thinkable." This whole approach encourages an emphasis on the limitation of intellectual options, "the set of constraints and limitations." Such an emphasis seems to me dangerous in regard to any historical period, since every period is likely to be less restricted in its range of intellectual options than this approach will suggest. With regard to the early modern period in Europe, however, such an emphasis seems especially inappropriate since the intellectual world of this period was bursting with manifold and contradictory views and positions, old and new, orthodox and heterodox—and all in print. Anyone who has read Burton's *Anatomy of Melancholy* will be unlikely to be impressed with the "constraints" on discourse in the period.[7] Stanley Fish's view of Burton and of the intellectual world of the period as essentially nihilistic is, as we have seen, false, yet it is a great improvement over the Tillyard-Foucault picture.[8] With regard to Donne, the view that ideas were not really important to him, that he was a merely an ambitious young would-be secretary or diplomat advertising his virtuosity to potential patrons produces a view of young Donne that seems to me (as it did to Empson) no more adequate than the view of him as always and everywhere orthodox.[9]

Empson was right, I think, that Donne—"Jack" Donne, that is—is a particularly important case (as is Marlowe).[10] If young Donne turns out to be merely orthodox or merely "political" in a very restricted, anti-ideological sense, this is indeed a significant finding. The essay that follows will take as its focus what has been plausibly called "the great, crucial poem of Donne's early manhood," the third Satire ("Of Reli-

7. The famous "Digression on Air" in the Second Partition of *The Anatomy* would be a good place to start; see Robert Burton, *The Anatomy of Melancholy,* ed. Holbrook Jackson (New York: Random House, Vintage, 1977), 34–61.

8. For a critique of Fish's view of Burton (and of the way Fish arrives at this view), see Essay 2 above.

9. The key work for seeing Donne's life and mind as dominated by ambition (and guilt over renouncing Catholicism) is John Carey's *John Donne: Life, Mind, and Art* (New York: Oxford University Press, 1981). Arthur F. Marotti develops Carey's themes in what is proclaimed as a "new historicist" manner in *John Donne, Coterie Poet* (Madison: University of Wisconsin Press, 1986). For the claim to New Historicism, see p. xiv.

10. It makes perfect sense in this context, which I think is indeed the relevant one, that Empson's last extended critical project was on Marlowe and *Dr. Faustus.* It has been published as *Faustus and the Censor: The English Faust-book and Marlowe's "Doctor Faustus,"* ed. John Henry Jones (Oxford: Blackwell, 1987). See n. 1 above for Marlowe as a test case.

gion").[11] Empson's wonderful essay on Donne's fantasy of freedom from repression, "Donne the Spaceman," is mainly concerned with the erotic poems, but in the preliminaries to his major argument, Empson makes some remarks *en passant* about Satire III. With his normal distrust of scholarly truisms and his desire for genuine historicism, Empson notes that although this poem "seems often to be regarded as a commonplace bit of Anglican liberalism," such "liberalism" was not commonplace or even safe in the mid-1590s. He notes, moreover, that despite some familiar rhetoric about fighting the devil, the third Satire seems "somehow also to give [an] inherent argument for freedom of conscience."[12] I think that Empson has, as usual, gotten to the heart of the matter. In this essay, I will try to demonstrate that Empson was right about the radicalism of the poem, historically right. I will try to demonstrate that such a view is not, after all, anachronistic. I will not argue that Donne's third Satire is consistent in its radicalism—it will, in fact, be part of my argument to deny this—but I will try to show that the radicalism in the poem is genuine, that it can be fully contextualized in the sixteenth-century world, and that it constitutes the poem's deepest and poetically most distinguished strain.

It seems worth stating outright that it would be surprising if a major text "Of Religion" by the young John Donne were a conventional piece. Donne's religious biography is extraordinary. What makes it so is not only his move from the militant Catholicism of his birth and upbringing to the Protestantism of the English Church, though this is interesting enough. Also extraordinary is the length of time it took Donne to make this move and, most of all, his recorded state of mind during the prolonged "in-between" period.[13] In a world where everyone was a religious something, often a militant something, Donne was, for a remarkably long time, a religious nothing. In the autobiographical "Preface to the Priestes and Jesuits" of *Pseudo-martyr*, written in 1609–10, Donne acknowledged his love of "freedome and libertie" in his studies, his tendency

---

11. Carey, *Donne: Life, Mind, and Art*, 26. The poem is entitled "Of Religion" in one manuscript and "Uppon Religion" in another. See *John Donne: The Satires, Epigrams and Verse Letters*, ed. W. Milgate (Oxford: Clarendon Press, 1967), p. 140. Citations of Satire III are to this edition (hereafter *Satires*) and will be given in the text by line number.

12. William Empson, "Donne the Spaceman," *Kenyon Review* 19 (1957): 341–42; Empson, *Donne and the New Philsophy*, 82.

13. For Donne's ancestry, childhood, and upbringing, see R. C. Bald, *John Donne: A Life* (New York: Oxford University Press, 1970), chaps. 2 and 3.

toward what he describes as an intellectual and religious bachelorhood, a temperamental unwillingness to "betroth or enthral my selfe, to any one science, which should possesse or denominate me."[14] The identification of commitment with enthrallment is a familiar feature of the erotic life that Donne represents in his lyrics ("Rob mee, but binde me not, and let me go"); in this preface to his most sober, important, and public piece of writing up to that time, Donne uses the identification of commitment with enthrallment to explain his intellectual and spiritual life.[15] He sees his unwillingness to espouse a single religious position as having produced a promiscuity in him, an "easiness" to afford "a sweete and gentle Interpretation, to all professors" of Christianity.

In the context of this candid but rhetorically complex self-characterization (is it praise or blame? or is it praise masquerading as blame?) Donne proceeds to an account of his religious history. He used, he says, "no inordinate haste, nor precipitation in binding my conscience to any locall Religion." "Binding" the conscience sounds negative here, as does the rather belittling "locall Religion." One would think that by the time of writing *Pseudo-martyr* in 1610, Donne had indeed "bound" his conscience to the "locall Religion" of England, but it should be remembered that it took five more years and considerable political pressure for Donne finally to take orders in this "local" church.[16] He presents his long period of what he calls "irresolution," which he acknowledges "bred some scandall," as having consisted of two phases. The work of the first phase was negative. Since Donne began his spiritual life with a heavily inscribed rather than a clean slate, to get to a position of neutrality he had "first to blot out certaine impressions of the Romane religion." Changing the image to make it more personal, Donne had, he says, "to wrastle both against the examples and against the reasons, by which some hold was taken, and some anticipations early laid upon my conscience" by "Persons who by nature had a power and superiority over my will" (parents and relatives) and by other Catholic adults who "by their learning and good life" made "impressions" on Donne's youthful psyche.[17]

14. John Donne, *Pseudo-Martyr* (London, 1610), B2r-v.

15. See "The Indifferent," line 16. All citations from Donne's poetry other than the Satires and verse letters are from *The Complete Poetry of John Donne,* ed. John T. Shawcross (New York: Doubleday, 1967).

16. See Bald, *Donne,* 204–20; Dennis Flynn, "Donne's Catholicism: II," *Recusant History* 13 (1976): 178–95; and Carey, *Donne: Life, Mind, and Art,* chap. 3.

17. On the significance of the coin imagery here, see John Carey, "Donne and Coins," in John Carey, ed., *English Renaissance Studies Presented to Dame Helen Gardner* (Oxford:

It is inaccurate, therefore, to say that Donne "would not abandon the religion of his youth until he had satisfied himself intellectually and morally that it was the right thing to do."[18] Donne presents abandoning the religion of his youth *as a prerequisite* for attaining intellectual satisfaction: "first to blot out certaine impressions." After the blotting out came a period of "search and disquisition" in which Donne attempted to survey and digest "the whole body of Divinity, controverted between ours and the Romane church." This was a lengthy process. As late as 1608, a friend who had converted to Roman Catholicism described Donne not as a committed Protestant but as (strikingly) "a mere libertine" in religion.[19] Donne saw *Biathanatos*, composed in 1607 or 1608, when he was at least thirty-four, as "written by Jack Donne."[20] And even in the preface to *Pseudo-Martyr*, Donne earnestly warned against thinking "that hee hath no Religion, which dares not call his Religion by some newer name than *Christian*." The third Satire was written in the mid-1590s, early in the period of Donne's suspension of commitment; I believe that its ultimate import is to stand as a defense of such suspension.

In interpreting Donne's account of his religious biography as I have above, and in taking this account, so interpreted, as providing a useful context for approaching Satire III, I am implicitly rejecting the claim, made by various scholars, that the *Satires* are fundamentally Roman Catholic in point of view and sensibility.[21] This claim tends in itself to produce a conservative Donne. Yet as R. C. Bald says, the biographical evidence makes it unlikely that by the mid-1590s Donne was "an unyielding Catholic."[22] The most important evidence is provided by the Satires themselves. The five Satires seem to have circulated in manu-

Oxford University Press, 1980), 151–63; and Richard Strier, "John Donne Awry and Squint: The 'Holy Sonnets,' 1608–10," *Modern Philology* 86 (1989): 357–84.

18. Marotti, *Donne, Coterie Poet*, 43.

19. See the excerpt from Sir Toby Matthew's *Relation* of his conversion to Catholicism in Bald, *Donne*, 188. In the essay cited in n. 17 above, I argue that the process of religious transformation was still incomplete in the period when Donne was composing the bulk of the "Holy Sonnets," and that this can be seen in the poems themselves.

20. See n. 1 above.

21. See, for instance, *The Poems of John Donne* , ed. Herbert J. C. Grierson, 2 vols. (Oxford: Clarendon Press, 1912), 2:117; Clay Hunt, *Donne's Poetry: Essays in Literary Analysis* (New Haven: Yale University Press, 1954), 170–72; and M. Thomas Hester, *Kinde Pitty and Brave Scorn: John Donne's "Satyres"* (Durham: Duke University Press, 1982).

22. Bald, *Donne*, 70.

script as a book or group in the order in which they appear in the first printed editions, and they were probably composed in this order.[23] The other Satires, then, especially the second and fourth, should throw some light on the third. In the second, Donne shows a detailed knowledge of Catholic institutional and intellectual structures ("Confession . . . Schoolmen . . . Canonists" [lines 33–38]), and in the fourth, as Erskine-Smith has suggested, Donne may well be drawing on the experience of danger and vulnerability of a Catholic in a Protestant state.[24] Yet what is most striking in the religious references of these satires is their independence from *any* established religious position.

Donne's aim (or fantasy) in these poems is to stand clear of the religious, political, and social pressures of his world. The second Satire is especially striking for its political daring, its references (censored in the first edition of the *Poems*) to lying "Like a Kings favorite, yea like a King" (line 70) and to bastardy "in Kings titles" (which is likened, in its abundance, to "Symonie' and Sodomy in Churchmen's lives" [74–75]).[25] With regard to texts, sacred and otherwise, Satire II is cynical about the procedures of all commentators and controversialists (99–102). The fourth Satire continues this detachment. It equates Catholic and Protestant persecutions ("protestation" at Rome could throw anyone "into the'Inquisition" while, in England, swearing an oath "by Jesu" can put one at the mercy of a Topcliffe).[26] This satire carefully balances Protestants and Catholics in contexts of both praise and blame: as lying historians ("Jovius or Sleidan" [47–48]) and as eminent scholars ("Beza . . . some Jesuites" [55–56]).[27] This is not the writing of a Catholic—or at least not of a normative post-Tridentine Catholic. It may well be the position of an Erasmian, but that was a very different matter. The Council of Trent was vehemently anti-Erasmian.[28] Erasmus was the

23. See Alan MacColl, "The Circulation of Donne's Poems in Manuscript," in A. J. Smith, ed., *John Donne: Essays in Celebration* (London: Methuen, 1972), 42, and *Satires,* xlv-xlvii.

24. Howard Erskine-Smith, "Courtiers out of Horace," in Smith, ed., *Donne: Essays in Celebration,* 283.

25. In Donne, *Poems, By J. D. with Elegies on the Authors Death* (London, 1633), p. 331, lines 69–70 and lines 74–75 are excised, with broken horizontal lines representing the number of lines missing. Hereafter cited as *Poems* 1633.

26. In later revisions, Donne changed "Topcliffe" to "Pursevant" (see *Satires,* 162).

27. The Protestant Sleidan was later replaced by the Catholic responder to Sleidan, Surius (see *Satires,* 152–53).

28. For a clear account of the history of Erasmus's reputation through the mid-eighteenth century, and especially for the radical devaluation of Erasmus by the Catholic

preeminent case of a figure who was frequently thought to have "no Religion" because he refused to "call his Religion by some newer name than *Christian*." Odd as it may seem to us, at the end of the sixteenth century, and perhaps throughout it, in many contexts to be an Erasmian was to be a radical.[29]

II

The remainder of this essay is devoted to a "close reading" of Donne's third Satire. This kind of sequential, nearly line-by-line reading, bearing as it does the taint of formalism, is no longer in fashion. Yet if one is interested in the "inside" perspective at all, it is the only way to enter into the emotional and intellectual tensions and eddies of a text, indeed, of the mind of a nonliving person.[30] Generalizations about a text are rarely helpful about that text, though they may be so for other purposes. With regard to individual texts, tracking their movements from beginning to end is our only hope for real engagement. To pick out bits and pieces of a text, and then to contextualize those bits and pieces as imaginatively as possible, can be exciting and extraordinarily illuminating. It creates the wonderful collage effects of New Historicism. But if you wish to see the mind of a particular historical individual at work (or play), there is no substitute for relatively thorough "close reading." It is only in the tiny details of a text—especially (but not exclusively) in a poem, where an extraordinary number of meaning-bearing elements are at work—that we can hope to capture the real complexity of lived experience and thought in the past.[31] To do "close reading" with as

Church after the Council of Trent, see Bruce Mansfield, *Phoenix of His Age: Interpretations of Erasmus, 1550–1750* (Toronto: University of Toronto Press, 1979), esp. chap. 2.

29. For a good sense of the potential and actual radicalism of Erasmus's religious views, see Marcel Bataillon, *Erasme et l'Espagne* (1937; rev. ed., 3 vols., Geneva: Droz, 1991); Lucien Febvre, *The Problem of Unbelief in the Sixteenth Century* (1942), trans. Beatrice Gottlieb (Cambridge: Harvard University Press, 1982), chap. 8; Roland H. Bainton, *Erasmus of Christendom* (New York: Scribner's, 1969); E. G. Rupp, *Patterns of Reformation* (London: Epworth, 1969); and Carlos M. Eire, *War against the Idols: The Reformation of Worship from Erasmus to Calvin* (Cambridge: Cambridge University Press, 1986).

30. On the importance of the "inside" perspective, see Essay 4 above.

31. I would defend the "close reading" of historical "documents" as well as poems. I have attempted such a defense, and such an activity, in "Describing and Curing a National

much knowledge but as few preconceptions as possible is, as I have suggested, the only way in which we will ever be able to come close to recreating the thought and lifeworlds of particular individuals. Ultimately we may well be interested in something larger than individuals, but we cannot properly get to the "something larger" without attending to what we can reconstruct of the intimate emotional and intellectual lives of individuals and of represented individuals. Even if we are prepared to dismiss much of what we find as "false consciousness" of one sort or another, it is historical data of immense importance nonetheless.

Donne is a great opener of poems. Where the first two Satires immediately establish a dialogical frame (their opening words are "Away thou" and "Sir, though" respectively), the third opens with the speaker in a state of puzzled yet highly stylized self-contemplation.[32] There is no clear interlocutor.[33] The speaker stresses both his emotionality and his bafflement as he watches his passions interfere with one another: "Kinde pitty chokes my spleene." This is strange and striking. We are thrown suddenly and uncomfortably not just into the speaker's mind but into his internal bodily processes, into (as Eliot hauntingly said) "the cerebral cortex, the nervous system, the digestive tract."[34] "Spleen" was a term with a range of reference simultaneously and ambiguously psychological and physiological. "Chokes" dominates the half line, making the kindness of pity seem purely ascriptive. The speaker seems splenetic toward pity.

The rest of the line is more stable and controlled: "brave scorn forbids." We are now in a world where the epithet and the verb cor-

---

Disaster: The Roots and Branches Petition and the Grand Remonstrance," in David L. Smith, Richard Strier, and David Bevington, eds., *The Theatrical City: Culture, Theatre, and Literature in London, 1576–1649* (Cambridge: Cambridge University Press, 1995).

32. In referring to "the speaker" of the poem, I do not mean to imply that I think that the poem is spoken by a "persona." I believe "the speaker" of Satire III to be a direct projection of the historical John Donne. I use the term only in a rhetorical sense. For the non-inevitability of the notion of a persona in lyric poetry, see the discussion of George Herbert's "The Church-porch" in Essay 5 above, especially pp. 96–101.

33. While N. J. C. Andreasen, "Theme and Structure in Donne's Satyres," *Studies in English Literature* 3 (1963): 59–75, sees Satire III as a soliloquy, Thomas O. Sloan, "The Persona as Rhetor: An Interpretation of Donne's Satyre III," *Quarterly Journal of Speech* 51 (1965): 14–27, sees the mode of the poem as that of deliberative oratory. I think that both scholars are right. I do not believe that persuading oneself and persuading others were seen as distinct activities by Renaissance persons.

34. T. S. Eliot, "The Metaphysical Poets," *Selected Essays* (New York: Harcourt, Brace, 1950), 250.

respond ("brave . . . forbids") rather than conflict ("kind . . . chokes"). We are far from physiology and have entered the realm of will and lordly control ("forbids"). The second line, however, brings us back to uncomfortable physical proximity. What "brave scorn forbids" is "Those teares to issue which swell my eye-lids" (line 2). We are awfully close to the speaker's face, and there is something (from the staunchly male point of view of "brave scorn") embarrassingly "feminine" and physiological in "swell my eye-lids." The image of a full pregnancy not allowed to "issue" into a birth is as uncomfortable as the image of choking.[35] The speaker (Donne?) really does seem mired in conflicting emotions. The spleen and scorn of the first line are convincing, but no more so than the extraordinary delicacy of the second.

It is a relief to encounter an ethical rather than a physiological subject at the beginning of the third line. We encounter an "I" with some moral distance from physiology: "I must not laugh, nor weepe sinnes" (line 3a). Why this speaker "must not laugh" [at] sins is easily apprehended, but why not "*weepe* sinnes"? Jesus, after all, wept for Jerusalem.[36] The rest of the line explains why this speaker cannot allow himself either of his contradictory responses. He cannot do so "and be wise" (line 3b). The desire to be "wise" in a strongly classical, distinctively Stoic sense is more important to this speaker than sorting out, tempering, or expressing his emotions.[37] The disconcertingly wet and physiological emotionality of the opening is perhaps meant to have the effect of leading us (presumed male) as well as the speaker to value the "dry light" and unemotionality of Stoic wisdom.[38]

The opening sentence ends with the speaker considering a response different from both laughing and weeping, an option that is presumably (but not assuredly) compatible with "wisdom": "Can railing then cure these worne maladies?" (line 4). "Railing" is a technical term. Donne

35. On pregnant tears, see "A valediction of weeping."

36. Here and in the rest of this paragraph, I am deeply indebted to Gregory Vlastos's remarkable comparison of Jesus and Socrates in "Introduction: The Paradox of Socrates," in Gregory Vlastos, ed., *The Philosophy of Socrates* (New York: Doubleday, 1971), 15–17.

37. Joshua Scodel in "The Medium is the Message: Donne's 'Satire 3,' 'To Sir Henry Wotton ("Sir, more then kisses"),' and the Ideologies of the Mean," *Modern Philology* 91 (1993): 482, asserts that Donne's speaker "does not seek Stoic impassivity." Scodel is committed to seeing the poem as embracing a consistent, if idiosyncratic, Aristotelian position (see n. 56 below).

38. For "dry light" (*lumen siccum*), see Francis Bacon, *The Advancement of Learning*, in *Selected Writings*, ed. Hugh G. Dick (New York: Random House, Modern Library, 1955), 165 (citing Heraclitus).

is contemplating Juvenalian satire conceived, as Sidney conceived it, in semimedical terms, with sins redescribed as "maladies." This is tentatively approached, and we can understand why. Even accepting the equation of sins with diseases, it seems a lot to ask from "railing" that it cure established maladies. This is more than Sidney credited to "bold but wholesome Iambic."[39] Donne's complex and conflicted proem to the Satire seems to end (fitly) by questioning the efficacy of a mode that it was about to adopt. Neither we nor the poet are sure that any satiric mode will be able to "cure these worne maladies" and enable the speaker to "be wise." It is not clear that "railing" should even be tried. Perhaps the moral essay would be the better genre. Already, within four lines, the poem is deeply self-conscious and self-questioning.

The second sentence is another question. Meant to be sarcastic, perhaps a form of "railing," it emerges as more baffled than biting. Donne reveals that the sins or "maladies" with which he is concerned are failures in spiritual commitment. Since his conception of wisdom is deeply classical, it is natural for this speaker to view "our" degree of spiritual commitment and its object against that of the pagans of the classical period and theirs, asking

> Is not our Mistresse faire Religion,
> As worthy'of all our Soules devotion,
> As vertue was to the first blinded age? (5–7)

Donne is saying (or at least implying) something remarkable in his presentation of "the first blinded age." The highest goal of pagan practical life, "vertue," is presented as having been an object of "Soules devotion," a term that normally designates a specifically Christian or at least biblical activity. The speaker is genuinely puzzled at the inefficacy of "faire Religion" to inspire an (at least) equivalent intensity. "Devotion," here, is a matter of commitment, not of religiosity. The "Soules devotion" of "the first blinded age" is unquestioned; it is the premise of the comparison. The sense in which this age was "blinded" is obvious—it was not privy to the sight of "faire Religion" (Christianity)— but this blindness seems merely technical. The point is the superiority, not the inferiority of the pagans. Donne tries the comparison again in the next sentence, explicitly measuring "our" failures (and their success) by the extent of our advantages: "Are not heavens joyes as valiant to

39. Sir Philip Sidney, *An Apology for Poetry*, ed. Geoffrey Shepherd (London: Nelson, 1965), 116.

asswage / Lusts as earths honour was to them?" (8–9). The test of "devotion" is, apparently, moral: its ability, as the enjambment insists, to "asswage / Lusts," to lead persons to suppress or (better) to redirect their appetites and passions.

In the midst of these questionings, the speaker stops to reflect. The tone shifts from scorn to sorrow as Donne contemplates the difference between "heavens joyes" and "earths honour": "Alas, / As wee do them in meanes, shall they surpasse / Us in the end" (10–11). This is elegantly compact and precise. The contrast blends the philosophical one between ends and means and the religious one between other ends and "the end." The mention of "heavens joyes" in line 8 generates a transcendental, even apocalyptic context. It follows from the speaker's argument that the pagans who gave "Soules devotion" to virtue will attain the transcendental "end." The idea of heaven seems regularly to have stirred the thought of fathers in Donne's mind. In the sonnet beginning "If faithfull soules," Donne fantasizes that his glorified father can behold Donne's spiritual athleticism ("valiantly I hels wide mouth o'rstride"). Here, Donne contemplates the possibility that "thy fathers spirit" shall

> Meete blinde Philosophers in heaven, whose merit
> Of strict life may be'imputed faith, and heare
> Thee, whom hee taught so easie wayes and neare
> To follow, damn'd? (12–15)

This is tricky, although its general outlines are clear: Donne is continuing his radically humanist line of thought. The "blind Philosophers" are unequivocally "in heaven," not in limbo or Purgatory.[40] They seem, in fact, more solidly and substantially there than does "thy fathers spirit."[41] We must stop and ask some questions here lest we take all of this too casually. One puzzle is how the philosophers got to heaven. They did so, it seems, on a strictly Catholic conception, through, as the line break suggests, "merit." The explication of "merit" as "strict life"

---

40. On the salvation of the virtuous pagans in humanist thought, see George Huntston Williams, "Erasmus and the Reformers on Non-Christian Religions and *Salus Extra Ecclesiam*," in Theodore K. Rabb and Jerrold E. Seigel, eds., *Action and Conviction in Early Modern Europe: Essays in Memory of E. H. Harbison* (Princeton: Princeton University Press, 1969), 319–70.

41. Carey's suggestion (*Donne: Life, Mind, and Art* , 28) that Donne is echoing *Hamlet* is fanciful and probably impossible (unless we accept the existence of a pre-Shakespearean ur-*Hamlet* with this phrase in it), but Carey is right about the strangeness and wraithlike quality of "thy fathers spirit," especially in comparison to the substantiality of the "blinde Philosophers."

is fully intelligible and fully in keeping with the stress in the poem on the capacity of devotion to "asswage / Lusts." But the situation is not so straightforward. As the enjambed sentence continues, it turns out that salvation is by faith, after all, and that Donne is speculating or postulating that "merit . . . may be'imputed faith." "Imputation" is a technical and loaded theological term central to Luther's theology. Donne is making startlingly un-Lutheran use of the key Lutheran terms of "imputation" and faith, since the force of the notion of imputed righteousness was precisely to *oppose* the philosophical, classical, and commonsense idea of achieved or actual righteousness.[42] Milgate sees Donne using the terms impudently here.[43] This is plausible and may be correct, but I wonder whether we ought to consider taking Donne at his word. Perhaps he is being boldly syncretic, trying to find a formula for the salvation of the philosophers that would include the key notions of both theologies. Donne is certainly playing, speculating ("*may*be imputed") but this may be serious play.

Other puzzles are how the father got to heaven and what the "easie wayes" are. It is unlikely that Donne is expressing the view (historically well-founded though it may be) that salvation by faith was meant to be an easy way.[44] It is also unlikely that Donne would present his father as having been saved by "faith alone." Biography works against this, as does the overall context of the poem, which is strongly moralistic. So the father must have gotten to heaven through some combination of "merit / Of strict life" and faith. But in that case where are the "easie wayes"? They are a chimera.[45] I would argue that the writing itself attests

42. On imputed versus actual or "philosophical" righteousness, see Luther's Preface to [his] Latin Writings; Preface to Romans; and 1531 Commentary on Galatians. The first two of these can be found complete, along with selections from the Galatians commentary, in *Martin Luther: Selections from his Writings*, ed. John Dillenberger (Garden City, N.Y.: Doubleday, 1961). Donne uses "imputed grace" in the "Going to Bed" elegy (line 42) in a way that relies on the Lutheran view.

43. See *Satires*, 141.

44. C. S. Lewis repeatedly explained that when Protestantism first emerged, it seemed not too grim but too glad to be true. See "Donne and Love Poetry in the Seventeenth Century," in *Seventeenth-Century Studies Presented to Sir Herbert Grierson*, preface by J. Dover Wilson (Oxford: Clarendon Press, 1938), 75; *English Literature in the Sixteenth Century, Excluding Drama* (Oxford: Clarendon Press, 1954), 33–35, 187–92. See also Strier, "John Donne Awry and Squint," 361–64.

45. Carey, *Donne: Life, Mind and Art*, has some shrewd comments on the oddness of "easie wayes" in the poem (28). We agree on the contradictions that this conception generates in the poem, but Carey sees "easie wayes" as playing a more important psychological role in the poem than I do.

to this. Donne's elaboration on "easie wayes" produces the weak en-jambment and redundancy of "and neare / To follow." What this signifies, I think, is that in the poem there is really no alternative to "merit/ Of strict life." But if that is the case, a central problem in Renaissance religious thought emerges here: where is the superiority—and distinctiveness—of Christianity?[46] Deconstruction can help us here. In the poem, the difference disappears. Donne does not want this to surface; he wants to pretend to maintain the difference, but the poetry and the argument are working, perhaps semiconsciously, in the other direction. A subtle sign of this is that, functionally, within the imagined narrative, the father's spirit could in fact be just as blind as the philos-ophers, since this spirit does not get to see but only to "heare" the special (bad) news. The privileging of sight that underwrites the denigration of the philosophers is never imagistically activated. "Close reading" here reveals ambivalence and potential heterodoxy. The distinction between Christian and philosophical salvation deconstructs itself.

With the reference to damnation, a new section begins. Courage becomes central (a theme, it should be noted, that further undermines the praise of "easie wayes"). In good Aristotelian fashion, the true cour-age is seen as involving proper fear: "O if thou dar'st, feare this, / This feare great courage and high valour is."[47] Nonetheless, despite the re-definition of courage as Christian fear, Donne admires the military and navigational daring, even the foolhardiness, of his generation.[48] The voice takes on Donne's characteristic wit (ships as "wooden sepulchres"), love of catalogues ("To leaders rage, to stormes, to shot, to dearth"), and range of reference ("limbecks"). The passage describes secular ac-tivities but, again taking a cue from deconstruction, we can see that the

46. On this problem in Renaissance religious thought, see the remarkable essay by Roland H. Bainton, "Man, God, and the Church in the Age of the Renaissance," in *The Renaissance: Six Essays* (New York: Harper and Row, 1962), 77–96.

47. On courage as a mean involving the appropriate amount of fear, with foolhardiness as an extreme, see *Nicomachean Ethics,* 1115b, trans. H. Rackham (Cambridge: Harvard University Press, Loeb Classical Library, 1934), 153–73. For a thoughtful exposition and analysis, see David Pears, "Courage as a Mean," in Amélie Oksenberg Rorty, ed., *Essays on Aristotle's Ethics* (Berkeley and Los Angeles: University of Calfornia Press, 1980), 171–87.

48. I think Hester is wrong to see the sailors, etc. merely as negative exempla. Hallett Smith seems to me more accurate in seeing the poem as basically admiring of Elizabethan courage (*Elizabethan Poetry* [Cambridge: Harvard University Press, 1952], 224). Emp-son, "Donne the Spaceman," said the same (342; *Donne and the New Philosophy,* 82). Hester (*Kinde Pitty and Brave Scorn,* 148) quotes Smith without acknowledgment that their views are different. Scodel ("The Medium is the Message," 484) also sees the explorers, etc. merely as negative exemplars.

realms refuse to stay apart. In considering his countrymen's relation to heat and cold, Donne's mind leaps with characteristic nimbleness and characteristic inability (or refusal) to keep the secular and the sacred distinct. In a dizzying flurry, he sees his contemporaries "for gain" bringing "couragious fire" to the cold north, and enduring equatorial heat and the "fires of Spain" better than "Salamanders" and "like divine / Children in th' oven" (21–24). "Fires of Spain" sounds Inquisitorial as well as geographical, and Milgate reminds us that in the Book of Daniel, the story of the "children" in the fire is an emblem of resistance to state-commanded idolatry.[49] So for a moment, the mercenary English sea-dogs are "divine" in resisting idolatrous tyranny. The poem seems to be proceeding on two different levels, with the associations established by the imagery not entirely consonant with the distinctions established by the discourse.

Imagery and discursive content are again at odds in the final instance of improper courage: "must every hee / Which cryes not, Goddesse, to thy Mistresse, draw . . . ?" (27–28). This is obviously meant to be an image of spurious, misapplied valor, but the imagistic context complicates this intention. The only mistress previously mentioned in the poem is "our Mistresse faire Religion." This connection suggests that perhaps violent defense of this Mistress against every other is "courage of straw" as well. Perhaps "faire Religion" is not to be defended by the sword, and perhaps other "mistresses" are fair—like virtue, for instance, or other, non-Christian religions. The poem does not, at this point, develop these suggestions, but they seem to be pressing on the surface of the argument. Despite some lively writing, the poem seems not yet to have found its thematic center.

At the end of the section, the imagery supports a distinction. In a strongly enjambed phrase, the divinely appointed duty "to stand" (30) contrasts sharply with all the frenzied motion that Donne has just evoked. The necessity to "stand / Sentinell" in this world and not desert one's post is familiar from the classical debate over suicide; it fits in nicely with the hint of Erasmian pacifism in "for forbidden warres, leave th' appointed field" (32) since from the perspective of spiritual combat, all material wars would be forbidden.[50] In treating the traditional spiritual

49. *Satires*, 142. On Daniel as a patron of resistance theory, see Essay 7, p. 194 below.
50. On the sentinel image in the argument against suicide, see *Phaedo*, 62b, *The Collected Dialogues of Plato*, ed. Edith Hamilton and Huntington Cairns (Princeton: Princeton University Press, 1961), 45; and Cicero, *De Senectute*, 20, text with a trans. by

foes, the writing comes alive only at the mention of the last of them, in Donne's order, the flesh.[51] The poetry gets more interesting as its topic recedes (or returns) from the specifically Christian ("the foule Devill") to the philosophical. Donne attempts a complex argument: to show his contemporaries that their behavior contradicts exactly the values they think it embodies, that they are unwittingly enacting a deep ontological and philosophical contradiction. The image of the second foe, the world, as a "worne strumpet" leads to the thought of sensual pleasure—which leads to linguistic and conceptual refinement:

> Flesh (it selfes death) and joyes which flesh can taste,
> Thou lov'st; and thy faire goodly soule, which doth
> Give this flesh power to taste joy, thou dost loath. (40–42)

Again we must recognize the unconventional. This is not a traditional argument against "the flesh," a phrase which Donne does not use. Despite the interjected parenthesis, it is not, in fact, an argument *against* "flesh" at all. "Joyes which flesh can taste" are never rejected or even devalued. They cannot be, since the argument for the amiability of the soul is precisely that it is what enables flesh to "taste" joy. The plea is not to renounce "joyes which flesh can taste" but to have a proper philosophical understanding of them, to see them, in Aristotelian fashion, as ontologically dependent on the "fair goodly soule." The soul should get credit for the body's joys. This is an argument not for asceticism but for holism. The conception of "tasting" joy, closely associated with the idea of nakedness, always led Donne in this holistic direction.[52] The

---

W. A. Falconer (Cambridge: Harvard University Press, Loeb Classical Library, 1923), 47. Redcrosse attempts to use this argument against Despair in *The Faerie Queene*, 1.9.41. For Erasmus's loathing of war, see (*intra alia*) "The Complaint of Peace," in *The Essential Erasmus*, ed. and trans. John P. Dolan (New York: New American Library, 1964), 177–204, and see Essay 2, n. 22 above. For the assertion that *"une guerre spirituelle doit etre menée par armes spirituelles"* ("a spiritual war should be conducted [only] by spiritual weapons"), see Sebastien Castellion [Castellio], *De l'impunité des hérétiques* (*De Haereticis non puniendis*), Latin text ed. Bruno Becker, French text ed. M. Valkhoff (Geneva: Droz, 1971), 289. English translation my own.

51. It was the conventionality of this section, I believe, that misled Empson into underestimating the interest of the poem as a whole: "the poem apparently is using the courage of the maritime adventurers simply to argue that we should be as brave in fighting the Devil" ("Donne the Spaceman," 342; *Donne and the New Philosophy*, 82).

52. For the holistic emphasis, see the parallel between the ways in which souls and bodies must both be "naked" to "*taste* whole *joyes*" in lines 33–35 of the "Going to Bed" elegy. The strange lines on the spiritual potential of nakedness in Satire I (lines 37–45)

argument is radically humanist and philosophical. The point is to love the soul, not to loathe the body. The status of the "faire goodly soule," however, has not been worked out in the poem. The relation between this "faire goodly" one and "our Mistresse faire Religion" has not been explicated. Is "Soules devotion" devotion to the beauty of the soul? *O sancte Socrate, ora pro nobis.*[53]

III

My argument throughout this book has been that we must attend at least as much to overt as to hidden structures. After the section on the soul, Donne's third Satire explicitly re-begins. Its focus becomes epistemological. The thought seems to be that merely ceasing from misguided uses of energy does not guarantee stability. It only puts one in a position to begin: "Seeke true religion" (43). This is the speaker's message to his pleasure-loving and desperately adventurous generation. Such a message would seem unexceptionable, but we must recognize that, in the context of late sixteenth-century Europe, it is odd. For most Europeans in this period, religion was not something to be sought; it was something given, something into which one was born or which was dictated to one from above. It was not the object of an intellectual quest. Donne's injunction requires a highly unusual detachment from existing commitments, a detachment like Donne's own in the mid-1590s. If courage is still at issue, it has become an intellectual matter, a matter of inquiry rather than of moral battle. The emphasis on truth keeps the focus intellectual, and the emphasis on seeking suggests a more active and unsettled position than does the image of the sentinel stoutly maintaining his post (though we will see that Donne returns to this image). The oddness of the injunction is intensified by what follows it. We must, as Stanley Fish has urged, attempt to be aware of logical and

---

show the power of the conceptions of nakedness and joy to elevate rather than to degrade the flesh in Donne's view. In those lines, the reference to a "plumpe muddy whore, or prostitute boy" leads Donne to contemplate Edenic innocence.

53. Desiderius Erasmus, "Convivium Religiosum," in *Opera Omnia,* 10 vols. (Hildesheim: Georg Olms, 1961–62), 1:683. See "The Godly Feast," in *The Colloquies of Erasmus,* trans. Craig R. Thompson (Chicago: University of Chicago Press, 1965), 68: "Saint Socrates, pray for us!"

semantic expectations.[54] Instead of detailed rules for the quest, Donne asks an abrupt and, for the first time in the poem, a fully genuine question: "O where?" Imagistically, the poem has already suggested that the answer to this question cannot be geographical. The answer, it would seem, must be, "Within the 'faire goodly soule' itself," but neither the poem nor the poet are willing as yet to make such a move.

The geographical possibilities must first be discursively rejected. We begin to get satirical portraits, and with these portraits, the poem finds its voice. Since the first is of a Catholic, we might think that we will be getting a typically "Anglican" scheme of extremes followed by a proper, modestly Protestant mean.[55] But this is not what Donne gives us.[56] Mirreus, the Catholic, is an Englishman, by birth presumably a Protestant, who leaves "here" and seeks "true religion" at Rome, "because hee doth know / That she was there a thousand yeares agoe" (45–46). What makes this choice irrational is the clear implication that true religion is no longer "there." The present situation is different from that of "a thousand yeares agoe." The substance is gone; "He loves her ragges" (47a). Just at this point, however, when "we" (as an English Protestant— and, as we have seen, male—audience) are smugly contemptuous of the misguided and relic-worshiping Mirreus, Donne asserts a continuity between Mirreus's behavior "there" and our behavior here: "He loves her ragges so, as we here obey / The statecloth where the Prince sate yesterday" (47–48). Suddenly idolatry is not some weird thing that they do "there" but a familiar thing that we do here, and it is suddenly and disconcertingly operative in a secular context, in a context not of bizarre religious practice but of political obedience. There is perhaps even an implication that Mirreus learned the habit of mind that sent him to the Roman church from the English attitude toward the state. Moreover if,

54. This is the (procedural) argument of "Literature in the Reader: Affective Stylistics," *Self-Consuming Artifacts: The Experience of Seventeenth-Century Literature* (Berkeley and Los Angeles: University of California Press, 1972), 382–427.

55. On the problems with "Anglicanism" as a term applying to sixteenth or seventeenth-century England, see Patrick Collinson, *The Elizabethan Puritan Movement* (Berkeley and Los Angeles: University of California Press, 1967), 13; and the same author's *The Religion of Protestants: The Church in English Society, 1559–1625* (Oxford: Clarendon Press, 1982), ix; also Nicholas Tyacke, *Anti-Calvinists: The Rise of English Arminianism, c. 1590–1640*, rev. paper ed. (Oxford: Oxford University Press, 1990), vii–viii, xviii; and Peter Lake, *Anglicans and Puritans: Presbyterianism and English Conformist Thought from Whitgift to Hooker* (Boston: Unwin Hyman, 1988).

56. Scodel, "The Medium is the Message," agrees that Donne undercuts the notion of the "mean" here, but argues that Donne reinvents an idiosyncratic version of the notion in the course of the poem. See also n. 145 below.

as I believe likely, there is a suggestion of menstrual rags in the picture of Mirreus's misplaced devotion to the "ragges" of an imagined Roman female, then there is a continuity from Rome to England in the imagery of unsavory devotion to objects associated with the lower body ("where the Prince sate"), a misogynist connection that is even tighter if "the Prince" in question is, as at the time of the composition of the poem it was, Queen Elizabeth. Elizabeth regularly referred to herself as a "Prince," and we recall Tribulation Wholesome's praise of "the beauteous discipline / Against *the menstruous rags of Rome*."[57] Donne's vision of how "we here obey" as repellent and demeaning state-worship was hardly part of the normal self-conception of English Protestantism.

Having complicated in this way his critique of Roman devotion, Donne can proceed to the other "extreme," the presbyterian. He now explicitly activates the erotic component of "true religion" as female and as (presumably) equivalent to "faire Religion," who should be "our Mistresse." The imagistic context becomes male heterosexual object-choice. While Crants refuses to be "inthrall'd" by gaudy rags, he does have an exclusive passion; he "loves her onely, who'at Geneva's call'd / Religion, plaine, simple, sullen, yong, / Contemptuous, yet unhansome" (49–52). This is perhaps a less perverse object-choice than that made by the fetishizer, but it still seems perverse, especially as an exclusive devotion, "her onely." The explanatory analogy, however, serves to make Crants's choice seem more rather than less intelligible to Donne's (male) audience. Donne presents Crants's behavior as familiar: "As among / Lecherous humours, there is one that judges / No wenches wholsome, but course country drudges" (52b-54). The trouble with this is that it really is familiar. One can imagine the case being made. It is Touchstone and Audrey. The plain and the rural can always be activated as morally su-

---

57. For Elizabeth referring to herself as a "Prince," see J. E. Neale, *Elizabeth I and Her Parliaments*, 2 vols. (New York: Norton, 1966), 1:50, 126–27, 146, 150, 173–76, 365–66; 2:99–100, 119, 213, 321, 389. For Tribulation's lines, see Ben Jonson, *The Alchemist*, 3.1.32–33 (emphasis mine), in *Ben Jonson: Three Comedies*, ed. Michael Jamieson (London: Penguin, 1966), 244. There is often, as here in Tribulation, a misogynist dimension to attacks on Rome (and on idolatry generally). On "a menstruous cloth" and idolatry, see Isaiah 30:22. The fact that, as Milgate points out (*Satires*, 144), the statecloth is a canopy does not alter the association with the lower body—"The statecloth where the Prince sate." For speculations on the anxieties aroused in Protestant Englishmen by the Virgin Queen, see Louis Montrose, "'Shaping Fantasies': Figurations of Gender and Power in Elizabethan Culture," *Representations* 1 (1983): 61–94; and Leah S. Marcus, *Puzzling Shakespeare: Local Reading and Its Discontents* (Berkeley and Los Angeles: University of California Press, 1988), 51–96.

perior, especially in contexts where wholesomeness (rather than, say, beauty) is the issue. And one can imagine Donne making the case. He comes close to doing so, in fact, in those moments, frequent in the Elegies, when he praises "use" over beauty, leather over silk and gold ("For one nights revels silk and gold we chuse, / But in long journeys cloth and leather use").[58] The erotic analogy undercuts the weirdness of Crants's choice. Again, the apparently balanced scheme breaks down.

If we were still (somehow) expecting the conventional scheme, the real surprise comes with the figure who stays home:

> Graius stayes still at home here, and because
> Some Preachers, vile ambitious bauds, and lawes
> Still new like fashions, bid him thinke that shee
> Which dwels with us, is onely perfect, hee
> Imbraceth her, whom his Godfathers will
> Tender to him, being tender, as Wards still
> Take such wives as their Guardians offer, or
> Pay valewes. (55–62)

This is powerful and passionate writing. There has been nothing in the poem quite like this straightforward attack on "some" established English preachers—the qualifier is perhaps self-protective—as "vile ambitious bawds." This is the first clear instance in the poem of "railing," of the Juvenalian mode of "bold and open crying out against naughtiness."[59] As the extraordinary lines on Mirreus and English state-worship implied, Donne has contempt for the whole system of state-enforced religion, with its ambitious preachers willing to sell "faire Religion" to the highest political bidder and with its associated legislative system constantly issuing new laws to regulate religious behavior. The idea of "ideological state apparatuses" would not have surprised Donne.[60] He does not, however, see its power over thought and behavior as irresistible.

---

58. "The Anagram," lines 33–34; and, for more elaborate development, see "Loves Progress," lines 11–16, 33–36. "The Anagram" was Donne's most popular poem in manuscript. See *John Donne: The Elegies and The Songs and Sonnets,* ed. Helen Gardner (Oxford: Clarendon, 1965), 138.

59. Sidney, *Apology,* 116. Scodel, "The Medium is the Message" (488), suggests that in the name "Graius," Donne is recalling the attack on Greeks as sycophantic mimics of their patrons in Juvenal's Satire 3. This is plausible, though there is no emphasis on mimicry in the Donne portrait.

60. The phrase, of course, is that of Louis Althusser in "Ideology and Ideological State Apparatuses," in *Lenin and Philosophy and Other Essays,* trans. Ben Brewster (New York: Monthly Review Press, 1971), 127–86.

His contempt for the individuals who are part of the "apparatus" is perhaps exceeded by his contempt for the individual who allows his thought to be controlled by the apparatus, who indeed thinks what the preachers and laws "bid him thinke," namely, "that shee / Which dwels with us, is onely perfect." In the erotic context, this figure is a child-groom: "hee / Imbraceth her, whom his Godfathers will / Tender to him, being tender." He willingly accepts whatever religion his official sponsors "Tender to him." He allows himself to be treated as an intellectual and spiritual "ward" of the state-church.[61] Donne has only contempt for such "tenderness." This may be the contempt of the "recusant," who refused to attend his parish church, but at this point some historical clarification is called for. It has been too readily assumed that this is the contempt of the *Catholic* recusant.

If, as I think we should, we take the reference to "new lawes" literally, the most likely reference would be to the activities of the 1593 Parliament. In the realm of religious regulation, what this Parliament did was to extend the anti-Catholic legislation of 1581 to the Puritans, who were punished more harshly than Catholics under its provisions. J. E. Neale sees the transformation in the 1593 Parliament of an anti-Catholic bill into "an Act against Protestant sectaries" as the most striking development of this parliament. Neale calls it "a revolution in parliamentary policy."[62] To speak of "the anti-Catholic legislation of the 1590s" (and to cite Neale as the source for this) is, therefore, extremely misleading.[63] "Recusants," in the mid-1590s, could be either Catholic or Protestant, although the new laws and ambitious preachers at the time were primarily anti-Puritan. Donne is speaking for recusants of all kinds. It is hard to see how these portraits could have been written by any sort of normative Catholic. The portrait of Mirreus is hardly flattering to Rome, and the main object of Donne's contempt seems to be lack of intellectual toughness and independence. An insistence on self-reliance, an equal contempt for the regulators of conscience and the willing objects of their endeavors—these are hardly the characteristics of institutional Catholicism, English or Continental, at the end of the sixteenth century. Many English Catholics resisted the English state-church, but they did so in the name of embracing the religion that their fathers and godfathers did

---

61. It may be relevant here that control over "wardship" was one of the great money-making operations of Elizabethan government. See Joel Hurstfield, *The Queen's Wards: Wardship and Marriage under Elizabeth* (Cambridge: Harvard University Press, 1958), especially chaps. 10 and 16.

62. Neale, *Elizabeth I and Her Parliaments*, 2:296–97.

63. Marotti, *Donne, Coterie Poet*, 304.

indeed tender to them. They believed that she which dwells at Rome "is onely perfect." The speaker of Donne's lines does not sound like a person whose aim is merely to claim one set of godfathers over another. He wants adulthood and autonomy, not dependence.

With Mirreus, Crants, and Graius, Donne would seem to have exhausted the major possibilities in the European world for locating "true religion." The series, however, continues. Again, we must work to recognize daring here. Critics tend to take the continuation of the portraits as obvious or inevitable, but the last two are utterly surprising. They are the most brilliant of the portraits and a tribute to the rigor and daring of Donne's inquiry. If each claim that true religion is "onely perfect" in a particular place is misguided, then two other logical possibilities present themselves—but only, it should be said, to a mind as rigorous and uninhibited as (Jack) Donne's. The first is enacted by "Carelesse Phrygius," who "doth abhorre / All, because all cannot be good, as one / Knowing some women whores, dares marry none" (62b-64). At first glance, Phrygius seems merely to be making a logical mistake. "All" (as so often in Donne) is the key word. It does not follow from the premise that all "cannot be good" that all must be bad, so it seems precipitous, therefore, to "abhorre / All." However, when Donne shifts to the erotic analogy and activates the pun on "abhorre," the situation becomes more complicated, and the context shifts from attitudes to behavior. The one who "Knowing some women whores, dares marry none" is not being precipitous; he is being timid or cowardly—a major failure in a poem committed to "great courage." On the other hand, maybe Phrygius is not being timid. Maybe he is merely being prudent. If Phrygius's view is not in fact that all women/churches are "whores"/impure, but that one (male) can't tell which are and which aren't, then his position, whether prudence or timidity, seems more intelligible. And if the consequences of making a mistake are disastrous, if divorce is not possible or (taking marriage to stand in for sexuality in general) if non-"wholesomeness" is fatal, then Phrygius's timidity edges closer to prudence.

In the view that I am suggesting, Phrygius is a skeptic, and here the erotic and the epistemological are strongly bound. There is some support here for Stanley Cavell's contention for a deep connection in the early modern period between philosophical skepticism and male anxieties about marriage.[64] Phrygius's problem with knowledge leads to a prob-

---

64. Stanley Cavell, *Disowning Knowledge in Six Plays of Shakespeare* (Cambridge: Cambridge University Press, 1987), 10, 20, and chap. 3 ("Othello and the Stake of the Other").

lem with commitment: he "dares marry none." He is unwilling, in Bacon's terms, "to fix a Beleefe," or in Donne's, to "betroth" himself (recall Donne's confessed unwillingness, with regard to religion, "to betroth, or enthrall my selfe").[65] It is important to see that Phrygius is not what, in philosophical terms, would be called a "negative dogmatist."[66] His position, to reiterate, is not that all women/churches are bad. In religious terms, this means that he is not a Separatist, one who thought all existing churches false, that is, impure, tainted.[67] The Separatists were indeed "negative dogmatists," but Phrygius is a skeptic in exactly the way Descartes was. He knows something—that "some women" are "false" (and some are not)—just as Descartes knew that some ordinary beliefs are false (and some true).[68] The problem is knowing which are which, and Phrygius, unlike Descartes, but like the erotic abstainer, treats this problem as insoluble.

It should not be surprising that the deepest moments in Satire III are produced by erotic analogies. Donne is, after all, our greatest lyric analyst of (at least) heterosexual male erotic psychology.[69] We have already seen how the erotic context complicates the criticism of Crants, with his quest for the "wholsome." Phrygius's worry is not infection but betrayal, and this seems to be an anxiety even more widespread in the early modern period than anxiety about infection.[70] The male who "doth abhorre / All" women is a familiar figure in Donne's erotic lyrics, where this figure's motive for adopting such an attitude is clear. The goal is to avoid vulnerability—in particular, to avoid the vulnerability to betrayal that would come with having made a commitment. In "Woman's Constancy," Donne's speaker avoids vulnerability by insisting on his knowl-

65. Francis Bacon, "Of Truth," in *Selected Writings*, ed. Dick, 7. See also p. 27 above.

66. See Richard H. Popkin, *The History of Scepticism from Erasmus to Spinoza* (Berkeley and Los Angeles: University of California Press, 1979), xvii.

67. For Phrygius as a Separatist, see Appendix A, "Careless Phrygius," in Hester, *Kinde Pitty and Brave Scorn*, 119–27.

68. For Descartes's project in the *Meditations*, see Harry G. Frankfurt, *Demons, Dreamers, and Madmen: The Defense of Reason in Descartes's "Meditations"* (Indianapolis: Bobbs-Merrill, 1970); and E. M. Curley, *Descartes against the Skeptics* (Cambridge: Harvard University Press, 1978).

69. In "Lesbian Erotics: The Utopian Trope of Donne's 'Sapho to Philaenus,'" Janel Mueller has argued that Donne's insights extend beyond male heterosexuality; see Claude J. Summers, ed., *Homosexuality in Renaissance and Enlightenment England* (San Francisco: Haworth, 1992) 103–32.

70. For anxiety about cuckoldry in early modern England, see Katherine Eisaman Maus, "Horns of Dilemma: Jealousy, Gender, and Spectatorship in English Renaissance Drama," *ELH* 54 (1987): 561–83.

edge of the addressee's (as yet unmanifested) intention to betray him and on his own full acceptance of the situation that he has postulated. In "The Indifferent," the speaker wishes on any woman who seeks to "stablish dangerous constancie" the ultimate horror, the experience of being committed to someone who will betray her. In "Loves Diet," the process of "ab-whoring" a threateningly devoted woman results in a happy state of psychological uninvolvement in which the speaker is even indifferent to sex ("negligent of sport").[71]

This last phrase brings us back to a striking formal feature in the characterization of Phrygius, his epithet: "Carelesse Phrygius." He is the only figure to have an epithet, yet the one that he has seems inappropriate. If anything, "Carelesse Phrygius" would seem to be overly careful. The only scholar until very recently to have puzzled over the epithet adopts the view of Phrygius as a Separatist, so that "as a separatist sectarian, he cares for no one else."[72] But this is neither lexicographically nor historically plausible. There is no instance of "careless" as "caring for no one else" in the *OED*, and the sectarians were notably clannish and group-oriented rather than individualistic. They were the brethren, and they attempted to establish "pure" churches.[73] Phrygius is a nonjoiner, a noncommitter; he is not in an enthusiastic "frenzy."[74] The most interesting possibility is that Phrygius is "careless" because he is free from care, *se-cura* (the first meaning in the *OED*). This is the *ataraxia* of the ancient skeptics, for whom skepticism, as Popkin reminds us, "was a cure for the disease called Dogmatism or rashness."[75] The state of indifference, of happy negligence, was a condition to which Donne, in the erotic context at least, was highly attracted (and again, I do not think that this should be moralized away or fobbed off on personae). Phrygius is, to be sure, a negative exemplum, but not, it turns out, unambiguously so.

71. See the fine reading of "Love's Diet" in Barbara Hardy's "Thinking and Feeling in the Songs and Sonets," in Smith, ed., *Donne: Essays in Celebration*, 79–80; also in Hardy, *The Advantage of Feeling: Essays on Feeling in Poetry* (Bloomington: Indiana University Press, 1977), 24. In this reading, Hardy does what Empson calls "attend[ing] to the story" (see Essay 1, n. 23 above), a procedure for which Hardy praises Empson in "The Critics Who Made Us: William Empson's *Seven Types of Ambiguity*," *Sewanee Review* 90 (1982): 430–39.

72. C. A. Patrides in *The Complete English Poems of John Donne* (London: Dent, 1985), 227.

73. For some actual Separatist texts, see George Huntston Williams, ed., *Spiritual and Anabaptist Writers* (Philadelphia: Westminster, 1957).

74. Hester's work on "Phrygian frenzies" (*Kinde Pitty and Brave Scorn*, 125) is interesting but not clearly relevant to Donne's portrait.

75. Popkin, *The History of Scepticism*, xv.

The final portrait is even more complex. It presents another version of indifference, but this time the positive rather than the negative version: "Graccus loves all as one." He is like "the indifferent" of the lyrics, who "can love both faire and browne," who can love "any"—so long as they do not try to "bind" him. Before telling us what Graccus believes, Donne gives us a coy enjambment ("he thinks that so"—line break), and we expect that what follows will be at least as fallacious as Phrygius's reasoning. Yet instead, Graccus thinks that "As women do in divers countries goe / In divers habits, yet are still one kinde, / So doth, so is Religion" (66–68). What is striking about Graccus's view is how sensible it is. It involves neither a false premise (like "she must be there because she used to be there") nor any obviously false reasoning (like moving from some to all). In one of his elegies, Donne holds it as obvious that entities are "still one kinde" in different clothing and in different conditions.[76] It's hard to see what's wrong with Graccus's view. But perhaps, in the religious context, we are being anachronistic; this is, as we have seen, the great club of the conservative historical scholar. Or perhaps, as Empson maintained, there were more attitudes available to a sixteenth-century intellectual than modern orthodoxy would like to allow.[77] After all, an eccentric Friulian miller of Donne's day held (and was burned for holding) that "the majesty of God has given the Holy Spirit to all, to all Christians, to heretics, to Turks, and to the Jews; and he considers them all dear, and they are all saved in the same manner."[78]

And perhaps this view was not merely eccentric. Menocchio went very far, but it might plausibly be said that the ultimate sponsor of Menocchio's view of the immense mercy of God was the figure of "the great Erasmus."[79] Erasmus held that "*whatever* is devout and contributes to

76. "Richly cloath'd Apes, are call'd Apes, and as soone / Ecclips'd as bright we call the Moone the Moone," "Elegie: On his Mistress," lines 31–32. The fact that these entities, apes and the moon, are famously unstable only intensifies the ontological identity claim. Compare Descartes's wax; see "Meditation 2" in *Meditations on First Philosophy*, in *The Philosophical Works of Descartes*, trans. Elizabeth S. Haldane and G. R. T. Ross, 2 vols. (Cambridge: Cambridge University Press, 1931), 1:154–57.

77. This is the point of most of Empson's essays on Donne (see n. 2 above).

78. See Carlo Ginzburg, *The Cheese and the Worms: The Cosmos of a Sixteenth-Century Miller*, trans. John Tedeschi and Anne Tedeschi (Baltimore: Johns Hopkins University Press, 1980), 9–10.

79. For "the great Erasmus," see "The Printer to the Reader," in John Donne, *Ignatius His Conclave*, ed. and trans. T. S. Healy (Oxford: Clarendon Press, 1969). For Erasmus on "The Immense Mercy of God," see *The Essential Erasmus*, ed. Dolan, 226–70. In this sermon, Erasmus does not reject Origen's view that everyone, including demons and the damned, will eventually be saved, though he does mention that this view has been

good morals should not be called profane" and that "perhaps the spirit of Christ is more widespread than we understand."[80] Another intellectual ancestor of this view was a great friend of the great Erasmus and a literal ancestor of John Donne: Sir Thomas More. Donne refers to More a number of times, and these references are always to the humanist, not to the hammer of Protestants. For Donne, More is the translator of Lucian and, especially, the author of *Utopia*.[81] In *Utopia*, the possibility is explicitly raised that religious diversity is perhaps a good rather than a bad thing.[82] Ficino entertained this view, and Nicholas of Cusa asserted it.[83] The greatest skeptic of the Renaissance held that "Of all the ancient human opinions concerning religion," that one "was most probable and most excusable which recognized God as an incomprehensible power, origin and preserver of all things, all goodness, all perfection, accepting and taking in good part the honor and reverence that human beings rendered him, *under whatever aspect, under whatever name, in whatever*

---

condemned (242). On the attractiveness of this view to Erasmus, see Bainton, *Erasmus of Christendom*, 194. Ginzburg, *The Cheese and the Worms*, 51, mentions the closeness of Menocchio's views to those of certain humanist scholars, but Ginzburg's programmatic antipathy toward high-to-low models of cultural transmission prevents him from exploring this closeness. Ginzburg's attempt (in n. 58, pp. 154–55) to defend his general procedures and, in particular, his occlusion of Ficino against Paola Zambelli's critique is, I think, disingenuous and unsuccessful; for the critique, see Zambelli, "Uno, due, tre, mille Menocchio?" *Archivo storico italiano* 137 (1979): 51–90. I would add to this critique the occlusion of Erasmus, and I would argue that on the matter of toleration, the difference between Menocchio and these culturally "higher" types lies only in the unself-consciousness of Menocchio's views, not in the content of those views.

80. "The Godly Feast," in *Colloquies of Erasmus*, 65 (emphasis mine). In *On the Providence of God (De Providentia)*, Zwingli virtually paraphrases this: "why call that 'philosophical' [in a pejorative sense—that is, *merely* philosophical] which is sacred and according to religion . . . [for] the truth, wherever found and by whomever brought out, is from the Holy Spirit"; *The Latin Works of Huldreich Zwingli*, trans. S. M. Jackson (Philadelphia: Heidelberg Press, 1929), 3:144.

81. For More as translator of Lucian, see *Pseudo-martyr*, 108; for admiring references to *Utopia*, see *Biathanatos,* facsimile (New York: Arno, 1977), 74 and 123.

82. Utopus, the founder of the Utopian polity, "was uncertain whether God did not desire a varied and manifold worship and therefore did not inspire different people with different views." St. Thomas More, *Utopia*, ed. Edward J. Surtz and J. H. Hexter (New Haven: Yale University Press, 1965), 221.

83. Ficino and Cusa are cited by Surtz (p. 522) in his commentary on the passage quoted in the previous note. On Cusa's religious universalism, see Ernst Cassirer, *The Individual and the Cosmos in Renaissance Philosophy* (New York: Harper and Row, 1963), 27–30. On Ficino, see Paul Oskar Kristeller, *The Philosophy of Marsilio Ficino* (New York: Columbia University Press, 1943), 315–22. Donne knew some of the writings of Cusa and discusses his *Cribratio Alcorani* in *Essays in Divinity*, ed. Evelyn M. Simpson (Oxford: Clarendon, 1952), 9.

manner."[84] Most of all, Graccus's view is close to that of the writer who insisted that "Synagogue and Church" named "the same thing," and that "Roman and Reformed, and all other distinctions of place, Discipline, or Person" named "but one Church." This same writer, in a work that he knew was going to be accused of "*Erasmiando*," called for a "humane indifferency," noting that "the free Spirit of God" blows "where it listeth, not tied nor imprison'd to any place or person." This writer proudly affirmed to his best friend that "I never fettered nor imprisoned the word Religion . . . immuring it in a Rome, or a Wittemberg, or a Geneva," and claimed that for him these churches were always "all virtuall beames of one Sun." This writer, of course, was John Donne.[85]

But there *must* be something wrong with Graccus's view. Donne's comment on it is ambiguous. In a violent enjambment, Donne says of the position that "this blind- / nesse too much light breeds" (68b–69a). The enjambment serves to establish, for a moment, "blind" as a noun. This might suggest that Graccus's view is a pretext, some sort of hypocritical concealment, but this possibility is left entirely undeveloped. In the actual context of the poem, what the unusual mid-word line break does is to connect Graccus, at least momentarily, with the other "blind" figures in the poem, the philosophers, whom Donne, like Erasmus and Zwingli, placed in heaven.[86] This association is appropriate, given Graccus's religious view, but it cuts against the moral condemnation of him. Will he end up a philosopher in heaven? Insofar as there is any moral condemnation of Graccus, it occurs in the half line that completes the thought about blindness: "this blind- / nesse too much light breeds." Yet in the tradition of Ficino and Cusa, the "blindness" that is bred from "too much light," from the "virtuall beames of

84. Michel de Montaigne, "Apology for Raymond Sebond," in *The Complete Essays of Montaigne*, trans. Donald M. Frame (Stanford: Stanford University Press, 1958), 380 (emphasis added). Montaigne's phrasing here ("most excusable") is typically careful.

85. For the references, see Donne, *Essays in Divinity*, 51; *Pseudo-martyr*, sig. B1r, 135; and *Letters*, 25. For another positive use by Donne of the notion of "indifferency" in the religious context (with an acknowledgment that this stance often breeds some scandal), see *Letters*, 87. For the Erasmian nature of one of the works that Donne probably drew on in *Pseudo-martyr*, see Dominic Baker-Smith, "John Donne's *Critique of True Religion*," in Smith, ed., *Donne: Essays in Celebration*, 420–23.

86. For Zwingli, see, most spectacularly, the list of "saints and sages" in *An Exposition of the Faith*, in *Latin Works of Huldreich Zwingli*, 2:272; also in *Zwingli and Bullinger*, ed. G. W. Bromiley (Philadelphia: Westminster Press, 1953), 275.

one Sun," is entirely positive.[87] But perhaps the primary reading is to follow the actual word order and take "blindnesse" as the subject rather than the object of "breeds," so that the blindness breeds "too much light." This would intensify the implication of promiscuity that is certainly meant to be here (as in "light" women), but even so this implication too is strangely undeveloped. Donne never translates Graccus's position into the description of a promiscuous lecherous humor. This would have been extremely easy (recall "The Indifferent"), but Donne does not do it.[88] The condemnation of Graccus remains perfunctory, abstract, and, most of all, ambiguous. As I have already suggested, it is at least odd, in an epistemological context, to complain about "too much light," and even in an ethical context, as the Wife of Bath suggests, and as Donne dramatizes in one of his most famous and spectacular images, promiscuity can be presented as a form of charity.[89]

IV

Yet Graccus's position does breed "too much light"—or rather, in the late sixteenth-century context, potentially too much heat. Donne is not prepared to endorse so heretically liberal a view. He did not know about Menocchio, but he certainly did know about Michael

87. On the "Orphic" reading of Blind Love, see Edgar Wind, *Pagan Mysteries in the Renaissance*, rev. ed. (New York: Norton, 1968), 53–58; 218–21.

88. Scodel, "The Medium is the Message," 492, calls attention to a portrait of a Gracchus together with a reference to "the Phrygian manner" (*"Phrygio . . . more"*) in Juvenal's second Satire (lines 114–26); see *Juvenal and Persius*, trans. G. G. Ramsay, rev. ed. (Cambridge: Harvard University Press, Loeb Classical Library, 1940), 26. This is an important discovery with regard to the names, but Scodel's attempt to connect Donne's Graccus substantively to Juvenal's is not convincing (his attempt to connect Donne's Phrygius to "the Phrygian manner," self-castration, works better). Donne's Graccus is simply not Juvenal's transvestite awaiting a husband. Moreover, apart from the name (on which see also Milgate, *Satires*, 145), to argue, as Scodel does, that Graccus cannot be a positive model because the poem's quest is not for Religion but for "true religion" is to beg the key question of whether the poem consistently maintains this distinction.

89. Geoffrey Chaucer, "The Wife of Bath's Prologue," lines 621–26, in *The Works of Geoffrey Chaucer*, ed. F. N. Robinson (Boston: Houghton Mifflin, 1957), 82. For Donne's image, see his Holy Sonnet on the church, where the church is most pleasing and faithful to God "When she'is embrac'd and open to most men."

Servetus, burned in Geneva in 1553, and many others.[90] Donne pulls back from Graccus's view, from the blindness of too much light. We can see here the pressure of history on a text. Dominic Baker-Smith, referring to the passage on "humane indifferency" and "the free spirit of God" in *Pseudo-martyr*, asserts wonderfully that "if Satire III is about anything it is about the free spirit of God."[91] Unfortunately, this is not completely true. Yet we need not go to the other extreme and accept Carey's view that the third Satire is fiercely intolerant of tolerance.[92] What we need to acknowledge is that the poem is more nervous and conflicted about its theological radicalism than Baker-Smith's wonderful asseveration suggests. When, in the third clearly marked section of the poem, Donne returns to the mode of direct, second-person singular address, he comments only on the final two options, those embodied by Phrygius and Graccus. "Unmoved" by these examples, "thou," unlike Phrygius, "Of force must one" position take, and unlike Graccus, when "forc'd" must "but one allow" (70). Why the individual "must one" take is never explained. The editors say that "Of force" means "of necessity," but they do not explain whence this necessity arises. Milgate cleverly suggests that the sense appears to be that "one cannot be religious without 'having a religion.'"[93] Yet perhaps this is too conservative. Even many years after the Satire, Donne imagined the possibility of a person who was religious without "having a religion," who believed in God but thought there was "a way to salvation without any particular religion."[94] And in the second half of the line, "forc'd" seems to represent mere coercion. Apparently the non-"tender" individual "but one" allows only under duress.

Donne seems to accept a position of forced choice, of, in the erotic analogy, marriage under duress, though with some resistance. We would seem to have come to a full stop here ("Of force must one, and forc'd but one allow") yet the beginning of the next line adds, with the loosest of connectives an afterthought that redirects the entire course of the argument: "And the right" (line 71a). This should, I think, come as a shock. Not only must the individual "allow" one religious position, and,

---

90. On Servetus, see Roland H. Bainton, *Hunted Heretic: The Life and Death of Michael Servetus, 1511–1553* (Boston: Beacon Press, 1953).

91. Baker-Smith, "Donne's *Critique of True Religion*," 431.

92. See Carey, *Donne: Life, Mind and Art*, 29.

93. *Satires*, 145.

94. *The Sermons of John Donne*, ed. George R. Potter and Evelyn M. Simpson, 10 vols. (Berkeley and Los Angeles: University of Calfornia Press, 1953–62), 3:276.

if forced, "but one," but that one must be "the right." Suddenly there is only one right answer. Suddenly it is not foolish to think that one church or position "is onely perfect." In pulling back from Phrygius and Graccus, Donne suddenly asserts the preeminence of ortho-doxy, right belief. The epistemological context of "true religion" is sheered off from the erotic context of "faire Religion" (which allowed for the praise of diversity, "both faire and browne"). This turn becomes even odder when we are told how to find "true religion": "aske thy father which is shee" (line 71b). Donne seems suddenly to be recommending Graius's obedient position. Only the suppression of the erotic analogy obscures the connection. A reasonably full reading of this poem must acknowledge the strangeness of this turn and must, I think, offer some account of it.

Here is one way to understand what has happened: in attempting to distance himself from the compelling heterodoxies of the "indifferent" figures, Donne has swung to an extreme conservatism.[95] One of the main reasons to work through a text in detail is to be able to chart such ebbs and flows. After "aske thy father," Donne begins to pull back from (as I see it) this protective lurch into conservatism. To "aske thy father which is shee" would seem to be a straightforward matter, but again it turns out that "easie wayes and neare" are not really available. If the historical Donne were to have imagined an answer from his father (or either of his stepfathers), there is no doubt whom "shee" would be, but to "aske thy father" turns out to be only the beginning of a process: "Let him aske his," and so on. The only guarantee against infinite regress that Donne offers is the very qualified assertion that "though truth and falshood bee / Neare twins, yet truth a little elder is" (72–73). This is hardly reassuring. "A little elder" does not seem very strong or immediately apprehensible; it seems an awfully small difference on which to base the status of truth. Yet the attempt, widespread in the scholarship, to see the poem as endorsing some familiar combination of "right reason aided by tradition" rests on these lines.[96] The lines themselves have barely been

95. I cannot agree with Carey that the tensions in the poem are to be seen as springing entirely (or even primarily) from Donne's ambivalence about adult independence (*Donne: Life, Mind and Art*, 28). The example of Servetus (and, later, of Bruno) suggests that there was truly something to be nervous about with regard to religious freethinking in the sixteenth century. Again, however, Carey is right to see the tensions. Our disagreement seems to me to be a model of agreeing on the facts (see p. 3 above).

96. The quotation is from Camille Wells Slights, *The Casuistical Tradition in Shakespeare, Donne, Herbert, and Milton* (Princeton: Princeton University Press, 1981),

analyzed. J. B. Leishman is the only critic to have put them under any pressure. Leishman seems to me correct in seeing these lines as untraditional in their rationalist and humanist emphasis: "This saving truth is, in a sense, factual rather than doctrinal, and to be attained not in some beatific vision, but as the result of a long and laborious process of historical, or semi-historical, research."[97] Even this account, however, suggests more reassurance than the very vexed and modest imagery of the poem does. Are truth and falsehood twins or not?

The next lines complete the swing back to autonomy. The fathers fall away, and again the emphasis is on personal effort: "Be busie to seeke her" (74a). In the rest of the couplet that completes this rededication, Donne (or his "speaker") underlines his commitment by strongly asserting his sincerity: "Beleeve mee this," he adjures (74b). What we are so solemnly adjured to believe is that "Hee's not of none, nor worst, that seekes the best" (75). This is a remarkable assertion; it insists on the religious standing of the seeker. And it is not clear what it means to say that such a figure is "not of none." The point of the line seems precisely to defend the earnest seeker who is "of none." Or perhaps there is a church of seekers, or a church that includes all the pious who are "without any particular religion." Donne's effort is to defend the figure who at least looks as if he is "of none." He returns to the viewpoint of Phrygius, who "doth abhorre / All," although now the context is purely epistemological, without the erotic analogy and with the skepticism precise and explicit: "To'adore, or scorne an image, or protest, / May all be bad" (76–77a). In propria persona Donne presents the possibility that "all" the major religious possibilities in Europe may "be bad." He does not say merely that any one of them may be bad but that it is possible that they all may be. Again, this would justify being "of none." The message of the poem becomes that of Socrates (surely one of the "blind Philosophers in heaven"), the great proponent of therapeutic skepticism: "Doubt wisely" (77b).[98] This may give us a perspective from

---

164; see also Sister M. Geraldine, "John Donne and the Mindes Indeavours," *Studies in English Literature* 5 (1965): 117; and many others.

97. J. B. Leishman, *The Monarch of Wit: An Analytical and Comparative Study of the Poetry of John Donne*, 5th ed. (London: Hutchinson, 1962), 116. Compare Carey, *Donne: Life, Mind and Art*: "The poem's effort is to make out that choosing a religion is a purely intellectual business" (p. 29).

98. Socrates distinguishes wise from unwise, productive from unproductive (*eristic*) doubt in *Meno*, 80d-81e, *Complete Dialogues of Plato*, 363–64. In *Biathanatos*, Donne

which to understand the true status of Phrygius (and perhaps Graccus) in the poem. Perhaps in their cases it is true that the trouble is not with their views but with the way they hold them. They are perhaps too tranquil in their positions. If the search for "true religion" takes place in the realm of opinion rather than that of knowledge, then (according to Donne much later), hesitation is appropriate, but "indifferency, and equanimity" are not.[99]

But does the search take place in the realm of opinion? This question haunts this section of the poem. In explaining wise doubt, Donne notes that "in a strange way / To stand inquiring right, is not to stray," while "To sleepe, or runne wrong, is" (77c-79a). This passage rests uneasily on two conflicting contrasts: right and wrong, on the one hand, and sleeping versus running on the other. The punctuation suggests that the contrast is between sleeping and running wrong, but semantically (with some help from the syntax) the contrast is between sleeping and running—what is wrong is running, that is, being precipitous. Socrates' daemon always told him not to do things.[100] In one reading, the emphasis is on finding the right way; in the other, it is on proceeding in the proper manner. One way to focus the problem would be to ask whether the passage would seem to approve (or conceive of) *running* right.[101] The same ambiguity exists in the phrase "inquiring right" itself. The traveler image suggests that the phrase means, "inquiring which is the right path," but the phrase can also be read as recommending "inquiring in the right manner." This same hesitation between emphasizing success and emphasizing effort, between result and process, is at work in the poem's most famous passage, the image of the hill of Truth:

> On a huge hill,
> Cragged and steep, Truth stands, and hee that will

---

speaks of "that successive Trinity of humane wisedome, *Socrates, Plato,* and *Aristotle*" (p. 58).

99. Donne, *Sermons,* 6:317.

100. "It always dissuades me from what I am proposing to do, and never urges me on," *Apology,* 31d, *Complete Dialogues,* 17.

101. The passage which Milgate *(Satires,* 146) quotes from the *Sermons* (8:54) on the relation between doubting and truth can be seen as a conservative recuperation (by "Doctor Donne") of this passage in the Satire. The emphasis in the sermon is on doubt as a step toward resolution. In the passage from Chrysostom that Donne there quotes, the soul that has first doubted is seen as accepting resolution more readily (*"facile solutionem accipit anima, quae prius dubitavit"*). This facility in accepting resolution is not in the poem.

> Reach her, about must, and about must goe;
> And what th'hills suddennes resists, winne so. (79b-82)

This image is neither as conventional as it seems nor, like the "truth as elder" trope, as reassuring as it is commonly taken to be. An abstraction on a hill is a familiar allegorical tableau, but none of the analogues cited by Milgate have the specific content of Donne's image. Normally, it is virtue or education on the hill. Again, "tradition" tends to blur rather than to clarify. Milgate himself acknowledges that an apparent analogue in one of Donne's sermons is strikingly different from the passage in the Satire. In the sermon, "we must leave our naturall reason . . . at the bottome of the hill."[102] Thomas V. Moore has offered a penetrating critique of the general tendency of critics to overstate the positive aspects of the satire and especially of this image.[103] He notes, for instance, that the emphasis in this passage is not, as Helen Gardner suggested, on the solidity and visibility of truth but on the difficulty of the quest.[104] Perhaps the most remarkable later instance of both the general and the particular tendencies that Moore discusses is this confident assertion: "the hill can be won and man one with God through His Son, the satirist confirms."[105] This is an assertion that leaves the poem entirely behind; Christ never appears in it. Rather than relying on "tradition" or "knowledge"—what *must* be there—we can trust the verse. It gives us stresses on "huge," "cragged," and "steep," and a most powerful evocation of repetitive circularity: "about must, and about must." There is no sense of progress in this line, only of effort. Poetically, the whole next line (82) is an afterthought. It comes as an addition, after a full stop, and its own structure is anticlimactic. Its final two words ("winne so") are weak; the energy of the line goes into the hill's resistance. The imagination of effort and resistance here is much more powerful than the imagination of success.[106]

102. See *Satires*, 292.

103. Thomas V. Moore, "Donne's Use of Uncertainty As a Vital Force in *Satyre III*," *Modern Philology* 67 (1969): 43.

104. Moore, "Donne's Use of Uncertainty," 47. For Gardner's claim, see *John Donne: The Divine Poems*, ed. Helen Gardner (Oxford: Clarendon, 1952), xix.

105. Hester, *Kinde Pitty and Brave Scorn*, 66.

106. In a comment on an earlier form of this essay given at a panel on resistance in the Renaissance, Annabel Patterson noted that it is only in this passage that any form of the word "resist" appears in the poem. If it is true (as I argue) that resistance is a crucial theme in the poem, the appearance of the word here would suggest that Donne in this image identifies more fully with the resistant hill than with the "winning" seeker. Psychological and political "resistance" would merge here.

We can trust the verse further. The poem proceeds as if the line about winning didn't exist. After "winne so," Donne continues, "yet strive so, that before age, deaths twilight, / Thy Soule rest" (83–84a). "Yet strive so" follows from "about must, and about must," not from "winne so." And what is the conception of "rest" here? It surely involves a notion of arriving at settled convictions sometime in one's lifetime before old age sets in, but whether the emphasis is on attaining a settled sense of one's own convictions or on attaining "the right" convictions remains unclear. Donne's revision of the lines may reflect this uncertainty. In a number of manuscripts (presumably reflecting earlier states of the poem), it is the mind rather than the soul that is to find rest before death approaches.[107] In shifting from "mynde" to "Soule," Donne may very well have been trying to push toward the more absolutist conception, since, as Milgate points out, Donne seems (at times, at least) to have used "mind" to designate a particularized subjectivity. In a letter to Good-yere, Donne distinguishes between, on the one hand, both the soul and the body—which both have preset ontological goals—and on the other "our third part, the minde, which is our naturall guide here, [and] chooses to every man a severall way."[108] The concern about "age, deaths twilight," would seem to call for "our naturall guide here," but I am not sure, in any case, that the change from "mynde" to "soule" eliminates the previous sense. The emphasis seems to be earthly rather than tran-scendental, and even the portentous reference to the gospel of John, "none can worke in that night" (84b), only serves to give more weight to a carpe diem for the intellectual life. The reference seems to be more to Catullus's everlasting night than to the apocalyptic context of the gospel.[109] . Protestantism made this classical view available to the Chris-tian by insisting that "none can worke" after death—that is, by elim-inating Purgatory from the cosmos (famously in Dante, a hill up which souls labor). Donne saw "all discourse of Purgatorie" as "but the *Mythologie* of the Romane Church."[110]

The carpe diem feeling dominates the line that follows. Intention and resolution will not suffice; what is necessary is action: "To will, implyes

---

107. *Satires*, 13; *Complete Poetry*, ed. Shawcross, 430.
108. *Satires*, 146; Donne, *Letters*, 62–63.
109. For *nox . . . perpetua* in the most famous of all *carpe diem* poems, see Catullus, *"Vivamus mea Lesbia,"* lines 11–12, in *Catullus, Tibullus, Pervigilium Veneris*, Catullus trans. F. W. Cornish, rev. G. P. Goold, 2d ed. (Cambridge: Harvard University Press, Loeb Classical Library, 1988), 6.
110. Donne, *Pseudo-martyr*, 106.

delay, therefore now doe" (85). But since the context is an intellectual one, Donne has to make clear what such "doing" consists of and what it can hope to accomplish. He reverts to his earlier appeal to physical heroism: "Hard deeds, the bodies paines; hard knowledge too / The mindes indeavours reach" (86–87a). This is bracing and highly reassuring, but it is almost too pragmatic and matter-of-fact. The context, after all, is not that of intellectual life in general but of the religious life in particular. Donne recoils from the view that Leishman has plausibly attributed to him, that saving truth is "factual" and to be attained by laborious scholarship and reasoning. After this picture of the inevitable success of "the mindes indeavours"—the Soul has dropped away again—Donne adds two words that return us to the religious realm: "and mysteries" (87b). Donne has to try somehow to reconcile his rationalism with an acknowledgment of "mysteries." The enjambment again creates an ambiguity. At first, taking "and mysteries" as continuous with the previous lines, it seems that "the mindes indeavours" can reach mysteries as well as "hard knowledge." But the next line denies this possibility: mysteries "Are like the Sunne, dazling, yet plaine to'all eyes" (88). No commentator has yet plucked out the heart of the mysteries in these "dazling, yet plaine" lines. The lines imply that "mysteries" are unequivocally *there*, that the existence of these mysteries cannot be denied—it is "plaine to'all eyes," even if the content of these mysteries is "dazling." But what is the relationship between the "dazling" of this sun and the "blind- / nesse" of Graccus and the pagan philosophers? The relationship between "the mindes indeavours" and "mysteries" is left thoroughly unclear.[111]

Perhaps Donne is suggesting that there are two different realms, in one of which, that of empirical truth and of diverse opinions, "the mindes indeavours" can work appropriately, whereas the other realm contains incontrovertible, nonempirical truths that are "plaine to'all eyes," including those of the philosophers. This is not a position unknown to the sixteenth century. "Doubt wisely" might suggest not only Socrates but the Erasmian (and Socratic) author of *De arte dubitandi*, Sebastian Castellio. Donne could not have known *De arte dubitandi*, but he could easily have read *Concerning Heretics*, Castellio's most famous work, and it is very unlikely that he would not at least have heard of

---

111. Helen Gardner again provides a reassuring and noncontextual gloss; see *Divine Poems*, xix.

Castellio and his views.[112] Castellio held, briefly, that, as Dryden later put it, "The things we must believe are few and plain": the existence and goodness of God, the immortality of the soul, the moral law.[113] These things can not rationally be doubted. On the other hand, everything else is in the realm of opinion, and can, indeed should, rationally be doubted (Castellio remarked that *"l'autheur principal de ceste opinion et secte a esté Socrates"*).[114] Prolonged controversy over a question is a sign of its dubitability, and it makes no sense to persecute someone for holding a particular view on an essentially contestable matter.[115] Castellio echoes and develops King Utopus's doubts about whether "God did not desire a varied and manifold worship and therefore did not inspire different people with different views." "Perhaps," Castellio speculated, "God is the better pleased not to be easily known and *to be glorified in different ways*."[116] Closer to home and to reality, a philosopher who was to become a close friend of Donne's, Edward (Lord) Herbert (George's older brother) came to hold a view of religious truth quite similar to Castellio's.[117]

112. *De arte dubitandi et confidendi, ignorandi et sciendi* remained in manuscript until it was edited and published by Elizabeth Feist in D. Cantimori and Elizabeth Feist, eds., *Per la storia degli eretici Italiani del secolo XVI in Europa* (Rome: Reale Accademia D'Italia, 1937), 307–430. Castellio is responsible for making Calvin's burning of Servetus into "the Servetus affair." Calvin and Beza both answered Castellio's attacks on the persecution of "heretics" (see nn. 50 above and 113 below). It is noteworthy with regard to the English context that Castellio dedicated his Latin translation of the Bible to Edward VI. The definitive study remains Ferdinand Buisson, *Sébastien Castellion: Sa vie et son oeuvre*, 2 vols. (Paris: Hachette, 1892). A useful collection, including Roland Bainton's "Sebastian Castellio, Champion of Religious Liberty," is *Castellioniana: Quatre études sur Sébastien Castellion et l'idée de la tolérance* (Leiden: Brill, 1951). Castellio's influence in the sixteenth and seventeenth centuries has not been fully explored. There is a beginning in J. Lindbloom, "La Place de Castellion dans l'histoire de l'esprit" in B. Becker, ed., *Autour de Michel Servet et de Sébastien Castellion* (Haarlem: Tjeenk Willink, 1953), 158–80.

113. Dryden, "Religio Laici," line 432, in *The Poetical Works of John Dryden*, ed. George R. Noyes (Boston: Houghton Mifflin, 1950), 167; Castellio, *De arte dubitandi*, 309–10, 351.

114. Castellio, *De l'impunité des hérétiques*, 224.

115. *De arte dubitandi*, 346–48; *De l'impunité des hérétiques*, 224–26.

116. Sebastian Castellio, *Concerning Heretics*, trans. Roland Bainton (New York: Columbia University Press, 1935), 237 (emphasis mine). For Utopus, see n. 82 above.

117. See Edward (Lord) Herbert of Cherbury, *De Veritate*, trans. Meyrick H. Carr (Bristol: Arrowsmith, 1937). In "The Grounds of Religious Toleration in the Thought of John Donne," *Church History* 11 (1942), Roy W. Battenhouse notes that Donne "sometimes reminds us of his friend, Lord Herbert of Cherbury" (233). I am not suggesting that Donne was already friends with Edward Herbert in 1595; they probably

One of the consequences of Castellio's position was the absoluteness of the individual conscience. In trying to contextualize Menocchio's view that "every man could be saved through his own religion," Carlo Ginzburg cites Castellio as an analogue.[118] Donne's advice to the life-long seeker of religious truth culminates in one admonition: "Keepe the truth which thou'hast found" (89a). This admonition precisely reca-pitulates the central ambiguity of this section of the poem: on one reading, the aim is to keep that part or aspect of the objective truth that you have managed to recognize ("Keepe *the truth* which thou'hast found"); on the other reading, you are to keep what has impressed *you* as the truth ("Keepe the truth which *thou'hast found*"). The first reading asserts the primacy of truth; the second the primacy of conscience—even over truth. The poem hesitates between these views, and it is important not dismiss the second as an anachronism, a Romantic innovation pro-jected back into the Renaissance. It was a genuine historical possibility. Luther meant to equate rather than to distinguish truth and conscience at Worms, but when he stated that "to act against conscience is neither safe for us, nor open to us," he necessarily provided a psychological and conceptual structure for the primacy of conscience.[119] Castellio took the next step. He noted that everyone feels his conscience to be compelled or captured by the truth he believes in; Castellio asserted, moreover, that God will love "those who with good intent defend that *which they conceive to be true*."[120] In the first Satire, Donne played lightly with the idea that the unpardonable "offense" is to sin against one's own con-science; with conscious hyperbole, he asked, "But how shall I be par-don'd my offense / That thus have sinn'd against my conscience?" (65–66). In a letter to Goodyere he again lightly alluded to the idea that "it is a sinne to doe against the conscience, *though that erre*"—exactly Castellio's position.[121] In *Biathanatos*, Donne expounds this position at length, arguing that "a conscience that erreth justly, probably, and *bona fide*, that is, after all morall industry and diligence hath been used" is "bound to doe according to that misinformation and the misperswasion

met in 1599 (see Gardner, ed., *Elegies and Songs and Sonnets*, 254). I am only suggesting that Castellio's views were less "outlandish" than they might seem.

118. Ginzburg, *Cheese and Worms*, 51.

119. H. Bettenson, ed., *Documents of the Christian Church*, 2d ed. (Oxford: Oxford University Press, 1947), 285.

120. "Reply to Calvin's Book in which he Endeavors to Show that Heretics should be Coerced by the Right of the Sword," in *Concerning Heretics*, 281, 223.

121. Donne, *Letters*, 76 (emphasis mine); Castellio, *Concerning Heretics*, 124, 215.

so contracted." Moreover, Donne adds, even if a conscience "erre negligently or otherwise vitiously, and *mala fide,* as long as that errour remains and resides in it, a man is bound not to doe against his conscience."[122]

V

Donne retreated from *Biathanatos.* In *Pseudo-martyr* he argued that "it is not conscience it selfe that bindes us," but rather "that law which the Conscience takes knowledge of."[123] Satire III and *Biathanatos* are major works by "Jack" Donne "Of Religion," and the latter is probably our best guide to the former. In *Biathanatos,* the assertion of the supremacy of "conscience it selfe" is tied to a strong anti-authoritarianism and assertion of the authority of the individual. The obligation that our conscience casts upon us, says Jack, is "of stronger hold and straighter band, *then the precept of any Superiour, whether Law or person.*"[124] Again and again in this text, Donne insists on the autonomy and autarchy of the individual: "in secret cases between the Spirit of God, and my conscience, of which there is not certainly constituted any exteriour Judge, we are our selves sufficient to doe all the Offices; and then delivered from all bondage, and restored to our naturall libertie, we are in the same condition as Princes are"; in private cases of conscience, "a private man is Emperor of himselfe."[125] Princes do but play us. Any reader of Donne's love poetry knows the hold that the idea of being "in the same condition as Princes are" had on Donne's imagination.[126] The final movement of the Satire is a defense of the individual

122. Donne, *Biathanatos,* 142.

123. Donne, *Pseudo-martyr,* 237. Even after *Pseudo-martyr,* Donne seems to have sometimes returned to his earlier position, at least in private. See the letter to the Duke of Buckingham in 1623 reproduced in Bald, *Donne,* 446, in which Donne writes that the Spanish divines, "though they say not true, yet they do not ly, because they speake their Conscience." I believe that Bald seriously misreads this letter.

124. Donne, *Biathanatos,* 143 (emphasis mine).

125. Donne, *Biathanatos,* 107, 47.

126. For some wonderfully suggestive writing on Donne and kingship, see Carey, *Donne: Life, Mind and Art,* 115; and Debora Kuller Shuger, *Habits of Thought in the English Renaissance: Religion, Politics, and the Dominant Culture* (Berkeley and Los Angeles: University of California Press, 1990), 165–76. Donne's status, even after *Pseudo-martyr,* as a devoted "king's man" has been questioned by Annabel Patterson in two essays, "All Donne," in Elizabeth D. Harvey and Katherine Eisaman Maus, eds., *Soliciting*

conscience in the face of political power. The culminating exhortation in the realm of epistemology ("Keepe the truth which thou hast found" [89a]) leads directly to this issue:

> men do not stand
> In so'ill case here, that God hath with his hand
> Sign'd Kings blanck-charters to kill whom they hate,
> Nor are they Vicars, but hangmen to Fate. (89b–92)

There are definite limits to what kings can legitimately do. As D. C. Allen pointed out, this passage echoes Luther's treatise on *Secular Authority—to What Extent It Should Be Obeyed*; the "hangmen" kings are Luther's.[127] This is not merely a verbal connection. Donne's fundamental emphasis, like Luther's and Castellio's, is on one's individual responsibility for one's spiritual state. "Every man," said Luther, in a passage prominently reproduced by Castellio, "is responsible for his own faith."[128] Donne's worry in this poem is not about the tyranny of kings and princes—which he, like Luther, seems to take for granted—but rather about the tendency of the individual to allow external authorities to dictate to the conscience, to forget how and where persons politically "stand."[129] Donne returns to Graius, to his attack on the "tender" and complaisant. With a sudden renewal of vehemence, he exclaims: "Foole and wretch, wilt thou let thy Soule be ty'd / To mans lawes, by which she shall not be try'd / At the last day?" (93–95a). There is real contempt here for "mans lawes" in the realm of the soul, but the emphasis here,

---

Interpretation: Literary Theory and Seventeenth-Century English Poetry (Chicago: University of Chicago Press, 1990), 37–67; and "John Donne, Kingsman?" in Linda Peck, ed., *The Mental World of the Jacobean Court* (Cambridge: Cambridge University Press, 1991), 251–72. Also in *Soliciting Interpretation*, see David Norbrook, "The Monarchy of Wit and the Republic of Letters: Donne's Politics," 3–36. I have contested the views of Patterson and Norbrook in "Donne and the Politics of Devotion" in Donna B. Hamilton and Richard Strier, eds., *Religion, Politics and Literature in Post-Reformation England, 1540–1688* (Cambridge: Cambridge University Press, 1995). I argue both that Donne was not a sycophant and that Carey's position retains much of its power.

127. D. C. Allen, "Two Notes on John Donne," *Modern Language Notes* 65 (1950): 103; *Satires*, 147; Luther, *Secular Authority—to What Extent It Should be Obeyed*, in *Luther: Selections*, ed. Dillenberger, 388–89.

128. Luther, *Secular Authority*, 385. Castellio's *Concerning Heretics* is largely a collection of excerpts; this segment from Luther's *Secular Authority* is the first and longest excerpt in the volume (pp. 141–53).

129. For "from the beginning of the world a wise prince is a rare bird indeed," see Luther, *Secular Authority*, 388.

as in *Biathanatos,* is on the soul's inherent freedom, on its proper refusal
to be tied, its special standing. The enjambment of line 93 allows "wilt
thou let thy Soule be ty'd" to exist for a moment as a question in itself.
The soul can only be "ty'd / To mans lawes" if, foolishly and wretchedly,
it allows itself to be so. "Wilt thou let" is the heart of the question.

The next lines continue the insistence on personal responsibility. In
attacking spiritual subservience, Donne is careful to include all forms of
authority in his purview, Catholic as well as Protestant, secular as well
as religious. Maintaining the apocalyptic context of "At the last day,"
he asks: "Will it then boot thee / To say a Philip, or a Gregory, / A
Harry, or a Martin taught thee this?" (95b-97).[130] The survey of conflicting possibilities leads back into the epistemological realm—"Is not
this excuse for mere contraries, / Equally strong? cannot both sides say
so?"—but this is only momentary.[131] Donne's focus remains on the
individual's relation to authority. He unpacks the political meaning of
"Keepe the truth which thou'hast found" by providing a parallel admonition and a monitory explanation:

> That thou may'st rightly'obey power, her bounds know;
> Those past, her nature and name's chang'd; to be
> Then humble to her is idolatrie. (100–102)

The issue here is not right belief but right obedience; religious truth may
be difficult, but this truth, the truth about "power," the conscientious
individual must "know." There is no room for doubt here. The essential
thing to know about "power" is "her bounds." Right obedience knows
these bounds; it is limited. Humility can be, as Milton puts it, "unsea-
sonable."[132] Some humility is "idolatrie." This is rich and complex
writing. Donne is invoking the great Protestant bugaboo, idolatry, in a
context that includes secular as well as religious powers, princes as well
as popes. As in the passage on obedience to "the statecloth where the
Prince sate," Donne wants to draw the Protestant horror of idolatry into

130. In a number of manuscripts, these lines are even stronger, beginning, "Oh will"
or "Oh, will"; *Satires,* 13; *Complete Poetry,* ed. Shawcross, 430 (Shawcross prints "Oh,
will").

131. The epistemological quandary is put even more sharply in one manuscript which
has "equally true" rather than "equally strong." See *Complete Poetry,* ed. Shawcross, 430.

132. *Of Reformation,* in *The Complete Prose Works of John Milton,* 8 vols. (New Haven:
Yale University Press, 1953–82), 1:523 (see also 1:522). See Richard Strier, "Milton
against Humility" (forthcoming).

the arena of political behavior. Milton will attempt the same in *Eikono-klastes*.[133]

The conception of right obedience as limited obedience is precisely the mechanism that allowed the radical English and Scottish resistance theorists of the sixteenth century, especially Ponet, Goodman, and Buchanan, to characterize resistance as true service in certain situations.[134] There is some confusion in the scholarship over whether this conception of limited obedience is a Catholic or a Protestant phenomenon. This is a classic example of "*une question mal posée*." As Cardinal William Allen pointed out in 1584, both Catholics and Protestants agreed "that princes may for some causes, and especially for their defection in faith and religion, be resisted."[135] Donne noted this convergence in *Biathanatos* (and again, in a different key, in *Ignatius his Conclave*).[136] The difference between the churches was not on whether resistance "for some causes" was allowable or necessary but rather on how such resistance was authorized. The Protestants, according to Allen, "do adjudge by their private folly and fantasy"—that is, by individual conscience—whereas the Catholics, "not trusting their own particular imaginations" do commit "the direction of matters so important to the church." Donne is certainly, in this respect, on the "Protestant" side; his conception of conscience is radically individualistic. He is not about to trust the direction of his soul or behavior to any institutional authority.

One critic has seen Satire III as ending with "a metaphysical plea for humble devotion," a "final 'act of self-immolation'"; the peroration is merely "an amplification of the commonplace Renaissance defense of 'right order.'"[137] This assertion, with its assured sense of the relevance of the great commonplaces, is precisely the move that Empson meant to warn against. A radical position is assimilated to a conservative (not to say "boot-licking") commonplace. An insistence that the individual must understand the limits of government is taken as an assertion that the individual "must understand his limitations"; an insistence on re-

133. The people, says Milton, "are prone ofttimes not to a religious only, but to a civil kind of idolatry in idolizing their kings." *Eikonoklastes,* in *Complete Prose,* 3:343.

134. For exposition and documentation, see Essay 7, pp. 174–75, below.

135. William Allen, *A True, Sincere, and Modest Defense of English Catholics,* ed. Robert M. Kingdon (Ithaca: Cornell University Press, 1965), 142. The quotation from Allen later in this paragraph is from the same page.

136. Donne, *Biathanatos,* 120; *Ignatius His Conclave,* 77.

137. Hester, *Kinde Pitty,* 57, 67, 69. The quotes from Hester in the rest of this paragraph are all from p. 69.

sistance, on not allowing oneself to be moved by external powers, is seen as a warning against being "led improvidently into rebellion." This reading is a classic case of knowing in advance, from an "historical" point of view, what the text *must* be saying. The critic has been misled by his awareness of the commonplaces into thinking that they must always be present. The extended analogy with which Donne ends the Satire is difficult, but we can catch what Milton would call its "drift and scope" if we attend to its structure and function.[138] Grammatically and rhetorically, the analogy must follow from the lines that introduce it. Whatever the peroration is doing, it must be amplifying the great final injunction about obeying power through knowing "her bounds." From a purely "internal" point of view, we can say that the peroration must be continuing Donne's critique of secular idolatry. This is not an a priori necessity, but one that derives from the local and immediate context.

The mention of "power" in collocation with "bounds" seems to have given Donne his image: "As streames are, Power is" (103a). From the history of this image in political discourse, we would expect a discussion of how the "stream" of power gets troubled or swollen.[139] But we must look. For the special purposes of this poem, Donne has started at the wrong end of the image. He wants to continue the discussion of power, but the poem, unlike the political tradition, is not interested in charting the ways in which power becomes abusive. Donne is interested in how the individual is to act once power has become so. That it will become so is, again, taken for granted. Immediately after announcing the analogy, Donne shifts his focus. The result is wildly disjunctive: "As streames are, Power is; those blest flowers that dwell" (103). Suddenly these hitherto unmentioned "flowers" are the focus. The puzzle is to find the

---

138. See *The Reason of Church-government Urg'd against Prelaty,* in *Complete Prose,* 1:750.

139. The image of the "rough stream" in a political context is familiar from classical poetry and drama. In Roman poetry, especially in Horace and Lucan, the image of the flooding river becomes specialized as the image of civil war; see D. C. Allen, *Image and Meaning: Metaphoric Traditions in Renaissance Poetry* (Baltimore: Johns Hopkins University Press, 1960), 132–33. Donne is not using the image in this way. It may be relevant to the way Donne does use the image that, in the political discourse of early seventeenth-century England, as John M. Wallace points out, the metaphor of a flooding river "was employed most often by the opposition [to the Crown]." In Coke and others, the flooding river is especially associated with the extension of royal prerogative. See John M. Wallace, "*Cooper's Hill*: The Manifesto of Parliamentary Royalism, 1641," *ELH* 41 (1974): 523. Donne's image, I would argue, tells us which tradition to link it to. We cannot know in advance what the image must mean.

tenor of this vehicle. The next line tells us that "those blest flowers that dwell / At the rough streames calme head, thrive and prove well."[140] One might think that "those blest flowers" are godly earthly princes who "dwell" close to the divine source of their power, but neither the general nor the local context of the poem supports this. The general context has been intensely concerned with the private subject in both the political and the psychological-philosophical sense. The local context goes on to discuss flowers that become the victims of the "tyrannous rage" of the stream (106), and in the final couplet the extended image as a whole is applied by Donne to individual "Soules" (109). It would seem then, that we need to interpret the "blest flowers" as private individuals who maintain a proper relation to "Power."

We should therefore be on (so to speak) firm ground, since we already know what the individual's relation to power should be: to know its bounds and not be improperly humble to it. Both of these are negative relations, however; both of them conceive of power as external, political, and coercive. "The rough streames calme head," however, seems to be different. It seems to suggest a divine source. The "blest flowers" thrive through dwelling at this source. But what does that mean? Here the meaning of "to dwell" in early modern English might help us. The word had a strong meaning, suggesting possession and full inhabitation, as at the end of Ben Jonson's "To Penshurst," "thy lord dwells." In Donne as in Jonson, the philosophical coloration of the word is Stoic; "Be then thine owne home, and in thy selfe dwell," Donne advises Sir Henry Wotton.[141] To "dwell" in this sense is an action, not a state; it is something that one consciously does, so that to say that those who act in this way "prove" (or "do") well is not merely to say again that they "thrive." The image takes its place with the other images in the poem of virtuous immobility, of figures who stand: the "Sentinell in this worlds garrison"; the wise doubter; and Truth, who "stands" on her hill. It is not insignificant, I would suggest, that in many manuscripts, including some very

140. There is major editorial disagreement about line 104. *Poems* 1633 and some manuscripts have "thrive and *do* well." This is the reading that Grierson and Shawcross adopt. The majority of manuscripts have "thrive and *prove* well," the reading that is adopted by Milgate. I have followed Milgate, though I think that here, as elsewhere in the poem, the textual ambiguity is significant and probably authorial.

141. "Sir, more then kisses," line 47 (*Satires*, 72). Scodel, "The Medium is the Message," is as concerned to downplay the Stoicism in this epistle as in the satire (see n. 37 above).

good ones, Truth does not stand on her hill but rather "dwells" there.[142] The deepest positive image in the poem is not of motion but of stasis. The image of inquiry, of repetitive and purposive motion "about . . . and about," takes place within a context of standing: "To stand inquiring right."[143] The flowers are "blest" through consciously remaining "At the rough streames calme head"—through maintaining, perhaps, their direct and unmediated relation to the divine source.

This reading is sustained (if not made inevitable) by the lines that follow. As the mention of the "calme head" in the context of the rough stream suggests, Donne is more eager in this poem (a satire, after all) to describe failures than successes, negative rather than positive exempla. Without any warning, and as if telling a continuous story (as, with regard to many individuals, he certainly thinks that he is), Donne shifts to describing the fate of those "flowers" that do not "dwell,"

> But having left their roots, and themselves given
> To the streames tyrannous rage, alas, are driven
> Through mills, and rockes, and woods,'and at last, almost
> Consum'd in going, in the sea are lost. (105–108)

The crucial fact is again volition: "having *left* their roots, and themselves *given*." Again, attention to verbal detail pays off. The rhyme tells the story; it is through having "given" themselves to the stream of Power that the flowers are "driven" by it. "Tyrannous," of course, is part of the tenor as well as the vehicle here. Those who are humble to tyranny become its victims. "Kind pity" seems truly to choke Donne's spleen here in his sorrowful evocation ("alas") of those (like devoted courtiers?) who are "almost / Consum'd in going" only to be finally "lost" when they reach their goal. I am not sure what to make of the "mills, and rockes, and woods." The concreteness seems misplaced. It is hard, however, not to hear in the thudding slowness and onomatopoetic structure of the line an echo of "about must, and about must goe." Donne is now, as I have suggested, occupying (dwelling in) the position of Truth. He does, as we have noted, know the truth about Power. The figures who are in motion here are not autonomously and diligently proceeding, though

---

142. *Satires*, 13; on the value of the different manuscripts, see pp. xli-lxii.

143. Part of the special horror of Graius is perhaps that he stays home without "standing," that he accepts "shee / Which dwels with us" rather than "dwelling" in himself. His immobility is pliant rather than resistant.

in circles, but being driven. Donne is now the Lucretian sage, watching from his secure height—though, as Bacon says "with pity and not with swelling pride"—the tribulations of sea-tossed others.[144]

Strained readings take special effort from the critic and the reader. It is hard to see in the vision of drowning a positive "act of self-immolation," since self-immolation is precisely what the foolishly humble and obedient souls who "in the sea are lost" endure. Loss of individuation seems to be the ultimate terror—giving up one's will. Again, the "given/driven" rhyme is crucial. There seem to be only two possibilities in this world: absolute self-containment and absolute other-dependence. The one is calm and "blessed," the other tumultuous and fatal. The ideal figure in this poem, like the triumphant soul in Herbert's "Vertue," "never gives." The obscurity of the image here might derive from the fact that while the feeling in this passage, as in Herbert's poem, is apocalyptic, the content is not. Being "lost" in this case is a temporal state; it has to do with a relation to earthly power "here" ("men do not stand / In so'ill case here"). The Lucretian image is Donne's way of conveying an inner-worldly and naturalistic version of losing one's soul.

In the final couplet, Donne explicates his image. All talk about flowers and streams disappears. Grammatically, as a continuation of the previous narrative, this couplet is descriptive; in tone, however, and in its relative syntactic independence (reinforced by its couplet status), it sounds like a grimly prophetic command or prayer:

> So perish Soules, which more chuse mens unjust
> Power from God claym'd, then God himselfe to trust. (109–110)

Donne's focus remains on the will, on what persons "chuse." The choice is between "mens unjust / Power" and "God himself." There is no conception of men's just power. This is the idea that Hester and Scodel assume, quite reasonably, *must* be in the poem but that does not actually exist in it. As we have seen so often, we can trust the verse. The enjambment is illuminating: "mens unjust" is a complete thought. This poem cannot imagine benign earthly power. There is no support in the poem for the view that human souls "can be nurtured rather than destroyed

144. See Lucretius, *De Rerum Natura*, 2.1–13, trans. W. H. D. Rouse, rev. Martin F. Smith, 2d ed. (Cambridge: Harvard University Press, Loeb Classical Library, 1982), 94; Bacon, "Of Truth," *Selected Writings*, 8. The pity, the attempt to avoid straightforward rejoicing at the destruction of the foolish, is part of the Lucretian topos. Milgate, *Satires*, 292, sees this Lucretian passage as contributing to the image of Truth on a hill, but I think that the passage is more deeply related to the conclusion of Donne's poem.

by worldly authority."[145] The "stream" is calm only at the head, which is divine. As soon as the stream becomes earthly power, it becomes "rough." Earthly power is a scourge that must be resisted: "Nor are they Vicars, but hangmen to Fate."

Power, in the poem, means power to bind or "tie" the soul. This sort of power is always illegitimate when exercised by anything but the Spirit of God. We recall *Biathanatos,* where "in secret cases between the Spirit of God, and my conscience, of which there is not certainly constituted any exteriour Judge, we are ourselves sufficient to doe all the Offices; and then delivered from all bondage, and restored to our naturall libertie." In this realm one has no superior but God—whatever divine source or sanction men's power may claim. As Luther said in *his* essay on the extent to which secular authority should be obeyed, "No one but God can have authority over souls."[146] The final words of the satire are "God himselfe to trust." To trust "God himselfe" in this context means to stand aloof from all earthly pressures on the conscience. To "dwell / At the rough streames calme head" is to maintain one's own integrity, to have a proper sense of one's own "naturall libertie" and individual access to the divine.

The integral soul, standing still, refusing to be bound, waiting for a personal revelation that may or may not come, is the final positive image of Satire III. To be such a figure is "not to stray." Jack Donne, the "mere libertine" in religion who thinks that the philosophers are in heaven and that "To'adore, or scorne an image, or protest / May all be bad," insists that he is "blest" and truly faithful. They also serve who resist and doubt. I do not see any criticism of or fetters on the autonomous self here. The individual depicted and represented in this poem does not seem to me "remarkably unfree"—though he is (potentially) in physical danger.[147]

---

145. Scodel, "The Medium is the Message," 500. Scodel needs this notion to locate a proper "mean" in relation to political authority in the poem. His scheme (the mean) is here, I think, dictating his reading.

146. *Luther: Selections,* 386. And see Castellio, *Concerning Heretics,* 124, 143 (an excerpt from Luther).

147. For Stephen Greenblatt's view of the Renaissance individual as "remarkably unfree," see *Renaissance Self-Fashioning from More to Tyndale* (Chicago: University of Chicago Press, 1980), 256. Scodel wants to soften this view, but nevertheless insists that the speaker imagined or projected in the third Satire is not "the fully autonomous person imagined by the Enlightenment" ("The Medium is the Message," 501). While it is true that the self is autonomous here "under God," I am not sure that this is felt in the poem (or the Enlightenment) as a constraint. I think, to reiterate, that we should resist (or at least be extremely wary of) such sharp period divisions.

In terms of intellectual history, Donne can be seen to have shown, in the strongest parts of the third Satire, the perhaps surprising compatibility of three of the most radical notions of the European sixteenth-century: Erasmus's "philosophy of Christ," Castellio's vindication of doubt, and Luther's conception of conscience. Informed "close reading" reveals this conjuncture.

Impossible Radicalism II
Shakespeare and Disobedience

I

We have seen from Donne's third Satire that radical thought on political and religious matters was indeed possible in the Renaissance (in England as elsewhere). The following essay continues this demonstration and provides a fuller context for the idea of limited and conditional obedience than the previous essay does. Just as we saw there that certain "modern" notions like liberty of conscience and religious toleration (even respect) were "thinkable" in the sixteenth century, so we will see here that certain other "modern" notions—like collective guilt and the moral responsibility of all individuals to oppose authorized evil—were also thinkable (and thought) in the period. I will argue that by the time that he wrote his first version of *King Lear* (circa 1605), Shakespeare not only agreed with "Jack" Donne that "rightly obey[ing]" power could sometimes mean not complying with its demands, maintaining one's own integrity in the face of it, but could also mean actively resisting and attempting to thwart it.[1] Shakespeare, I will argue, pushed the paradox of right obedience as sometimes consisting

1. I accept the view that Shakespeare wrote two distinct versions of *King Lear*. For a group of essays supporting this view (and providing various arguments for it), see Gary Taylor and Michael Warren, eds., *The Division of the Kingdoms: Shakespeare's Two Versions of King Lear* (Oxford: Clarendon Press, 1983). This volume will henceforth be cited as *Division*. See also Steven Urkowitz, *Shakespeare's Revision of "King Lear"* (Princeton: Princeton University Press, 1980).

of disobedience as far as it would go. He adopted the most radical possible position on the issue of obedience to wicked authorities.

This assertion runs squarely counter to two widely held beliefs about Shakespeare. These beliefs are, at least on the face of them, logically incompatible with one another, yet I think, however odd this seems, that they are often both held by the same persons. The beliefs in question are: (1) that Shakespeare's social and political views were deeply conservative (not to say, reactionary); and (2) that Shakespeare did not (as a playwright, at least) have "views." I am not sure how one can logically reconcile these positions (they might be called the Burkean and the Keatsian views of Shakespeare).[2] A possible way of reconciling them is to say that Shakespeare's conservatism consisted of instincts, antipathies, and sympathies rather than something so abstract as "views." Another way of putting these positions together is to fold the "Keatsian" into the "Burkean" by suggesting that "views" are themselves radical, and that not having them means cherishing particular forms of life that exist without having, desiring, or needing explicit justification for them.[3] Greenblatt's crypto-Catholic and nostalgic Shakespeare is a figure rather like this, as is C. L. Barber's quite similar Shakespeare.[4]

But how would one go about showing that Shakespeare had views, let alone radical ones? We have no pamphlets or tracts by him, and, of course, it would not necessarily settle the issue if we did (though it would certainly establish presumptions). The following procedures seem reasonable. We must see whether certain views are expressed by characters of whom, it seems clear, we are meant to approve or with whom we are meant to sympathize; we must see if there is a *pattern* of such views being expressed, so that they seem to be something that the playwright was truly interested in; and, finally, we must see whether such views are expressed

2. Annabel Patterson usefully shows how Coleridge seems to have been the earliest progenitor of both these views. See the foreword to her *Shakespeare and the Popular Voice* (Cambridge, Mass.: Blackwell, 1989), 6–7. Coleridge's extraordinary influence in creating "English Literature" as a whole as a domain of conservative values would be very much worth a major study.

3. See, for instance, Burke's defense of "prejudices" in *Reflections on the Revolution in France* (New York: Doubleday, Anchor Books, 1973), 100–101.

4. On Greenblatt's "Shakespeare and the Exorcists," see Essay 3, pp. 57–59, above. For C. L. Barber, see "The Family and the Sacred in Shakespeare's Development" in C. L. Barber and Richard P. Wheeler, *The Whole Journey: Shakespeare's Power of Development* (Berkeley and Los Angeles: University of California Press, 1986), 1–38. Barber's view of the late Elizabethan religious situation is more fully presented in the essay on Marlowe's *Dr. Faustus*, in *Creating Elizabethan Tragedy: The Theater of Marlowe and Kyd*, ed. Richard P. Wheeler (Chicago: University of Chicago Press, 1988), 87–130.

in a number of plays, whenever contexts arise where they might be appropriate. If all these conditions are met, it seems reasonable to think that we have found something that Shakespeare believed. I do not think that Shakespeare is "the less Shakespeare" for having had beliefs that he expressed in his plays.[5] When Sidney said that the poet "nothing affirms," he had in mind factual claims, not ethical and political ones.[6] Only a peculiar version of post-Romantic poetics could lead to the view that the poet "nothing affirms" in general. But let me proceed now to context.

The question of whether there were limits to the obedience that inferiors owed their social and political superiors was one of the great issues for both Renaissance and Reformation political thinking. It was a highly vexed issue, not one on which a stable consensus or even, in many cases, stable individual positions existed.[7] Both the humanist and the Reformation traditions were ambiguous and self-contradictory on the matter. Let us begin with the humanist tradition. A crucial moment for that tradition occurs in the second book of *The Courtier*. When Federico Fregoso describes the ideal courtier as turning "all his thoughts . . . to love, and (as it were) to reverence the prince hee serveth, and . . . to be altogether plyable to please him," Pietro da Napoli interrupts with the bitter remark that such a "plyable" courtier is not an ideal but a reality ("of these . . . now adayes ye shal finde ynow"), since what Federico has described is, according to Pietro, "a joly [*jolie*] flatterer."[8] Federico is thus forced to attempt to distinguish the courtier from his wicked shadow. He attempts this first by an appeal to motives (flatterers do not truly love their lords), and then by insisting that when he speaks of the courtier's obedience to his prince, he means obedience only to "commandements that are reasonable and honest" (106).

Federico does not pursue this momentous assertion. He goes on instead to define and exemplify a category of morally neutral commands;

5. For "the less Shakespeare," see the last line of Browning's "House" in *The Poems and Plays of Robert Browning*, introduction by Saxe Commins (New York: Random House, 1934).

6. Sir Philip Sidney, *An Apology for Poetry*, ed. Geoffrey Shepherd (London: Nelson, 1965), 123.

7. For an overview of the whole period, see Quentin Skinner, *The Foundations of Modern Political Thought*, 2 vols. (Cambridge: Cambridge University Press, 1978). For a brief overview of the English context at the end of the sixteenth century, see Richard L. Greaves, "Concepts of Political Obedience in Later Tudor England: Conflicting Perspectives," *Journal of British Studies* 22 (1982): 23–34.

8. Baldassare Castiglione, *The Book of the Courtier*, trans. Sir Thomas Hoby (London: Dent, Everyman's Library, 1928), 106. All further page references to *The Courtier* will appear in the text.

the issue of wicked commands is dropped. The problem of limits to obedience returns, however, with the discussion of how the courtier is to advance himself. Vincentio Calmeta denies Federico's claim that courtiers can rely on virtue to succeed and eschew "any naughtie way" or "subtill practise." Federico asserts (with, presumably, unintended satire) that it is not totally impossible to find a prince who rewards virtue. He concedes, however, that if the courtier finds himself serving a prince who only values "naughtie" practices, "as soone as he knoweth it, let him forsake him" (112). But Calmeta dissents from this as well. He argues that wicked princes are not only normal but must be endured: "Wee must take them with all their faultes." He appeals to "infinite respectes" that "constraine a gentleman after he is once entred into service with a Lord, not to forsake him." When Federico continues to insist on the priority of moral duties, the question again arises "whether a gentleman be bound or no, while he is in a princes service, to obey him in all thinges which he shall commaund, though they were dishonest and shameful matters." Federico stoutly maintains that "in dishonest matters we are not bound to obey any bodie," and another interlocutor (Ludovico Pio) bursts in to register the full shockingness of the view Federico has articulated. The terms in which the question of obedience is now posed are brutally realistic: "And what? . . . if I be in service with a prince who handleth me wel, and hopeth that I will doe any thing for him that may bee done, and he happen to command me to kill a man, or any other like matter, ought I to refuse to doe it?" (112). Federico insists that a prince is to be obeyed only in "thinges that tend to his profit and honour" (which are, presumably, virtuous things), and that he must be disobeyed in things that do not so tend. This immediately raises the issue of private judgment, from which Federico weakly backs off with the obfuscatory remark that it is often hard to distinguish ill from good things, especially with regard to killing.

In the course of this dialogue, a clear sense of moral imperative has been muddied by the "infinite respectes," presumably prudential and practical, that would recommend loyalty regardless of the situation, and by the sudden and highly unsettling emergence of the issue of epistemological uncertainty.[9] Lauro Martines has argued that while "the relation between the prince and the courtier" is at the conceptual center

---

9. On the unsettling quality of this epistemological uncertainty, see Wayne A. Rebhorn, *Courtly Performances: Masking and Festivity in Castiglione's "Book of the Courtier"* (Detroit: Wayne State University Press, 1978), 188.

of *The Courtier*, from the political point of view, "Castiglione, who insists on this relationship, has no clear view of it."[10] The humanist tradition did not offer a clear mandate. Neither the philosophically explicit fourth book of *The Courtier* nor the similar dialogue in Book I of More's *Utopia* moved beyond the impasse in which Castiglione's Federico left the question of service to the wicked. The fourth book of *The Courtier* deepens the distinction between the courtier and the flatterer (the former is a truth-teller, the latter a liar), and it sees all the courtier's accomplishments as a means of establishing a human context in which he can speak truth. Yet it returns to Federico's view that if the prince's nature is utterly unredeemable, the courtier must flee, lest he feel, in words repeated verbatim from Book II, "the hartgriefe that all good men have which serve the wicked" (301; 112).[11] Tyrannicide is praised in passing (289–90), but not mentioned in the practical context.

In More, the issue of "pliability" versus moral rigor is extremely vexed. The alternative to rigor is not passive endurance but active accommodation, making the best of every bad situation; the guiding program is purely pragmatic: "Whatever play is being performed, perform it as best you can [*Quaecunque fabula in manu est, eam age quam potes optime*]."[12] This "other philosophy, more practical for statesmen" ("*civilior*") put forth by "More/Morus" is then subjected to a devastating critique by the traveler and Platonist, Raphael Hythlodaeus. To be, adopting Federico Fregoso's term, a "pliable" moralist at a wicked—that is, normal—court, would not only cause the courtier or counselor "hartgrief," but it would be dangerous to him ("He would be counted a spy and almost a traitor who gives only faint praise to evil counsels"), and it would be morally disastrous. Such a "pliable" or "civil" courtier would either be forced into wickedness himself or "made a screen" for the wickedness of others (103). At this point the topic is dropped.[13]

10. Lauro Martines, "The Gentleman in Renaissance Italy: Strains of Isolation in the Body Politic," in Robert S. Kinsman, ed., *The Darker Vision of the Renaissance* (Berkeley and Los Angeles: University of California Press, 1974), 89.

11. For an explanation of the tightness of this connection between the fourth book and the second, see Lawrence V. Ryan, "Book IV of Castiglione's *Courtier*: Climax or Afterthought?" *Studies in the Renaissance* 19 (1972): 156–79.

12. St. Thomas More, *Utopia*, ed. Edward Surtz and J. H. Hexter (New Haven: Yale University Press, 1965), 99; Latin, p. 98. Further page references will appear in the text.

13. For an excellent account of the tensions in More—although an account that tends to be overly sympathetic to "Morus"—see Stephen Greenblatt, *Renaissance Self-Fashioning from More to Shakespeare* (Chicago: University of Chicago Press, 1980), chap. 1, esp. pp. 34–36.

The Protestant tradition was equally unresolved on the question of obedience to the wicked. On the one hand, the reformers extolled (over against the papacy) the God-given legitimacy of secular rulers; on the other hand, they insisted on the God-given legitimacy and inviolability of individual conscience. In the first decade of the Reformation, this tension was resolved by a sharp distinction between nonobedience and resistance. To the question, "When a prince is wrong, are his people bound to follow him then too," Luther answered, "No, for it is no one's duty to do wrong," and cited Acts 5:29, "we ought to obey God rather than men"—always a potentially explosive text.[14] Ultimately, for Luther, the decision whether to obey or not was a matter for the individual conscience enlightened by the Word, but he distinguished sharply between nonobedience and active resistance ("disobedience" blurs the distinction). In the case of immoral commands, Luther as strongly condemned resistance as he insisted upon nonobedience. Nonobedience led to the glory of martyrdom; resistance to the sin of rebellion. In *The Obedience of a Christian Man*, Tyndale followed Luther closely, emphasizing nonresistance even more strongly than Luther did: "Neither may the inferior person avenge himself on the superior, or violently resist him, for whatsoever wrong it be."[15] In his summary at the end of the treatise, however, Tyndale added a crucial reservation: "[Princes] may not be resisted: do they never so evil. . . . Neverthelater, if they command to do evil, we must then disobey, and say, 'We are otherwise commanded of God.'" We are still, however, "not to rise against them" (332).[16]

The Edwardine Homily on "Good Order and Obedience to Rulers" echoes Tyndale. Its opening paragraph on order and degree as a metaphysical principle is often quoted as an example of the Renaissance *episteme* or world-picture. We can get a clearer sense of what mattered to most actual English Renaissance minds when we note that, after the

14. *Secular Authority: To What Extent It Should Be Obeyed*, in *Martin Luther: Selections from his Writings,* ed. John Dillenberger (Garden City, N.Y.: Doubleday, 1961), 399.

15. *The Obedience of a Christian Man*, in *Doctrinal Treatises and Introductions to Different Portions of the Holy Scriptures by William Tyndale,* ed. Rev. Henry Walter (Cambridge: Cambridge University Press, 1848), 175. Further page references will appear in the text.

16. This is the passage that led More to refer to Tyndale's "holy book of disobedience." See Sir Thomas More, *The Dialogue concerning Tyndale,* ed. W. E. Campbell (London: Eyre and Spottiswoode, 1927), 273. It nicely dramatizes the tensions in Tyndale's position to compare More's characterization with Henry VIII's alleged delight in the *Obedience* as a "book for me, and all kings to read" (quoted from Strype in *Doctrinal Treatises . . . by Tyndale,* 10).

flourish of its opening paragraph, the homily does not make its argument on cosmological grounds. It proceeds entirely through biblical citation. The cosmological opening was merely a flourish. On the basis of scripture, the homily asserts the unlawfulness of inferiors and subjects "in any case" to resist superior powers.[17] Christ taught that all rulers, including wicked ones, have their power from God; Peter "bringeth in the patience of our Saviour, to persuade obedience to governors, yea, although they be wicked" (109). In the example analyzed at greatest length, David "did know that he was but king Saul's subject, though he [David] were in great favour with God, and his enemy king Saul out of God's favour" (111). The homily also includes, however, a very strong exhortation to principled nonobedience, an exhortation even stronger than Tyndale's: "Yet let us believe undoubtedly, good Christian people, that we may not obey kings, magistrates, or any other, though they be our own fathers, if they would command us to do any thing contrary to God's commandments." Nevertheless, "we may not in any way resist violently" (112–13). The tension between nonobedience and nonresistance is at its highest here.

The later homily "Against Disobedience" (rather than on obedience) eliminates the tension. Written in 1570, in the immediate aftermath of the rebellion of the northern earls, it takes us all the way from Tyndale to Hobbes. Centrally acknowledging the existence of wicked as well as virtuous rulers, it asks the vital question, "What shall subjects do then? Shall they obey . . . wise and good princes and contemn, disobey, and rebel against . . . undiscreet and evil governors?"[18] God forbid, it responds, and its first move is to deny the validity of that dangerous thing, individual conscience: "What a perilous thing were it to commit unto the subjects judgment, which prince is wise and godly . . . and which otherwise." As in Hobbes, private judgment is seen as leading to perpetual unrest.[19] Every prince is thought to be ungodly by some subjects, and "If therefore all subjects that mislike of their prince should rebel, no realm should ever be without rebellion" (556). This homily is a brilliant piece of writing, and it faces the obvious next question directly: what if there is no epistemological problem? "What if the prince be undiscreet

17. *The Two Books of Homilies Appointed to be Read in Churches* (Oxford: Oxford University Press, 1859), 109. Further page references in text.

18. "An Homily against Disobedience and Wilful Rebellion," *The Two Books of Homilies,* 555.

19. See *Leviathan,* ed. C. B. Macpherson (New York: Penguin, 1968), 365.

and evil indeed, and it [is] also evident to all men's eyes that he is so?" The answer is unequivocal even in this case: "let us patiently suffer" (557). As in the earlier homily, David is invoked as an especially edifying model, an example of the irrelevance of either superior virtue or explicit divine favor in justifying rebellion against the anointed and obviously wicked. A good man is an obedient subject. There is no possible tension. David was "so good a subject that he obeyed so evil a king" (566). Conscientious nonobedience vanishes as either an option or an obligation.

There is, however, a strand within the Protestant tradition that expanded rather than withdrew the doctrine of conscience, that intensified nonobedience into resistance rather than diminishing it into endurance. To locate this radical strand, we must turn to the English Protestant writers who faced what was to them something like the equivalent of the Nazi occupation of France, the reign in England of a Catholic queen married to the king of Spain. The Marian exiles John Ponet and Christopher Goodman, along with the Scots John Knox and George Buchanan, were the most radical political theorists of the century. By 1530, Luther had rejected his earlier opinion that resistance to an established secular ruler was always wrong. He argued that certain kinds of immoral magistrates (i.e., Catholic crusaders against Protestants) *are themselves rebels*, and therefore opposition to them is not rebellion.[20] Melanchthon argued similarly, and this will become, as we shall see, an extremely important form of argument.[21] It did not, however, address the question of on whom the duty of resistance falls. Within the Lutheran and (later) Calvinist theory of proper and mandated resistance, there remained an unwillingness to assign this duty to every member of a society ruled by an immoral and ungodly prince. Most of the major Reformers of the mid-century, like the Huguenots later, located the duty of active resistance in "lesser magistrates" and withheld it from private individuals.[22]

---

20. *Dr. Martin Luther's Warning to His Dear German People*, trans. Martin Bertram, in *Luther's Works*, American Edition, ed. Franklin Sherman (Philadelphia: Fortress Press, 1971), 47:18–20.

21. On the change in Luther's views, on Melanchthon's views, and on Bucer's retreat from these positions, see Skinner, *Foundations*, 2:200–206.

22. For Calvin, see the final two sections of the *Institutes* (4.20.31–32). For a classic Huguenot statement of the distinction between lesser magistrates and private persons (with a very cautious allowance for divinely inspired exceptions to the distinction), see the *Vindiciae contra Tyrannos*, in *Constitutionalism and Resistance in the Sixteenth Century*, ed. and trans. Julian H. Franklin (New York: Western Publishing Co., 1969), 149–56.

Ponet, Goodman, and Buchanan did not so limit the scope of resistance.

A striking, unremarked, and very "modern" feature of the political thought of Ponet and Goodman is their conception of collective responsibility. They insist that the passive allowance of wickedness is itself wickedness. Ponet is particularly emphatic that not only "the doers" but also "the consentours to evil," shall be punished.[23] He recognized that, as Hannah Arendt puts it, "in politics, obedience and support are the same."[24] Of Nero's crimes, Ponet asks, "who were to be blamed for these cruell actes? He for doing them, or others for flattring him, or the senate ād people of Rome in suffring him?" Ponet's conclusion is: "Surely there is none to be excused, but all to be blamed." Ponet concedes that "he is a good citezin that dothe none evil," but insists that "he is a better that letteth [prevents] others, that they shall not doo hurt nor uniustice." The blood of innocents will be demanded of those who consent to or even passively allow atrocities—on the part of their political "head" as well as others. Ponet has no patience with prudence ("O faynte heartes" [Biir]), equivocation (Eviiiv), or with Morus-like adapting to the play at hand (he parodies one of his contemporaries as saying "If the Turke ruled in Englād, I wold frame mi selfe to live according" [Lviv -viir]).[25] Goodman, in a striking parabasis, warns those who merely follow orders that not only the commanders of evil shall feel "Gods heavy wrathe," but "*so shalt thou, being made an instrument* of their impietie."[26] Ignorance is no excuse in moral contexts (167); nor are examples of the great (180); or the teachings of conservative political theory: "comon and symple people" think that they must be obedient "because their doinges are counted tumultes and rebellion." They therefore wrongly "suffer themselves like brute beastes rather than reasonable

23. *A Shorte Treatise of Politicke Power* (1556), facsimile, The English Experience, no. 484 (New York: Da Capo Press, 1972), sig. Dviir. Further references will be cited in the text.

24. Hannah Arendt, *Eichmann in Jerusalem,* rev. ed. (New York: Penguin, 1965), 279.

25. In the first of the Admonitions to Parliament (1572), corrupt established divines in the Church of England are seen as approving of "men for all seasons." See *Puritan Manifestoes,* ed. W. H. Frere and C. E. Douglas (London: Society for Promoting Christian Knowledge, 1907), 9.

26. Christopher Goodman, *How Superior Powers Ought to Be Obeyed* (Geneva, 1558), facsimile, The English Experience, no. 460 (New York: Da Capo Press, 1972), 167 (italics mine). Further references will be cited in the text.

creatures, to be led and drawen where so ever their Princes commandements have called" (145–46). Again, as in Donne's third Satire, the
doctrine of conscience is paramount. "Thou thy self must answer for thy
self," says Ponet (Diiir)—and for those around and above you too.[27]

An example that Ponet treats at length is Saul's commandment to "his
owne household wayters and familiar servantes" to kill Ahimelech (1
Samuel 22:17). With typical verve and dramatic imagination, Ponet
presents the servants as having had the option of being pliable, of saying
to Saul, "we wilbe your true obedient servauntes, we will believe as the
king believeth, we will doo as the king biddeth us." But Saul's waiters
did not do this. Instead, recognizing God as the supreme power and
using their own judgment regarding Ahimelech, they explicitly and
absolutely ("playnly and utterly") refused to obey "the kinges unlawfull
commaundement." In acting thus, Ponet not only insists (with Luther)
that the servants were not rebels, but makes the further claim that they
were "yet the kinges true servauntes and subjectes" (Dvr). On the
question of whether Christians are as free as "Ethnicks" to kill male-
factors, "yea, though they were magistrates," Ponet at first asserts that
"in som cases" Christians are equally free (as "when a governour shall
sodainly with his sword rune upon an innocent"), then seems to espouse
a conservative general principle that denies such freedom ("all
things . . . according to ordre"), and then lists five sorts of exceptions
to this apparently absolute principle (Gviiir-v).[28] Later in the *Shorte
Treatise*, Ponet tells the story of one of these exceptions (Ehud killing
Eglon in Judges 3) and notes that the deed is specially commended in
scripture—even though Ehud was "a private person" authorized "only
by the spirite of God" (Hvir).[29] From Ehud, Ponet moves to the case
of Matathias, the first leader of the Maccabean revolt (1 Maccabees
2:17–28), who not only personally refused to obey Antiochus's commandment to worship an idol but also slew a Hebrew he saw obeying
the law and then fell upon "the ordinary commissioners" sent from

27. When, later in the sixteenth century, Catholics took up resistance theory, they did
not endorse this conception of conscience. See Essay 6 above, p. 158.

28. For his conception of the freedom of "Ethnicks" (pagans) with regard to tyran-
nicide, Ponet is unquestionably thinking of Cicero's views, especially in the *Oratio pro
Milone*, from which Ponet quotes. See Winthrop S. Hudson, *John Ponet, Advocate of
Limited Monarchy* (Chicago: University of Chicago Press, 1942), 85.

29. On the importance of the model of Ehud for a later tyrannicide tract, Edward
Sexby's anti-Cromwellian *Killing No Murder* (1657), see James Holstun's "Ehud's Dagger: Patronage, Tyrranicide, and *Killing No Murder*," *Cultural Critique* 22 (1992):
99–142.

Antiochus to announce the law (Hvir). "These examples," Ponet rather coyly states, "need no further exposition."

Goodman provides the "further exposition" that Ponet pretends to think unnecessary. Goodman notes that it might seem "a strange doctrine" and "a great disorder" that "the people" should "take unto them the punishment of transgression" (185, 191), but he assures the reader that it is, nonetheless, the true doctrine of scripture polity. This is the line that Buchanan develops. In *De Jure Regni apud Scotos*, many of the positions of Ponet and Goodman attain their most lucid and perhaps most radical exposition. Classical and scriptural views are identical for Buchanan (as they will be for Milton later). Buchanan joins what he sees as a scriptural injunction "to cut off wickedness and wicked Men, without any exception of rank or degree" to a classical conception of tyrannicide: "a Tyrant is a publick Enemy, with whom all good men have a perpetual warfare."[30] Buchanan sees God as "many times" stirring up "from amongst the lowest of the people some very mean, and obscure men to revenge Tyrannical Pride" (54). Most importantly, Buchanan develops the assertion in Ponet that disobedience is true loyalty to an immoral commander. "Doth he seem to respect the Good of a mad Man," Buchanan asks, "who looseth his Bonds?" This is an important analogy for Buchanan, and he develops it at length. He notes that "they who are restored to Health do render thanks to their Physitian, whom before they hated, because he would not grant their Desires whilst they were sick." He then makes the political application: "if Kings continue in their Madness, whoever doth most obey them, is to be judged their greatest Enemy." The disobedient servant is the good Physician; the obedient cherish the disease (57–58). Buchanan's spokesman ("B") returns to the physician conceit later in the dialogue. B's interlocutor, "M," is worried, like Castiglione's Calmeta, over the "hazards and inconveniences" that attend on such radical views. Like Ponet, B is serenely untroubled by prudence and timidity. The good physician, says B, knows when and how to administer his medicines (68).

Kenneth Muir has noted a possible imagistic and conceptual borrowing from Ponet's *Shorte Treatise* in *Lear*, and there is a striking, probably anti-Catholic, and fairly unusual metaphor for flattery ("court

---

30. George Buchanan, *De Jure Regni apud Scotos, or, A Dialogue, concerning the due Privilege of Government in the Kingdom of Scotland* (London, 1689), 51, 66. Quotations and page references in the text are from this translation (the date of which is surely significant). There is a modern translation by Charles Flinn Arrowood under the title, *The Powers of the Crown in Scotland* (Austin: University of Texas Press, 1949).

holy-water") common to both works, but my aim has been less to suggest sources for *Lear* than to establish the range of ideas about obedience that were readily available to Shakespeare.[31] My analysis will try to demonstrate that in both versions of *King Lear* Shakespeare dramatized and espoused the most radical of these ideas (the Folio will emerge as developing the ideas). Agreeing with Muir, I would see *Lear* as the culmination of a development in Shakespeare's political thinking from a focus on the problem of order to a focus on the problem of corrupt (and corruption-inducing) authority.[32] *Hamlet* marks the turn, though Shakespeare had touched on some of the issues earlier. The most interesting of the earlier treatments are in *Richard III* and *King John.* In *Richard III*, the murderers of Clarence present their "commission" to a jailer who "will not reason what is meant thereby"; the murderers see themselves as loyal, dutiful, and absolved of responsibility because "What we will do, we do upon command." Clarence disputes this evasion of responsibility, calling them "erroneous vassals," reminding them of a higher law ("the great King of Kings / Hath in his law commanded / That thou shalt do no murder") and asking, "Will you then / Spurn at his edict, and fulfil a man's?" (1.4.190–93). Later in *Richard III*, Sir James Tyrrel, who supervises the murder of the princes

---

31. For the possible imagistic borrowing, see *King Lear*, ed. Kenneth Muir, The Arden Shakespeare (London: Methuen, 1972), 146 (note on 4.2.49–50). For "court holy-water" (meaning flattery), see *Lear*, 3.2.10 in the Arden edition, and Ponet, *Shorte Treatise,* Miir ("This is not holy water of the court"). Muir (100) cites two other sixteenth-century occurences of the phrase (he does not seem to be aware of Ponet's use of it). For the rest of this essay, in quoting from *King Lear*, I will, unless otherwise indicated, cite *King Lear* by Through Line Number (TLN) from the Folio version (F) as presented in *The Norton Facsimile of The First Folio of Shakespeare*, ed. Charlton Hinman (New York: Norton, 1968). For the Quarto text of *Lear* (Q), I have used *King Lear 1608 (Pied Bull Quarto)*, Shakespeare Quarto Facsimiles, no. 1 (Oxford: Clarendon Press, 1939). All other Shakespeare plays are cited from *William Shakespeare: The Complete Works*, gen. ed. Alfred Harbage (Baltimore: Penguin, 1969). On the two versions of *Lear*, see n. 1 above. To locate equivalents of TLN references in the Arden *Lear*, see p. 202 below.

32. Kenneth Muir, "Shakespeare and Politics," in Arnold Kettle, ed., *Shakespeare in a Changing World* (New York: International Publishers, 1964), 72. That corruption at court was a problem that came to the fore in England in the first decade of the seventeenth century is argued in a famous and widely influential essay by J. E. Neale, "The Elizabethan Political Scene," in *Essays in Elizabethan History* (New York: St. Martin's, 1958), 59–84. Neale's conclusions are supported in modified form in Joel Hurstfield, "Political Corruption in Modern England: The Historian's Problem" and "The Political Morality of Early Stuart Statesmen," in *Freedom, Corruption and Government in Elizabethan England* (Cambridge: Harvard University Press, 1973), 137–62, 183–96; and in Linda Peck, *Court Patronage and Corruption at the Early Stuart Court* (London: Routledge, 1990).

in the tower, presents himself as Richard's "most obedient subject" (4.2.66).

In *King John*, a play that has a number of connections to *Lear*, Hubert must weigh his "warrant" and oath ("I have sworn to do it") against the human meaning of blinding the young prince on whom he has attended (4.2.38–124). The case of Rosencrantz and Guildenstern is perhaps closest to that of Sir James Tyrrel, but these courtiers do not seem (like Tyrrel) "discontented," merely and utterly venal and obsequious. As Guildenstern says, they obey Claudius and give themselves "in the full bent" to lay their service freely at Claudius's feet to be commanded (2.2.29–32). I think that we are meant fully to share in Hamlet's disgust at Rosencrantz and Guildenstern's making love to their employment— even if this does not fully justify Hamlet's treatment of them. In *Othello*, when Emilia explicitly asserts the limits of her duty to be an obedient wife to Iago, "'Tis proper I obey him, but not now" (5.2.197), we come, both chronologically and conceptually, to the very threshold of *Lear*. After *Lear*, in the Romances, as I will show in a brief final section, the distinction between virtuous disobedience and improper loyalty becomes axiomatic for Shakespeare—something he believes.

II

The methodology of this section of the essay will be that of close reading for a particular theme.[33] The opening scene of *Lear* raises the issue of obedience, proper and improper, almost immediately, but before turning to this aspect of the scene, a larger issue about the political orientation of the play must be addressed. If the spring of the entire tragic action, or at least of the Lear plot, is seen to be the division of the kingdom as such or Lear's abdication as such, then the entire play would seem to be oriented in a conservative direction, toward the ideology of order and degree—"The specialty of rule hath been neglected." The assumption that this is true, that the division and abdication are the great mistakes from which the tragic action flows, is one of the most well-entrenched assumptions in Shakespearean scholarship. It is regularly

33. For how this procedure escapes my own indictment of critical "schemes," see Essay 3, n. 14 above.

taught to countless students under the guise of "scholarship" (and proper moralism), and it is a tribute to the power and persistence of the conservative view of Shakespeare. The "scholarly" assumptions that division of a kingdom and abdication would necessarily have been perceived as disastrous mistakes by an early seventeenth-century audience are among those "truths" that hardly need proving anymore—that hardly, in fact, need to be supported by evidence. Reference to *Gorboduc* and to the theory of hierarchy (as enunciated in Hooker or in the first paragraph of the homily on Good Order) seems to stand in for evidence.

Yet internally, Shakespeare's play (in both versions) is quite clear on the initial political situation, and contextually the actual social and political history of Europe in the sixteenth century does not support the normal view. The key to understanding—or rather, merely to seeing—what actually takes place in the opening scene is to distinguish between Lear's initial plan (call it Plan A) and his revised plan. As the opening lines of the play make clear, the actual plan had been very carefully worked out. The first words that we hear are about the proposed division and how impartial and careful the king has been in the process of determining and negotiating it ("in the division of the Kingdome, it appeares not which of the Dukes hee valewes most, for qualities are so weigh'd, that curiosity in neither, can make choise of eithers moity"). Lear's chief counselors, Gloucester and Kent, are familiar with the terms of the division and do not register any anxiety about it. They are very calmly discussing the situation, which has, presumably, been in process for a while.

There is no reason why they should feel any anxiety, since the plan, insofar as we can infer its details, was a sensible and politically astute one. From a truly historical point of view, we can see that an Elizabethan or Jacobean audience would have recognized Lear's situation, with regard to the inheritance of his kingdom, as a very unfortunate and perplexing one.[34] He was in the situation of Henry VIII prior to the birth of Edward. Lear had only daughters. This was bad enough, but the elder two of Lear's three are married to powerful and potentially antagonistic dukes. One is tempted to ask the critics who think of the division of the kingdom as inherently disastrous what they think Lear ought to have done. It is

---

34. In *The True Chronicle Historie of King Leir,* there is explicit concern over the issue that God has not granted Leir, with his three daughters, "an heyre indubitate" (line 44). See Geoffrey Bullough, ed., *Narrative and Dramatic Sources of Shakespeare* (New York: Columbia University Press, 1973), 7:338.

clear, however, that the facts of Lear's situation as we are given them are never considered before the Grand Scholarly Generalization clicks in.[35] If we are seriously going to attempt imaginative historical realism, we have to recognize that the choices open to a monarch in Lear's situation were (1) to proceed by primogeniture, so that Goneril would inherit the kingdom; or (2) to devise some sort of arrangement—that is, a division. Fathers with exclusively female heirs often made such arrangements, and they were free to do so. Primogeniture did not apply to women.[36] It is hard to see that naming Goneril sole heir was a desirable or politically workable solution given the power and known temperament of Regan's husband, the Duke of Cornwall. In order to prevent civil war Lear had to divide his kingdom, a motive that the Folio emphasizes ("that future strife / May be prevented now" [TLN 49–50]).[37] And in order to give Cordelia anything, Lear had to divide the kingdom into three rather than two segments.

So far, none of this is truly speculative. The further details of "Plan A" might seem to be so, but they are also quite clearly implied by the text(s). The plan had further provisions for keeping the peace, though here we might seem to be speculating. The texts tell us both that the "moieties" are of equal extent and that Cordelia's share will be "more opulent."[38] Unless this is a simple contradiction (or Lear is just encouraging Cordelia), the answer to this puzzle would seem to reinforce a picture of the initial plan that would follow from the seats of the potentially warring dukes (Albany in the north, Cornwall in the south): Cordelia's equal but "more opulent" share would be in the middle of the kingdom. Lear would live there with Cordelia and her husband (almost certainly intended to have been Burgundy) in what would amount to a buffer state.[39] This plan seems to have every advantage. It

<hr/>

35. For reference to an immediate political context in which Shakespeare's audience would have been strongly for "the division of the kingdomes" (Q has the plural), see n. 47 below.

36. See Joyce Youings, *Sixteenth-Century England*, The Pelican Social History of Britain (New York: Penguin, 1984), 113; and Lawrence Stone, *The Crisis of the Aristocracy, 1558–1641*, abridged ed. (Oxford: Oxford University Press, 1967), 274, 290. Rosalie Colie sees the relevance of this in "Reason and Need: *King Lear* and the 'Crisis' of the Aristocracy," in Rosalie L. Colie and F. T. Flahiff, eds., *Some Facets of "King Lear": Essays in Prismatic Criticism* (Toronto: University of Toronto Press, 1974), 196–98.

37. This line does not appear in the Quarto (Q).

38. The Quarto has "equalities are so weighed" where the Folio has "qualities."

39. For Burgundy as the intended husband of Cordelia (he is given right of first refusal), and for some shrewd remarks on the intended division ("Plan A"), see Harry V.

would (as far as is humanly possible) guarantee political and military stability and it would also take special care (and advantage) of Cordelia. But what about the abdication issue? First ("internally"), it seems reasonable to think that the tripartite division plan would have had the best chance of success if it was begun while Lear was still alive and could supervise it. Second, historically, the most famous case of a reigning monarch in the sixteenth century abdicating his throne in order "To shake all Cares and Businesse from [his] Age" (TLN 44), was a spectacular success. Charles V, the most powerful ruler by far in sixteenth-century Europe, retired to a monastery and passed the kingship of Spain to his absent son (who was in the Netherlands at the time) with no problem whatever.

What we witness in the opening scene, then, is not a disastrous plan being made yet worse, but a set of spontaneous bad decisions on Lear's part supervening on a plan that might well have been a workable one—a true crisis.[40] Reading the scene in this way helps us better understand Shakespeare's presentation of the behavior of both Cordelia and Kent. They are both to be seen as caught by surprise. Cordelia was not planning to disappoint Lear in public, nor was Kent planning to protest the arrangements Lear was making. Kent's concern for Lear's "safety" (TLN 168) is a response to the revised plan. What this means is that the love-test cannot have been part of the initial design, since, as we have seen, the shares to go to each of the sisters had already been carefully worked out. In the anonymous *Leir*, the love-test has a function, but in Shakespeare's play, it is a kind of game that Lear is playing ("Which of you *shall we say* doth love us most") while waiting for Gloucester to return with Cordelia's suitors. The real business of the scene was to make the division of the kingdom official through public proclamation and, the one actual piece of business, to declare which of Cordelia's suitors has succeeded (the rival princes "heere are to be answer'd" [TLN 53]). The love-test is purely ceremonial, and the suggestion that it is part of

---

Jaffa, "The Limits of Politics: *King Lear*, Act I, scene i," in Allan Bloom and Harry V. Jaffa, *Shakespeare's Politics* (1964; rpt. Chicago: University of Chicago Press, 1981), 113–45. I should add that this essay also contains, I think, a number of egregiously forced assumptions about Lear's "perfection" as a king, about politics, and about the supposed moral or "Aristotelian" structure of Shakespearean tragedy.

40. For the greater and more coherent dramatic effect of reading the scene in this way, see G. R. Elliott, "The Initial Contrast in *Lear*," *Journal of English and Germanic Philology* 58 (1959): 251–63.

the division merely a flourish. As Stanley Cavell has argued, all three of the daughters understand perfectly what is being asked of them.[41]

Goneril participates in the ceremony brilliantly. Realizing that Lear is calling more for word than matter, her inspired use of inexpressibility topoi allows her to fulfill her ceremonial role and free herself entirely from matter. Goneril has, in fact, performed so brilliantly and upped the rhetorical ante so high that Regan can only echo her and Cordelia can only commit herself to matter *rather than* to words. Cordelia's initial act is mere refusal, nonobedience ("Nothing my Lord"). She insists on distinguishing herself from her sisters and from the terms of the ceremony. When drawn into speech, she fills in the content of her present and future relations to her father, while the occasion calls only for form. She commits herself to a "plain" rhetoric of concrete enumeration, rather than to a ceremonial rhetoric of comparatives and superlatives. As is well known, the relation of a child to a parent was an essential part of the general nexus of hierarchical subordination in conservative Renaissance social and political discourse as well as a major source for political analogies.[42] It is crucial to the value structure of *King Lear* that, from the point of view of conservative moral and political thinking, Goneril is entirely correct in saying to Cordelia, "you have obedience scanted" (TLN 304).[43] Regan has just said: "Prescribe not us our dutie" (TLN 301). Goneril and Regan are the mouthpieces for "duty" and "obedience" straightforwardly conceived.[44]

We recall that the Homily on Order reminded us that although we may not "in any wise" resist violently, we must believe undoubtedly that there are circumstances in which we "may not obey kings, magistrates, or any other, *though they be our own fathers*." Yet we cannot help

41. Stanley Cavell, "The Avoidance of Love: A Reading of *King Lear*," in *Disowning Knowledge in Six Plays of Shakespeare* (Cambridge: Cambridge University Press, 1987), 62.

42. For a powerful and (more or less) typical example, see William Gouge, *Of Domesticall Duties*, in *The Workes of William Gouge*, rev. ed. (London, 1627). For this type of discourse, see Gordon J. Schochet, *Patriarchalism in Political Thought* (Oxford: Blackwell, 1975).

43. The assignment of this speech to Goneril is a Folio alteration. Randall McLeod is correct in noting that the Folio adds to Goneril's part, and that Goneril is "cooler" in the Folio, but I think that he very much mistakes the nature of cruelty in the play in seeing this coolness as making Goneril "milder" in the Folio; "*Gon.* No more, the text is foolish," in *Division*, 155–93.

44. This helps explain why, as Edwin Muir elegantly puts it, Goneril and Regan "have a good conscience, even a touch of self-righteousness"; "The Politics of *King Lear*," in *Essays on Literature and Society*, rev. ed. (Cambridge: Harvard University Press, 1965), 40.

wondering whether Cordelia's situation was truly one of these special circumstances (which the Homily against Disobedience disavows). Goneril's condemnation is not enough in itself, at this point in the play, to lead us to approve wholeheartedly of Cordelia's behavior. Perhaps some honorable form of compliance would have been possible.[45] "Duty" and "obedience" are rendered problematic by the contrasting actions (that is, speeches) of Cordelia and her sisters, but disobedience is not fully valorized by Cordelia's behavior. For this, we must turn to Kent. It is in Kent's behavior in this scene that the theme of virtuous, morally mandated disobedience, even interference, is fully articulated.

Kent is normally thought of as a feudal retainer. This captures some central elements of his characterization, but obscures his identity as a Renaissance courtier. In scene 1, Kent attempts exactly what the revised "schoolmaster" courtier of Castiglione's fourth book is supposed to do: to speak truth to power, to use his personal skills and the relationship to the ruler that these skills have brought him to tell his prince unpalatable truth. One function of the opening prose interlude is to give us a sense of Kent's normal behavior as a courtier. Although critics are often confused about this, Shakespeare does not present Kent as naturally or habitually boorish or even plain-spoken. With regard to what we are to understand as Kent's normal behavior, the striking feature of the opening interlude is how exquisitely Kent handles the almost impossible social situation in which he is placed by Gloucester's crudely jocular introduction of Edmund-as-bastard. "I cannot wish the fault undone, the issue of it, being so proper" is truly magnificent, responding without stuffiness to Gloucester while managing to acknowledge and compliment Edmund. This is courtliness at its best, humanly and morally graceful without being in any way greasy.[46] And Kent's initial addresses to Lear are both courtly. "Good my Liege," he begins, after the astounding curse on Cordelia (TLN 128). Lear immediately shuts him up with a threat and announces the new division and abdication plan. Kent tries the courtly mode again (though subtly echoing Cordelia's concrete enumeration): "Royall *Lear*, / Whom I have ever honor'd as

45. Bradley states this view strongly. See A. C. Bradley, *Shakespearean Tragedy* (1904; rpt. New York: Meridian, 1955), 256.

46. In his superb essay on "*King Lear* and its Language," Sheldon P. Zitner has noticed the morally alert courtliness of this initial exchange (in Colie and Flahiff, *Some Facets of "King Lear,"* 6). In their pioneering essay on "'Service' in *King Lear*," *Shakespeare Quarterly* 9 (1958): 347–55, Jonas Barish and Marshall Waingrow note that Edmund shrewdly "takes Kent as his model in the forms of service" (350).

my King, / Lov'd as my Father . . . As my great Patron" (TLN 148–51).
Only when Lear again cuts him off with a threat does Kent alter his style
(his counterpart in *Leir* falls silent at this point). Shakespeare wants to
present Kent as knowing exactly what he is doing—to the point of having Kent explicitly call attention to the relation between the extremity
of the situation and his abandonment of verbal decorum. "*Be Kent
unmannerly,* / When Lear is mad," he formally announces (TLN 154b-
155a). Only after this announcement does Kent address Lear uncere-
moniously, that is, without a prologue, in the familiar form, and with a
generic, nonhonorific description: "What wouldest thou do old man?"
(TLN 155b).

Kent's rudeness is chosen, under pressure, as a moral stance. He is
operating at a borderline where Castiglione merges into Ponet (Annabel
Patterson has suggested that it is analogous to the world of Parliamentary
privilege).[47] Again "thouing" Lear, Kent explains that in interfering, he
is acting out of faithfulness: "Think'st thou that dutie shall have dread
to speake / When power to flattery bowes?" Kent's anticourtly style (like
Cordelia's, he implies) is not an option but a moral obligation: "to
plainnesse honour's bound / When Majesty falls to folly" (TLN 158–
59). Kent is acting like Buchanan's "physician" in refusing to acknowledge as legitimate the wishes of the king-as-madman. He is attempting
to recall Lear to reason ("in thy best consideration, checke / This
hideous rashnesse") and to recollection ("Thy yongest Daughter do's
not love thee least"). Yet he keeps speaking long after it is clear that Lear
is only being incensed by his resistance; he ignores direct commands and
interrupts Lear mid-oath. This final move produces, in the Folio only,
a small act of resistance by Albany and, if Beth Goldring is right, Cordelia, in checking Lear from physical violence to Kent (TLN 175).[48]

---

47. See *Censorship and Interpretation: The Conditions of Writing and Reading in
Early Modern England* (Madison: University of Wisconsin Press, 1984), 71. Patterson
argues for the political indeterminacy of the play, but if *Lear* can be seen as supporting
parliamentary privilege, especially with regard to the king's highly unpopular plan for
"Great Britain," then this provides a contemporary context in which the division of the
kingdom(s) would have been positively rather than negatively conceived. Parliament
wanted the kingdoms divided. On the parliamentary opposition to the union of the
kingdoms, see Wallace Notestein, *The House of Commons, 1604–1610* (New Haven: Yale
University Press, 1971); for the history of the project of the Union, see Brian P. Levack,
The Formation of the British State: England, Scotland, and the Union (Oxford: Clarendon
Press, 1987). Patterson seems to see *Lear* as more sympathetic to political radicalism in
Shakespeare and the Popular Voice, 111–12.

48. Beth Goldring, "*Cor.*'s Rescue of Kent," in Taylor and Warren, *Division*, 143–51.

Kent's attempt at schoolmaster courtiership receives precisely the "re-ward" (TLN 186) that More's Hythlodaeus or Castiglione's Calmeta would have predicted, banishment, and in the final speech before his fate is sealed, Kent combines Buchanan's analytical image with Ponet's pro-phetic stance, presenting himself more as bearing witness than as ad-vising:

Kill thy Physition, and thy fee bestow
Upon the foule disease, revoke thy guift,
Or whil'st I can vent clamour from my throate,
Ile tell thee thou dost evill. (TLN 177–80)

The structure of values established in the first scene continues throughout the play. Plain speech and conscientious breaches of deco-rum remain touchstones of value and are richly developed as such. Kent, manifesting his characteristic awareness of style ("I other accents bor-row"), reenters the play in 1.4 in the role of a non-gentle servant, a menial who is incapable of courtly speech (he can only "marre a curious tale in telling it" [TLN 363–66]).[49] The introduction of Kent as Caius is immediately followed by a brief and haughty appearance by a gen-tlemanly servingman, Goneril's steward Oswald, and by a brief inter-jection by one of Lear's retainers. This retainer, raised from Servant to Knight in the Folio, takes it on himself to comment, directly to Lear, on the developing situation; he emphasizes that he is relying solely on his own judgment and conscience in making these remarks: "to my judge-ment, your Highnesse is not entertain'd with that ceremonious affection as you were wont" (TLN 587–88). The quality captured in this knight's wonderful phrase, "ceremonious affection," is the quality of normative or ideal courtliness, and it is entirely missing from the world of this play. Given its lack, unceremonious affection, loving plain-spokenness, is the only alternative.[50] In the face of Lear's anger, the Knight explains his presumptuous and unmannerly behavior thus: "I beseech you pardon me my Lord, if I bee mistaken; for my duty cannot be silent, when I think your Highnesse wrong'd." Again, as in scene 1, in unusually negative

49. For the distinction between menials and gentlemanly "serving-men," see I. M., *A Health to the Gentlemanly Profession of Serving-Men*, Shakespeare Association Facsimiles, no. 3 (London: Oxford University Press, 1931).

50. See Kenneth J. E. Graham, *The Performance of Conviction: Plainness and Rhetoric in the Early English Renaissance* (Ithaca: Cornell University Press, 1994), chap. 6.

or perilous situations, "duty cannot be silent"—even at the risk of breaching decorum.

Oswald reenters at this point, dutifully following the instructions that (in the Folio) we have seen Goneril issuing to him in the previous scene ("Put on what weary negligence you please" [TLN 519]), and Kent intervenes. Shakespeare now introduces the last of the lovingly rude truth-speakers in the play, the Fool, whose first action is to identify with Kent (or Kent with himself). We can see what Shakespeare is doing in this scene. He is lining up the characters: Kent, the Fool, and the nameless Knight on the one hand, Oswald and Goneril on the other. As in the equivalent scene in *Twelfth Night* (1.5), willingness to tolerate the Fool is a way of making the crucial division.[51] The Fool is a licensed plain-speaker who presents an utterly cynical, Hythlodaeus-like view of court life: "Truth's a dog must to kennell; hee must bee whipt out, when the Lady Brach may stand by th' fire and stinke" (TLN 641–43). A "brach" is a very high-class dog, and in the great dramatic moment of the scene, Lady Brach herself, Goneril, enters.[52] Here, as usual, Goneril speaks for decorum.

Goneril begins her reproof of Lear with a comment on the Fool. His license is typical of the "rank and not to be endured riot" with which Lear's retinue threatens to "infect" the manners of her sober court (TLN 712–15, 752–55). She does not appreciate it when Lear adopts something like the Fool's "pranks" to make a point (TLN 746). The elaborately suspended and complexly subordinated syntax that Shakespeare gives to Goneril allows her to present her own desires as objective necessities: "The shame it selfe doth speake / For instant remedy" (TLN 755–56). Lear reacts to the personal threat behind the impersonal rhetoric, and at this point Albany enters. The question becomes where Albany stands. "Is it your will, speake Sir," Lear demands (TLN 770). Albany pleads ignorance, is horrified at the excess of Lear's curse, and then, after Lear rushes out, begins a weak protest. Goneril cuts him off,

51. Goneril's initial complaint against Lear concerns Lear's defense of his Fool (1.3). In the Folio, where Goneril is addressing Oswald ("Steward") in this scene (1.3), it is unlikely that Oswald was the "gentleman" who struck the Fool. If it were Oswald (as is more likely in the Quarto, where "Gentleman" is interlocutor), the situation would exactly parallel that in *Twelfth Night*: Fool versus Steward. In any case, the general structure is identical. For a sustained meditation on "Fool in *Lear*," see Empson's chapter by that title in *The Structure of Complex Words* (London: Chatto and Windus, 1964), 125–57.

52. On the class implications of dog versus "brach," see Muir's note (quoting Duthie) on this line, the Arden *Lear*, 39–40.

appealing (in the Folio) to political prudence, and tasking him for foolishness or at least "want of wisedome" (TLN 867).[53] Albany weakly accepts the possibility of Goneril's superior politic prudence, weakly recommends leaving well enough alone, and, when Goneril is about to counter, exits with, "Well, well, the'vent" (TLN 872). At this point, we are surely meant to see Albany as, in Buchanan's words, one of those who "albeit they are not ignorant what is lawful and just or right, yet prefer a quiet sloathfulness to honest hazards, and hesitating in their minds, do frame their consultation on the expectation of the Event."[54]

Throughout the exchange with Albany, Goneril is constantly calling for Oswald (an effect that is intensified in the Folio). She relies on Oswald to be totally instrumental to her purposes; Oswald is not only to warn Regan about Lear's retinue but "thereto [to] adde such reasons of [his] owne, / As may compact it more" (TLN 862–63). Kent is sent off to Regan by Lear, and in 2.2 the inevitable confrontation occurs. In the structure of the play, Kent and Oswald are *systematically* contrasted.[55] The sight of Oswald sends Kent into a Fool-like aria of virtuoso imprecation (TLN 1087–95). Contra Jonathan Dollimore, and despite the references to Oswald being "beggerly," and "three-suited," Kent is not insulting Oswald for being poor and in service.[56] As I have already suggested, although *Lear* is set in the legendary past, its social world is that of Shakespeare's England. A figure like Oswald, a steward in a major noble household, was not at all poor, but actually quite grand. He would probably have had a steward himself.[57] Unless Oswald is finely, even ostentatiously dressed in a very grand version of Goneril's livery, many of Kent's insults make no sense, nor does Lear's remark about Oswald's "borrowed pride" (TLN 1472). Oswald should certainly be

53. TLN 842–57, from "This man hath had good counsel" to "When I have show'd th' unfitness" are a Folio addition.

54. *De Jure Regni apud Scotos*, 61.

55. See Barish and Waingrow, "'Service' in *Lear*," 353.

56. Jonathan Dollimore, *Radical Tragedy: Religion, Ideology and Power in the Drama of Shakespeare and his Contemporaries* (Chicago: University of Chicago Press, 1984), 201. The quotation from Dollimore in the next paragraph also appears on this page. On the sociology of Kent's insults, see Muir's notes (Arden *Lear*, 65).

57. See, for instance, the biography of William ffarington, Esq., steward until 1594 to Lord Ferdinando Strange, Earl of Derby, in *The Stanley Papers, Part 2: The Derby Household Books*, ed. F. R. Raines (Manchester: Chetham Society, 1853), xviii-xcviii. See also Paul V. B. Jones, *The Household of a Tudor Nobleman, Univ. of Illinois Studies in the Social Sciences* 6 (1917); and Mark Girouard, *Life in the English Country House* (New Haven: Yale University Press, 1978), 82–83.

much better dressed than Caius-Kent. Kent mixes phrases that suggest that Oswald is poor with ones that suggest that he is foppish. Kent is insulting Oswald by promiscuously alluding both to the kind of servant Oswald is ("proud . . . glasse-gazing . . . finicall") and to the kind of servant that Kent is pretending to be and that Oswald would disdain ("beggerly . . . filthy").

The major criticism of Oswald is, in fact, moral rather than social. If this be what Dollimore would call "humanism," so be it. Kent, in his own guise or as Caius, has not simply internalized the play's "dominant ideology of property and power." The dominant ideology of the play (and the of period) is much less successfully dominant and much less consistently conservative than Dollimore suggests. Dollimore down-plays the role of critical ideology in the play (since only a "materialist" perspective can be positive in his scheme). Yet the central point of Kent's tirade is that Oswald is, as the Folio puts it, "superserviceable": "one that would'st be a Baud in way of good service" (TLN 1091, 1092–93).[58] The essential picture is of a man who would do anything on command, "in way of good service." In explaining his anger at Oswald to Cornwall, Kent expounds on the point, now in high verse. He is incensed that "such a slave as this should weare a Sword," that is, should *look like* a gentleman and true courtier (sword bearing was a class privilege), and yet be among the "smiling rogues" who

> smooth every passion
> That in the natures of their Lords rebell,
> Being oile to fire, snow to the colder moodes;
> Revenge, affirme, and turn their Halcion beakes
> With every gall, and varry of their Masters,
> Knowing naught (like dogges) but following. (TLN 1148–53)

This is the figure Pietro da Napoli discerned in Federico Fregoso's "plyable" courtier; it is the smiling client in Juvenal's third Satire and in Jonson's *Sejanus*.[59] This is Frank Whigham's "ordinary courtier" (as opposed to extraordinary principled types like Kent or Sir Philip Sid-

---

58. One of the most telling pieces of evidence for the Folio's greater clarity about the themes that I have been tracing is its substitution of "super-serviceable" for the Quarto's "superfinicall" (Q E1r).

59. See *Sejanus, his Fall*, 1.34–41, *Ben Jonson*, ed. C. H. Herford and Percy Simpson (Oxford: Clarendon Press, 1932), 4:356; and see 9:598 for the Juvenalian source. The passage in *Lear* is closer to Jonson than to the original. Muir, Arden *Lear*, xxi, notes the connection.

ney).[60] Such an "ordinary" figure encourages rather than, as Kent did in scene 1, stands against irrational passions in social superiors. Kent's characterization suggests that Shakespeare knew the dialectic of Luther and Buchanan in which the improperly obedient participate more truly in "the name and quality that is termed rebellion" than do the disobedient, since here the submissive servants are those who aid and abet a rebellion ("smooth every passion / That in the natures of their Lords rebell").[61] The culminating dog image suggests an essential difference between brute and reasonable service, between those who are capable of loyal disobedience and those who, in Goodman's words, "suffer themselves like brute beastes rather than reasonable creatures, to be led and drawen where so ever their Princes commandements have called." The fundamental "antipathy" Kent posits between himself and Oswald (TLN 1160) is between two conceptions of obedience: one conscientious and limited, that "rightly obey[s]" power by knowing its proper bounds; the other "naught . . . but following."[62]

In the scene between Kent and Oswald, Cornwall replaces Goneril as the voice of propriety. "Know you no reverence," he asks the railing Kent. "Yes Sir," Kent politely answers, but appeals, first, to the (nonsocial) "privilege" of righteous anger (TLN 1143)—a moral use of a key social term—and then to something like the Fool's licensed *parrhesia*: "Sir," he says, "'tis my occupation to be plaine."[63] Cornwall's response to this is extremely interesting. He detects the element of wilfullness in Kent's behavior and offers a brilliant, Astrophil-like parody of affected

60. For Oswald as an "ordinary courtier," see Frank Whigham, *Ambition and Privilege: The Social Tropes of Elizabethan Courtesy Theory* (Berkeley and Los Angeles: University of California Press, 1984), 20–21.

61. For the quotation, see Luther, *Warning to his Dear German People*, 20. Jonson's treatment does not suggest this dialectic (nor does Juvenal's); their focus is on mimicry.

62. For "That thou may'st rightly obey power, her bounds know" (line 100 of Donne's third Satire), see Essay 6, pp. 157–58ff. above. As the OED indicates, Shakespeare is an early user of "antipathy" in a metaphorical (nonphysical) sense.

63. With regard to the political meaning of the defense of "folly" and plain-speaking in the play, it is worth recalling that Ponet, in the *Shorte Treatise*, presents himself as a kind of Fool. He speaks, he says, "not so finely as som others can, but boisteously after my rude maner" (Kiiv). Luther adopted the persona of a court fool in the Preface to the *Appeal to the Ruling Class [of Germany]*, *Luther: Selections*, ed. Dillenberger, 404. For a powerful meditation on the function of this persona, see Robert Weimann, "History and the Issue of Authority in Representation: The Elizabethan Theater and the Reformation," *NLH* 17 (1986): 456. On *parrhesia*, freedom of speech in the Athenian assemblies, see Victor Eherenberg, *From Solon to Socrates* (London: Methuen, 1968), 181, 217, 271 (and comedy).

plainness: "He cannot flatter he, / An honest mind and plaine, he must speake truth; / And they will take it so; if not, hee's plaine" (TLN 1173–75). Parody then turns into moral critique. Cornwall recognizes the contrast between Kent and Oswald, but sees Kent as worse, as one of "These kinds of Knaves . . . [who], in this plainnesse / Harbour more craft, and more corrupter ends / Than twenty silly-ducking observants" (TLN 1176–78). The moral moorings of the play threaten to come loose here. Yet while it is generally true that, as Zitner puts it, "no verbal style is self-validating,"[64] the ethic of *Lear* is so deeply anticourtly that there is in fact no plain knave in the play. For the figure Cornwall describes, we must look to *Othello*, not to *Lear*. We must look to Iago rather than to Kent (though it surely helps us understand Iago's power to recognize that he is pretending to be a figure like "Caius"). As is the case with the association of plainness with pride in the opening scene (Lear speaks of "pride," which Cordelia "cals plainnesse" [TLN 137]), the play does not support the critique. The plain style remains a locus of value. Significantly, Kent defends his "dialect" (TLN 1185) and his sincerity by asserting his willingness to disobey and alienate Cornwall on moral grounds: "he that beguild you in a plaine accent was a plaine Knave; which for my part I will not be, though I should win your displeasure to entreat me to't."

In the name of the particularly thin conception of propriety and decorum that Cornwall shares with Goneril and Regan, he commands the deeply indecorous step of putting "Caius," the King's messenger, in the stocks. At this point, the moral pressure shifts to Gloucester. He was offstage, fetching "the Lords of France and Burgundy," during the great explosion of scene 1, and therefore was not available for protest; the pressure was all on Kent there, as it was on Albany in 1.4. In acts 2 and 3, the pressure, as Maynard Mack puts it, "to take some sort of stand," is on Gloucester.[65] Gloucester's initial protest is polite but nonetheless real: "Let me beseech your Grace, not to do so" (TLN 1220).[66] He disobeys a direct command (from Cornwall, in the Folio) in staying with

---

64. "*Lear* and Its Language," in Colie and Flahiff, *Some Facets of King Lear,* 9.

65. See Maynard Mack, *"King Lear" in Our Time* (Berkeley and Los Angeles: University of California Press, 1972), 90.

66. The Folio perhaps weakens Gloucester's protest at this point by cutting the Q lines (E2v) about the social meaning of the "low correction" that Cornwall proposes (in the Arden conflation, the Q-only lines are approximately 2.2.137–41a). It should be noted, however, that Gloucester's conciliatory acknowledgment of Kent's "fault" is also cut in the Folio.

Kent, and he does not palliate or equivocate in his judgment: "The Duke's to blame in this" (TLN 1235).[67] Yet when Lear enters the scene, Gloucester finds himself bearing messages back and forth between Lear and his daughter and son-in-law. As the purposeful quality of the behavior of Cornwall and Regan begins to dawn fully on Lear, Gloucester utters the great cry of the appeaser—"I would have all well betwixt you" (TLN 1396)—but the rest of the scene makes it clear that there is no middle position in this world. Gloucester says nothing during the successive interchanges between Lear and Cornwall, Lear and Regan, and finally, Lear and Goneril. Yet Gloucester follows Lear into the storm. The line that notes Gloucester's absence, however, also announces his return (TLN 1597). It is a brilliant stroke; he is still temporizing. Despite his compassionate evocation of Lear's situation, despite his reservations about the actions of Cornwall and company, Gloucester seems prepared to obey the command he has received: "Shut up your doores my Lord" (TLN 1612).

To assess Gloucester's behavior in act 3, we must be aware of his social and political status vis-à-vis Cornwall and Regan. To Gloucester, Cornwall is "the Noble Duke my Master,/ My worthy Arch and Patron" (TLN 995–96); it is only through Cornwall's authority that Gloucester has access to state power and can issue his proclamation against Edgar ("The Duke must grant me that," Gloucester avers [TLN 1019]). Difficult as this is for us to perceive, there is a great distance in social and political status between Gloucester and Cornwall. Cornwall rules half of England (including the region in which Gloucester has his house); he is Gloucester's acknowledged sovereign, his "master" (recall "Let me beseech *your Grace*, not to do so").[68] Yet in act 3, by the next time we see Gloucester, he has made his choice. Authority and humanity have definitively split apart, and Gloucester has lost the former in the name

67. David Bevington has pointed out to me that Gloucester's not following Cornwall offstage could be played as "dithering" rather than as defiant noncompliance. In either case, however, Gloucester does not comply. Perhaps "dithering" too can be a form of resistance.

68. Muir's assertion (Arden *Lear,* 63) that Cornwall is subordinate to Regan is based on a very dubious reading (and editing) of Regan's continuation of Cornwall's line to Gloucester at TLN 1061 ("You know why we came to visit you"). Muir punctuates this as an interruption by Regan (2.1.117; p. 63), but both Q and F punctuate Cornwall's line as a question, so that there is continuation but no interruption. Muir is (literally) making the text fit his theory here. Lear twice speaks of "the Duke of Cornwall and his wife" (2.4.94, 113), and it should also perhaps be noted (as Elliott, "Initial Contrast," 261, does) that in 1.1, after the disinheriting of Cordelia, Lear seems to see himself as dividing the kingdom between Cornwall and Albany, his "Beloved Sonnes" (TLN 146).

of the latter: "When I desired their leave that I might pity him, they tooke from me the use of mine owne house" (TLN 1752–53).[69] Gloucester was "charged," in true regal idiom, "on paine of perpetuall displeasure," not to aid Lear. Charity has become a crime, but Gloucester now feels in the grip of a moral imperative: "If I die for it, (as no lesse is threatned me) the King, my old Master, must be relieved" (TLN 1768–69). It is important to read "old" here as "former" as well as "aged." Gloucester is insisting on a duty that does not depend on the immediate political situation. When he finds Lear on the heath, he reemphasizes the point, speaking the language of morally mandated disobedience to superior powers, the language of higher than immediate, narrowly political duty. "Go in with me," he says to Lear, "my duty cannot suffer / T'obey in all your daughters' hard commands" (TLN 1926–27). Gloucester means his duty to Lear, but he could also mean his duty to Cornwall and company, as we shall see. In any case, Gloucester flags his disobedience: "Though their Injunction be to barre my doores . . . Yet have I ventured" (TLN 1926–30). As in all the moments of moral courage in the play, duty and obedience are opposed.[70]

It is important to be clear on Gloucester's political as well as his social situation. In sending Lear to Dover, Gloucester is aiding an invading enemy (and, perhaps, a popular rebellion).[71] The letter that Edmund, in his major act of loyalty, passes on to Cornwall proves Gloucester "an intelligent partie to the advantages of France" (TLN 1981). Cornwall and company are not misusing language in speaking continually of "the traitor Gloucester."[72] Gloucester cannot, ultimately, deny the charge when it is specifically put to him; "I am tyed to th' Stake," he says, "and I

69. For a very similar discussion of the opposition between authority and humanity in the play, see Weimann, "History and the Issue of Authority," 473.

70. A striking feature of the way in which moral obligations are conceived of in the play is that they are always put in terms of "duty," never in terms of "conscience." This perhaps reflects the play's stress on concrete human relations as the source of morality. It perhaps also reflects the thoroughgoing secularism of the play. "Conscience" appears both in Holinshed (Bullough, 7:317), and in *Leir* (line 880; Bullough, 7:359).

71. Elimination of references to a French invasion is one of the most consistent departures of the Folio from the Quarto. Urkowitz has argued that in the Folio substitution of "a power already *footed*" (TLN 1764) for "a power already *landed*" (Q G1r) in 3.3, rebellion rather than invasion is suggested; *Shakespeare's Revision of "King Lear,"* 73. Gary Taylor sees the Folio alterations to the latter part of the play as systematically emphasizing rebellion rather than invasion, and he notes that, with regard to Jacobean politics, this made the Folio more rather than less radical ("Monopolies, Show Trials, Disaster, and Invasion: *King Lear* and Censorship," *Division*, 80).

72. This is emphasized in the Folio, in which Gloucester is called a "traitor" or "treacherous" twice more than in the Quarto.

must stand the Course" (TLN 2125–26). Yet though Gloucester is indeed a traitor, the scene of his mutilation is not presented as a judicial one. Shakespeare has Cornwall explicitly declare the extrajudicial, purely private nature of his actions: "Though well we may not passe upon his life / Without the forme of Iustice, yet our power / Shall do a curt'sie to our wrath" (TLN 2084–86). There is no legal or political point to torturing Gloucester.[73] They already know what he knows. The presentation of a world "upside down" is made literal in the procedure Cornwall announces for the mutilation of Gloucester: "Upon these eyes of thine, Ile set my foote." Cornwall blinds Gloucester in one eye; Regan urges him on, appealing, characteristically, to decorum: "One side will mocke another: Th'other too" (TLN 2143). At this moment, one of the most remarkable and politically significant episodes in the play occurs. A character designated in both the Quarto and the Folio merely as Servant interrupts Cornwall with an imperious command, "Hold your hand, my Lord." Regan and Cornwall are astonished. Regan says, "How now, you dog"; Cornwall exclaims, "My villain," meaning "my menial," but the Servant appeals, as Kent had earlier, to the special social "privilege" of righteous anger, and fights with Cornwall. "Nay then come on, and take the chance of anger" (TLN 2153). Regan takes hold of a sword and, in the Quarto stage direction, stabs the servant in the back, exclaiming, with the full weight of outraged decorum in her words, "A pezant stand up thus!"[74]

Regan is right. The menial's behavior is outrageous. It is unthinkable—but not, as we have seen and as we see here, literally so. Shakespeare

73. For the theory of judicial torture, see John H. Langbein, *Torture and the Law of Proof* (Chicago: University of Chicago Press, 1977).

74. Where F has merely "Killes him" (TLN 2155), Q has "Shee takes a sword and runs at him behind" (H2r). It is interesting to contemplate the Quarto stage direction in relation to the Dürer design to which Stephen Greenblatt has called attention, the monument to a "Victory over the Rebellious Peasants," which features at its apogee a peasant stabbed in the back with a sword. Shakespeare's scene here does not seem to involve the "genre problem" that Greenblatt emphasizes in Dürer's design. There is no comedy or ambivalence in this depiction, in *Lear*, of a "peasant" stabbed in the back. See Stephen Greenblatt, "Murdering Peasants: Status, Genre, and the Representation of Rebellion," *Representations* 1 (1983): 1–29; also in *Learning to Curse: Essays in Early Modern Culture* (New York: Routledge, 1990), 99–130. Greenblatt does not discuss the *Lear* scene in his essay, but he does discuss Shakespeare's depiction of the death of Jack Cade in 2 *Henry VI*, where the "genre problem" is quite intense. Since 2 *Henry VI* is one of Shakespeare's very early plays, the different depiction of "murdering peasants" in *Lear* supports the suggestion that Shakespeare's politics change, become less conservative, in the course of his career. Annabel Patterson adopts this view in *Shakespeare and the Popular Voice*, 10 and passim. On Greenblatt's difficulties with allowing for the possibility of genuine radicalism in Shakespeare and in the period, see Essay 6, n. 1 above.

is presenting the most radical possible sociopolitical act in a way that can only be interpreted as calling for his audience's approval. This is Ehud killing Eglon in Ponet; this is Matathias. The servant is obviously not a "public person," and his action is one of militant interference; it transcends and does not even involve nonobedience, since it is not clear that he has been directly commanded to do anything (in performance, a director has to decide whether this servant is to be one of those holding the chair to which Gloucester is bound). The scene is that which Buchanan describes and endorses: "[when] from amongst the lowest of the people some very mean, and obscure" person is stirred up to revenge Tyrannical Pride. From the legal point of view, it should be noted, the servant, like Gloucester, is committing treason—though in the servant's case the treason is "petty." As Michael Dalton explains, "Pety treason is when wilfull murder is committed (in the estate Oeconomicall) upon any subiect, by one that is in subiection, and oweth faith, duty, and obedience, to the party murdred."[75] The punishment for Petit Treason was the same as for High.[76] Recognizing the political radicalism of this scene, which is entirely a Shakespearean invention, perhaps helps solve a long-standing puzzle: Why did Shakespeare have the mutilation take place onstage? Dr. Johnson and most nineteenth-century critics and directors found this scene improper and excessive. Theatrical convention demands that this sort of thing happen offstage. The political helps explain the theatrical radicalism. Shakespeare perhaps felt that only through the extreme moral revulsion brought on by having to witness such a scene could he rely on his audience to approve rather than to recoil when they saw "A pezant stand up thus" and mortally wound a prince. To the question in the Homily against Disobedience—"But what if the prince be . . . evil indeed, and it [is] also evident to all men's eyes that he is so?"—Shakespeare offered an answer very different from that of the Homily.[77]

The rationale the servant offers for his act is as remarkable as the act itself. After commanding the Duke of Cornwall to desist from what he

---

75. See Michael Dalton, *The Countrey Justice* (1619; facsimile New York: Arno Press, 1972), 213. As far as I know, the first critic to point out that "as late as 1728, for a servant to kill his master or mistress was counted a specially heinous crime, far worse than ordinary murder," and to identify this "specially heinous crime" as Petit Treason, was Mary Hallowell Perkins in *The Servant Problem in English Literature* (Boston: R. G. Badger, 1928), 75.

76. On the punishments for treason, see Dalton, *Countrey Justice*, 215, and Essay 8, p. 218 below.

77. Compare Sidney Shanker, *Shakespeare and the Uses of Ideology* (The Hague: Mouton, 1975), 144: "Passivity could be no response desired for *Lear*."

is doing, the servant characterizes his own behavior toward the duke as an instance of loyalty rather than of rebellion:

> I have serv'd you ever since I was a Childe:
> But better service have I never done you,
> Then now to bid you hold. (TLN 2146–48)

This is the clearest articulation and most extreme case in the play of the paradox of service through resistance. Armed resistance is presented as good service. We recall Ponet's insistence that when Saul's "household wayters and familiar servauntes" refused to obey Saul's commandment to kill Ahimelech, they were "yet the kinges true servauntes and sub-jectes." In the Geneva Bible, Daniel, flouting a royal decree, assures Darius that "unto thee, O King, I have done no hurt" (6:26). The marginal gloss explains that since Daniel "did disobey the Kings wicked commaundement [in order] to obey God," he "did no injurie to the King."[78] Buchanan would see the Servant as another political "physi-cian." We can begin to appreciate how important this conception was to Shakespeare by reflecting that he could have gotten the same plot effect, but not the paradox, if he had made the militant servant one of Gloucester's rather than one of Cornwall's retinue. The scene takes place, after all, in Gloucester's house, as Gloucester keeps saying. Shakespeare wanted the servant to be Cornwall's in order to make the paradox possible, to emphasize the genuineness of the loyalty involved ("I have serv'd you ever since I was a Childe").[79]

In a world where atrocities like the blinding of Gloucester occur, there is no room for temporizing. When we next see Albany, "never," as Oswald says, "[was] man so chang'd" (TLN 2270). In the encounter that the puzzled Oswald reports to Goneril, he and Albany found one another (morally) unintelligible: "he call'd me Sot, / And told me I had turn'd the wrong side out." As far as Oswald can see, "what most he

78. *The Geneva Bible*, A facsimile of the 1560 edition, introduction by Lloyd E. Berry (Madison: University of Wisconsin Press, 1969), 361a. According to Peter Heylin, King James found this translation extremely unsatisfactory and held that "the Notes upon the same in many places savour of Sedition" (quoted in Hudson, *Ponet*, 185). In the Au-thorized Version, the verse is translated *"before thee*, O king, I have done no hurt."

79. In their extremely interesting essay, "The Language of Social Order: Individual, Society and Historical Process in *King Lear*," David Aers and Gunther Kress see the servant here (like Cordelia in scene 1) taking "the traditional ideology" so literally that "it becomes a subversive force in itself "; David Aers, Bob Hodge, and Gunther Kress, eds., *Literature, Language and Society in England 1580–1680* (Totowa, N.J.: Barnes and Noble, 1981), 87. This is of a piece with taking Kent as a feudal retainer. Again, I feel the force of this suggestion but would point to more contemporary (Renaissance and Reformation) ideological formations.

[Albany] should dislike, seemes pleasant to him" (TLN 2277). In the Folio, which drastically cuts Albany's condemnation of Goneril, the condemnation remains strong but the focus of the scene is Albany's reaction to Gloucester's story rather than to Lear's—or rather, to a traditional Messenger's narrative of the scene that we have in fact just witnessed. The focus is precisely on the narration and on Albany's reactions, the kinds of reactions that Oswald, in his role as messenger, found so odd. This second messenger is another Oswald. He is entirely concerned with the business at hand (which is perhaps why, in the Folio, he is Messenger rather than Gentleman, a function rather than a social status). "Oh my good Lord," he begins, "the Duke of *Cornwals* dead, / Slaine by his Servant, going to put out / The other eye of Glouster" (TLN 2313–15). The news is the death of Cornwall; what he was doing at the time is almost irrelevant. The Messenger's casualness about the moral content of his message ("going to put out / The other eye") is dramatized by Albany's response: "Glousters eyes[!]" The Messenger takes no account of this response; he continues the story of how Cornwall was killed. Albany's response to the account of Cornwall's servant "bending his Sword / To his great Master" is to see the action as divinely sanctioned, perhaps even inspired.[80] He does not worry about the servant's social status. He also does not lose track of the human situation: "But (O poore Glouster) / Lost he his other eye?"[81] The Messenger clarifies the point and turns immediately to Goneril with his business: "Both, both, my Lord. / This Letter[,] Madam, craves a speedy answer." This messenger is another "good servant."[82]

The major "good servant" in this sense, however, continues to be Oswald. He was largely absent in act 3, though present in Lear's reference to "servile ministers" and in "Tom o' Bedlam's" imagined past

80. Albany's response is metaphysical and pagan—"This shows you are above, / You Justices" (F)—rather than Biblical. This serves to defuse or cushion somewhat the potential radicalism of his comment. For the systematic quality of the paganism of *Lear*, see William R. Elton, *"King Lear" and the Gods* (San Marino: The Huntington Library, 1968). It is also worth noting that the Messenger's account differs slightly from what we saw. The Messenger emphasizes the purely affective side of the Servant's intervention, seeing him as acting only out of a private feeling, "thrill'd with remorse," rather than out of the complex understanding of conscientiously limited duty that, as we have seen, the Servant articulated.

81. The way in which the play consistently calls attention to the immense difference between losing one and losing both eyes strongly supports the literalist rejection of the "sight pattern." See Essay 3, n. 23 above.

82. In the Quarto, this Gentleman's narrative is clearly meant to contrast with that of the compassionate Gentleman in the following scene (4.3 in a conflated text), which the Folio cuts. In the Folio, the Messenger's account of Gloucester's blinding is the only extended narration in the play.

as a proud servingman (who "serv'd the Lust of my Mistris heart, and did the acte of darkenesse with her"), but he reemerges quite prominently in act 4.[83] Kent's view of him proves true. Oswald is present when Goneril makes her adulterous and murderous plans with Edmund, and she assures Edmund that "This trustie Servant / Shall passe betweene us" (TLN 2286–87). Having become "a bawd in way of good service," Oswald remains a trusty servant to Goneril. He refuses to allow Regan to unseal Goneril's letter to Edmund. "I may not Madam," he says to Regan, "My Lady charg'd my dutie in this busines" (TLN 2403–4). For Bradley (as, more recently, for Marvin Rosenberg), this is a typically Shakespearean humanizing touch, showing that Oswald "is not wholly worthless"; Dr. Johnson was frankly puzzled: "I know not well," he wrote, "why Shakespeare gives to Oswald, who is a mere factor of wickedness, so much fidelity."[84] Johnson's puzzlement is more helpful, I think, than Bradley's sentimentality and Rosenberg's "tough-mindedness." This is hardly a moment in which we are meant to admire Oswald. At the end of the scene, Regan, who has recognized the strategic folly of sparing the blinded Gloucester's life, reminds Oswald that "If you do chance to heare of that blinde Traitor, / Preferment fals on him, that cuts him off" (TLN 2426). "Would I could meet [him]," says Oswald chillingly, "I should shew / What party I do follow."[85]

83. Oswald does appear, in propria persona, in act 3. At the beginning of scene 7, he makes a brief appearance with some "intelligence," and then goes off with Goneril and Edmund, who also make brief appearances. Shakespeare seems to want all the wicked characters to appear in this scene. As to whether the imagined sexual "service" of "Tom" is meant to suggest that Oswald performs the same service for Goneril, I think that the texts leave this genuinely open, and I am myself agnostic on the question. It is certainly a possibility. It would fit into the view of Oswald as vain, ambitious, and "superserviceable," and it helps clarify Oswald's social status by reference to the fantasies of Malvolio, that other steward of a great lady's house. On the other hand, Goneril is a very grand figure and might not consider it suitable to her greatness to be "served" in this way. If a director chooses to hint at this possibility, it makes Goneril's lust for Edmund less surprising. Whether this latter result is desirable or not is itself a matter for interpretation.

84. *Shakespearean Tragedy*, 238 (including the Johnson quote); Marvin Rosenberg, *The Masks of King Lear* (Berkeley and Los Angeles: University of California Press, 1972), 93.

85. F's substitution of "party" for "Lady" in this line not only clears up an ambiguity (which "Lady" at this moment, when Oswald is speaking to Regan, does he mean?), but shows the Folio's typical predilection for more explicitly political terminology. I do not mean to suggest that "party" is used in the modern political sense here, but on the other hand, I do not think the modern sense completely irrelevant here. "Party" as "faction" was normal in the seventeenth century; see, for instance, the constant reference to a "malignant" or "ill-affected" party in The Grand Remonstrance, in *Constitutional Documents of the Puritan Revolution*, 1625–1660, ed. S. R. Gardiner, 3d ed. (Oxford: Clar-

The next scene gives Oswald his chance; it is the only moment in the play when we see Oswald on his own. We are confirmed in the view that there was more than class snobbery in Kent's rage "That such a slave as this should weare a Sword." For Oswald, the blind Gloucester is "a proclaim'd prize," a way to that greatest of all goals, "preferment." As Goneril's most intimate follower, he adopts the unctuous impersonality of her style: "the Sword is out / That must destroy thee," he tells Gloucester grandly (TLN 2679–80). Edgar, now playing "a most poor man" rather than Tom o' Bedlam, interposes. Oswald calls attention to the indecorousness, the illegality, and the imprudence of the (apparent) poor man's intervention: "Wherefore, bold Pezant / Dar'st thou support a publish'd Traitor? Hence, / Least that th'infection of his fortune take / Like hold on thee." Edgar suddenly breaks into dialect, and Zitner is certainly correct that "what releases Edgar's dialect manner is Oswald's courtly one, his succession of coldly turned phrases, his lofty epithets."[86] Oswald is speaking as a great man here—"Let go Slave, or thou dy'st"— while Edgar's dialect is intended as a specifically lower-class version of the plain style: "Good Gentleman, goe your gate, and let poore volke passe. . . . Chill be plaine with you" (TLN 2690–95). They fight, and Edgar's peasant cudgel defeats Oswald's sword. This episode is clearly meant to recall the intervention of the other, actual "bold Pezant" of the blinding scene. The language—"Pezant . . . Slave . . . Dunghill" ("Out Dunghill," says Oswald)—is filled with echoes of the earlier scene (recall "throw this Slave / Upon the Dunghill"). The effect is to reinforce the image of this sort of "peasant rebellion" as a paradigm of moral action.

Edgar's epitaph for Oswald bears attention. With his dying breath, Oswald attempts to see his duty to Goneril fulfilled; Edgar comments:

I know thee well. A serviceable Villaine,
As duteous to the vices of thy Mistris
As badnesse would desire. (TLN 2704–6)

"Duteousness" in the play is not a virtue in itself. It is morally neutral. The question is duteous to whom or to what? Unlike Bradley, the play

---

endon Press, 1906), 203, 204, 227. The development of the term seems to me a happy circumstance for this line, and one harmonious with its historical meaning and general intent. This is a good case, I think, of the delicacy with which the notion of anachronism needs to be handled, since the normal heavy-handed prohibition of our "modern" meaning would shrink the line's meaning as well as its resonance.

86. *"Lear* and Its Language," 10.

does not admire mere doglike fidelity. "Serviceableness," mere instru-
mentality, is always negative. It is part of Shakespeare's portrayal of what
it means, in Johnson's great phrase, to be a "factor of wickedness" that
Oswald has "so much fidelity." He cannot rightly obey power because
he thinks that it has no bounds. As Arendt remarks, "total loyalty is
possible only when fidelity is emptied of all concrete content."[87] The
critique of doglike fidelity is precisely a critique of "good service" literally
conceived. Shakespeare calls it "superserviceableness." Despite the fact
that, as Barish and Waingrow note, Edmund's specialty is good service,
he is not at the center of the play in this regard.[88] Edmund manifests
hypocrisy and opportunism, the Fool's targets, but not superserviceableness, Kent's target and, as Edgar recognizes, Oswald's specialty.

In the final act, we are given one more example of immoral "good
service." We get to see how a dog's obeyed in office. After Lear and Cordelia are captured, Edmund enlists an unnamed "Captain" into his service. Edmund offers preferment, gives a lesson on "pliability"—"know
thou this, that men / Are as the time is"—and then describes the
essential feature of the service he is asking: "thy great imployment / Will
not beare question: either say thou'lt do't, / Or thrive by other meanes"
(TLN 2973–77). No thought about the content of the command is
acceptable. The Captain must agree to "do't" before he knows what
"it" is. The Folio version of this interchange omits the Captain's ironic
claim to humanity ("I cannot draw a cart 'nor eate dride oats; / If it bee
mans worke, Ile do't").[89] The effect of this omission is to dramatize what
it means for a human being to make himself into a mere instrument. This
Captain allows himself to be, in the wonderful Elizabethan phrase,
entirely Edmund's "creature." He has no independent consciousness.
His only words are to say, respectfully, what Edmund tells him to:
"either say thou'lt do't, / Or thrive by other means." "Ile do't[,] my

---

87. Hannah Arendt, *The Origins of Totalitarianism*, expanded ed. (New York: Harcourt, Brace, 1968), 324.

88. "'Service' in *Lear*," 350.

89. Urkowitz seems to me mistaken in characterizing the Captain's exit lines in the
Quarto (the lines on "not being able to "draw a cart") as rationalization or self-justification
(*Shakespeare's Revision of King Lear,* 104). The lines are an expression of determination
to duty. They are perhaps based on some lines in *Leir*, in which a very eager-to-serve
Messenger tells Gonorill: "use me, trust me, commaund me: if I fayle in anything, tye me
to a dung cart, and make a Scavenger's horse of me" (lines 1014–16, Bullough, 7:362).
This figure from *Leir* lies somewhere behind the Captain and Oswald, but the *Leir*
Messenger is a comic-melodramatic villain ("A purse of gold giv'n for a paltry stabbe!"),
as Shakespeare's figures are not.

Lord" is his entire speaking part. He is not given an exit line. He goes off silently and obediently, like a proper dog, suffering himself like a brute beast rather than a reasonable creature to be led and drawn wheresoever his master commands.[90] Through this moment we realize that the mad Lear's Fool-like or Hythlodaean view of his society is true only under certain conditions: a dog's obeyed in office only when its followers are also dogs.

As Barish and Waingrow observe, the final speech of the play "reiterates the note of service."[91] Yet what is recommended is quite paradoxical:

The waight of this sad time we must obey.
Speake what we feele, not what we ought to say.

Here, in the final moment of the play, proper obedience is defined as breaching decorum.[92] We "obey" the "waight" of *Lear* by not doing and saying what, in normal times, "we ought." Martines, who characterizes the Renaissance as a period in which "the thrust of political power [was] such that it afforded men few choices," notes that "personal integrity must have been doubly rare then."[93] In *King Lear,* integrity is all.

III

If, after *Lear,* Shakespeare never again so clearly espoused active resistance, the distinction between the good servant who disobeys immoral commands and the wicked who will do anything becomes a fundamental axiom. The Romances prior to *The Tempest* are explicit on

90. Aers and Kress suggest that the Captain here is to be seen as an "employee" in the newly modern (capitalist) sense ("The Language of Social Order," 88). Here I do not think that modern sense of "employment" is relevant, since in this case (as opposed to the case of "party" discussed in n. 85 above), the modern sense seems to me to distract from rather than to enhance the immediate context. The bond between the Captain and Edmund seems to be a personal rather than an impersonal one ("One step I have advanc'd thee").

91. "'Service' in *Lear,*" 355.

92. For the speech as a rationale for the anticonventional, see Zitner, "*Lear* and its Language," 4.

93. "The Gentleman in Renaissance Italy," 77.

this point.[94] Shakespeare explicitly thematizes it. In *Pericles*, the conversation between Antiochus and Thaliard echoes that between Edmund and the Captain:

> *Ant.*: We hate the prince of Tyre, and thou must kill him: It fits thee not to ask the reason why: Because we bid it. Say, is it done?
> *Thal.*: My Lord, 'tis done. (1.1.157–60)

When Thaliard arrives at Tyre to do his task, he explains his conception of duty. It is rather like that of Ludovico Pio in *The Courtier*: "if a king bid a man be a villain, he's bound by the indenture of his oath to be one" (1.3.7–8). These themes are reiterated later in the play. In suborning Leonine to kill Marina, Dionyza admonishes him, "Thy oath remember; thou hast sworn to do it" (4.1.1). In the (would-be) murder scene, Leonine keeps returning to this rationale: "I am sworn / To do my work with haste," he tells Marina (4.1.68–69). When she asks (quite sensibly), "Why will you kill me," he responds, in lines that echo Antiochus's charge to Thaliard, "My commission / Is not to reason of the deed, but do't." As he seizes Marina, Leonine explains, "I am sworn, / And will despatch" (90–91). The final obedient servant that we see in *Pericles* is worse than "a bawd in way of good service," he is the trusty servant of a bawd. With regard to selling Marina's virginity, the Bawd admonishes Boult, "Get this done as I command you." Boult, ever the good servant, replies, "Performance shall follow" (4.2.57–59).

In *The Winter's Tale*, Shakespeare's fullest portrayal of a king behaving as a madman, all the virtuous characters adopt either Buchanan's militant perspective or Federico Fregoso's defensive one on such a situation. Camillo, the king's most trusted counselor, is enjoined to murder a man (also a king) whom Camillo, on the basis of his own perception, believes to be innocent. Shakespeare gives Camillo full awareness that, if he were to comply with Leontes' command, he could appeal for justification to a fundamental premise of orthodox social thinking: "I must be poisoner / Of good Polixenes; and my ground to do't / Is the obedience of a master" (1.2.351–53). Camillo, however, sees his master, in Buchananesque terms, as one "Who in rebellion with himself will have / All that are his so too." Instead of smoothing this passion that in the nature of his lord rebels, and thereby participating "in

---

94. *The Tempest* is more complicated. On the "dual politics" of that play (European and colonial), see Richard Strier, "'I am Power': 'Normal' and Magical Politics in *The Tempest*," in Derek Hirst and Richard Strier, eds., *Destinies and Choices: Politics and Literature in Seventeenth-Century England* (forthcoming).

the name and quality which is termed rebellion," Camillo decides instead, with Castiglione's Federico and Ottaviano, to forsake his master's service. He first subverts and then deserts Leontes in order not to take part in Leontes' "rebellion with himself."

The Kent-like figure in *The Winter's Tale* is another plain and rude speaker, Paulina. This character is the culmination of Shakespeare's increasingly positive treatment of "shrews" in his plays.[95] In *The Winter's Tale*, the "shrew" is transformed into the figure of the prophetic truth-teller. Paulina describes herself to the mad king as

> your loyal servant, your physician,
> Your most obedient counsellor, yet that dares
> Less appear so in comforting your evils
> Than such as most seem yours. (2.3.54–57)

She says of the more complaisant court figures, "You that are so tender o'er his follies / Will never do him good" (2.3.127–28). This is pure Buchanan: "If Kings continue in their Madness, whoever doth most obey them, is to be judged their greatest Enemy." Interestingly, the play also contains a scathing description (albeit misapplied) of a "hovering temporizer, that / Canst with thine eyes at once see good and evil, / Inclining to them both (1.2.301–3). The figure in the play who does act like this, who attempts to occupy a middle position and commits an inhuman act because he is "by oath enjoin'd" (3.3.52) exits famously pursued by a bear.

In *Cymbeline*, perhaps written immediately following Shakespeare's revision of *Lear*,[96] the theme of virtuous disobedience is almost obsessive. Cloten, the tragicomic villain-prince of the play, exfoliates at length to Pisanio, a truly virtuous servant, his (Cloten's) view of the obedience that inferiors owe him. Since Cloten is a prince,

Sirrah, if thou wouldst not be a villain, but do me true service, undergo those employments wherein I should have cause to use thee with a serious industry—that is, whatever villainy soe'er I bid thee do, to perform it directly and truly—I would think thee an honest man. (3.5.109–13)

None of the virtuous servants in the play consider acting in this way—performing "whatever villainy" they are bid—to do "true service" or to

95. For a sketch of this development, see Valerie Wayne, "Refashioning the Shrew," *Shakespeare Studies* 17 (1984): 159–187.

96. For this hypothesis, see Gary Taylor, "*King Lear*: The Date and Authorship of the Folio version," *Division*, 386.

be "an honest man." When Cornelius, the queen's physician, disobeys the queen's commands and substitutes a soporific for poison, he claims that he is "the truer, / So to be false with her" (1.5.43–44). In a situation that parallels that of Camillo in act 1 of *The Winter's Tale*, Pisanio is commanded by a master he believes to be acting madly to, in Ludovico Pio's words, "kill a man" (or, in this case, a woman). Speaking of and to his absent master, Pisanio recalls that he has been charged to obedience "Upon the love and truth and vows which I / Have made to thy command." Pisanio's meditation on his duty to commit murder on this basis recalls a key word from *Lear*: "If it be so to do good service, never / Let me be counted serviceable" (3.2.14–15). Shakespeare's firm opinion on this matter is stated by Posthumus at the opening of the fifth act, when he begins to attain moral clarity:

> Every good servant does not all commands;
> No bond, but to do just ones.

Ponet would have agreed—along, presumably, with Mr. John Bate, the wealthy merchant who, in 1606, refused to pay what he considered an illegal tax.[97]

97. For "Bate's case," see *Cobbett's Complete Collection of State Trials* (London, 1809), 2:371–519. For commentary, see Johann Sommerville, "Ideology, Property, and the Constitution," in Richard Cust and Ann Hughes, eds., *Conflict in Early Stuart England: Studies in Religion and Politics, 1603–1642* (London: Longman, 1989), 47–71; Clive Holmes, "Liberty, Taxation, and Property," and Charles M. Gray, "Liberty, Property, and the Law," in J. H. Hexter, ed., *Parliament and Liberty from the Reign of Elizabeth to the English Civil War* (Stanford: Stanford University Press, 1992), 122–54, 155–200.

TEXTUAL POSTSCRIPT: Through Line Numbers (TLNs) in the Folio *Lear* correspond—roughly—to the Arden edition as follows:

1–332	= 1.1	1251–72	= 2.3	1969–95	= 3.5	2382–2428	= 4.5
333–504	= 1.2	1273–1613	= 2.4	1996–2056	= 3.6	2429–2742	= 4.6
505–28	= 1.3	1614–53	= 3.1	2057–2176	= 3.7	2743–2843	= 4.7
529–872	= 1.4	1654–1750	= 3.2	2177–2265	= 4.1	2844–2917	= 5.1
873–925	= 1.5	1751–75	= 3.3	2266–2347	= 4.2	2918–36	= 5.2
926–1073	= 2.1	1776–1968	= 3.4	2348–81	= 4.4	2937–3302	= 5.3
1074–1250	= 2.2						

Impossible Radicalism
and Impossible Value
Nahum Tate's King Lear

"Everyone knows" two things about Nahum Tate: (1) he was a fool; and (2) he was a Tory (though these "facts" are rarely correlated). He was a fool because he—Nahum Tate!—had the temerity to rewrite *King Lear*, Shakespeare's grandest creation. Persons of all sorts take a pride to gird at Tate's *Lear*. Tate was a Tory because, among other things, he was the author (or coauthor) of the continuation of Dryden's *Absalom and Achitophel*. In the essay that follows, I mean to defend Tate's version of *Lear* on the basis of its literary value—a concept that I believe in. I do not mean to argue that Tate's play is an improvement over Shakespeare's—though I do think that in at least one detail it is—but I do mean to suggest that Tate's *Lear* is an intelligent, interesting, and well-written work on its own. I mean to establish this indirectly in the course of reexamining the politics of Tate's play. There is as striking (and, unfortunately, unsurprising) unanimity on the matter of the politics as there is on the matter of the literary value of Tate's play. All recent scholars agree that adaptation of Shakespeare's plays in the Restoration was part of a single political agenda, "royalism's last stand," an agenda that was profoundly conservative and committed to portraying "all civil unrest as butchery."[1] The political content of Tate's play,

---

1. See J. Douglas Canfield, "Royalism's Last Dramatic Stand: English Political Tragedy, 1679–89," *Studies in Philology* 82 (1985): 234–63; Matthew Wikander, "The Spitted Infant: Scenic Emblem and Exclusionist Politics in Restoration Adaptations of Shakespeare," *Shakespeare Quarterly* 37 (1986): 340–58; and the critics cited in nn. 2, 12, and 24 below.

in other words, is known in advance. No wonder, then, that the play is a wonderful example of a work that has never really been read—not only by those who (mindlessly) mock it, but also by those who have professed to study it.

The largest questions that this essay raises are how one establishes the political, or other, immanent meaning of a work, and how one establishes literary value. While this essay will primarily be concerned with the first of these questions, it implicitly assumes that if a work can be shown to address a significant issue in a substantial way (these terms, of course, need to be defined, but can be fairly readily), and if the work is, at the same time, interestingly written at the micro-level, it is a work of genuine literary value. In demonstrating the care with which the political strand of the play is developed, the general carefulness and power of the work will, I trust, emerge. As will be obvious in my treatment, I think that the passages that manifest the political content of the play constitute some very powerful writing.

I

_____

Let me begin by examining the arguments that have been made for the Toryism of Tate's *Lear*. I will start from what seem to me to be the weakest and proceed to what seem to me to be the strongest of them. This involves, roughly, to move from "external" to "internal" considerations, and I will argue for what might be called "close contextualization" as well as for close reading. Perhaps the most external way of establishing the politics of Tate's play is by relying on one's "knowledge" of Shakespeare and seeing the choice of a Shakespearean framework as itself indicative. If Shakespeare's "loyalty to hierarchical structures" and "strong sense of order, loyalty, and obedience" are taken for granted, this establishes a presumption in itself.[2] I hope to have shown in my previous essay how dubious this assumption is, especially in relation to *King Lear*. An apparently less dubious way of establishing a presumption about the politics of Tate's *Lear* is to look at the preface

2. See Nancy Klein Maguire, "Nahum Tate's *King Lear:* 'The King's Blest Restoration,'" in Jean I. Marsden, ed., *The Appropriation of Shakespeare: Post-Renaissance Reconstructions of the Works and the Myth* (New York: Harvester Wheatsheaf, 1991), 36; Christopher Spencer, *Nahum Tate* (New York: Twayne, 1972), 68.

to his next adaptation of Shakespeare, that of *Coriolanus,* where Tate explicitly attacks "the busie Faction of our own time," the Whigs, and says that the point of the play is "to recommend Submission."[3] The politics of *Absalom and Achitophel* seem to be similar to this.[4]

But, putting aside possible problems with these very confident readings of *The Ingratitude of a Common-wealth* and *Absalom and Achitophel,* what is the argument that these works are relevant to Tate's *Lear?* In the preface to his first adaptation of Shakespeare, *The History of King Richard II,* Tate tells us that his *Lear* was written "just before" his *Richard II,* though it was produced and published later.[5] This means that Tate's *Lear* was written in the summer or fall of 1680, about a year before his version of *Coriolanus* and about two years before his continuation of *Absalom and Achitophel.* Tate may have had the same position in the summer of 1680 that he had in the fall of 1681, but then again he may not have. As every historicist scholar has (rightly) seen, the context of Tate's adaptations of Shakespeare is the Exclusion Crisis of 1679–83, the parliamentary and popular movement to exclude Charles II's Catholic brother, James, the Duke of York, from succession to the throne. The "Whigs" were defined by being the "party" or movement for exclusion (and perhaps by nothing else).[6] The historians have taught us that the "Exclusion Crisis" really was a crisis, and was perceived as such by contemporaries. In the general elections held in August and September of 1679, many were contested, itself a significant fact.[7] Moreover, while local issues and family connections still determined most of the contests, many elections were fought on national issues; one pamphlet of the time spoke of *England's Great Interest in the Choice of this New Parliament.* This was a period in which "politics as usual" was not going on. Things happened suddenly and rapidly between 1679 and

3. N. Tate, *The Ingratitude of a Common-wealth: Or, the Fall of Caius Martius Coriolanus* (London, 1682), sig. A2 r-v .

4. See, for instance, Bernard N. Schilling, *Dryden and the Conservative Myth: A Reading of "Absalom and Achitophel"* (New Haven: Yale University Press, 1961).

5. On the dates of composition, Tate says in the prefatory letter ("To my Esteemed Friend, George Raynsford, Esq.") to *The History of King Richard II* (London, 1681) that his adaptation of *Lear* was written "just before" his *Richard II.*

6. The term is notoriously hard to define in this period, but a pro-Exclusion position is its incontrovertible core. This is more reliable as an indicator than is support for a particular candidate, including the Duke of Monmouth, for the post-Exclusion succession.

7. J. R. Jones, *The First Whigs: The Politics of the Exclusion Crisis, 1678–1683* (London: Oxford University Press, 1961), 96. See also Mark Kishlansky, *Parliamentary Selection: Social and Political Choice in Early Modern England* (Cambridge: Cambridge University Press, 1986).

1681. It was the kind of "moment" in which thoughtful persons could and did change their views in a short period of time. For instance, in the second Exclusion Parliament (in the fall of 1680), Sir Henry Capel, who had voted against the exclusion of James from the succession in the Parliament of May 1679, had decided that although he thought of himself as a moderate, Exclusion "was a case in which there was no room for moderation," and he became a strong spokesman for it.[8] There is nothing inherently unlikely, therefore, in Tate having a different view of politics in his version of *King Lear*, when the parliamentary movement for Exclusion was at its highest tide (the summer and fall of 1680), than he came to have in his version of *Coriolanus* a year later, when both the parliamentary and the popular movement had been defeated. Nicholas Rowe collaborated with Dryden on a Tory play (*The Duke of Guise*) in 1682, but in 1680 had written *Lucius Junius Brutus*, which was suppressed as antimonarchical.[9] And it is worth recalling that, as Phillip Harth has shown, prior to the publication of *Absalom and Achitophel* in November of 1681, Dryden's anti-Whig sympathies were not at all clear (and may not have existed—though Harth, I hasten to add, would deny this suggestion).[10]

So if we cannot use Tate's *The Ingratitude of a Common-wealth* and continuation of *Absalom and Achitophel* to establish any strong presumption with regard to his *Lear*, where can we turn (if we are not

8. See Jones, *The First Whigs*, 139.

9. I owe this information to a communication from Professor Phillip Harth, for which I am very grateful.

10. See Harth's "Dryden in 1678–1681: The Literary and Historical Perspectives," in John M. Wallace, ed., *The Golden and the Brazen World: Papers in Literature and History, 1650–1800* (Berkeley and Los Angeles: University of California Press, 1985), 55–77. Harth argues for recognition of the *lateness* of Dryden's entrance (with *Absalom and Achitophel*) into the Exclusion Crisis. Dryden emerged, as Harth puts it, "at the eleventh hour as a Tory spokesman" (67). Harth's essay demonstrates the importance of attending to the precise dating of works written during the Exclusion Crisis, and of not reading backwards within an author's canon in the period. Harth shows that until November 1681, Dryden was taken, not without reason, to have had Whig sympathies. Harth characterizes "the impression that Dryden was leaning toward the Whigs" before the fall of 1681 as having been "mistaken" (71); he sees Dryden as having been truly neutral in this period, though consistent in his commitment to the English constitution as a "mixed government." Harth's own evidence, however, allows for the view that Dryden's contemporaries were not entirely mistaken in their view of him prior to the end of 1681 as pro-Whig. It is difficult to believe that, for most of the Exclusion Crisis, Dryden was living in "apparent obliviousness to the political inferences that could be drawn from some of his actions" (72). This is surely an odd state of mind to impute to as public and political a writer as Dryden.

prepared to argue on purely "internal" grounds) to establish some sort of reasonable presumption? The obvious answer is to turn to *The History of King Richard II*, which, as we have already noted, was written in very close proximity to *The History of King Lear*. There is a reason why the scholars who are certain of the conservatism of Tate's politics have not done this. Both *The History of King Richard II* and its history are an embarrassment to them. The topic is a very odd one for a Tory to have chosen, and Tate's play was both denied a license as a text (in December 1680) and banned as a (slightly disguised) production in January of 1681.[11] This should give us pause in the assignment of Tory meaning to Tate's *Lear*. The scholars have been remarkably hamhanded in the face of Tate's *Richard II*. Explanations for the existence of this work (as produced by a Tory author) have ranged from the claim that Tate's mind was profoundly "unpolitical" to the claim that his mind was profoundly deficient ("plain stupidity").[12] But what if, as his work certainly suggests, Tate was neither unpolitical nor stupid? The only other term that has entered into the discussion is "disingenuousness." This is an alternative to "stupidity" that Robert D. Hume gives in accounting for Tate's surprise that his *Richard II* (or *The Sicilian Usurper*) was suppressed. "Disingenuousness," however, is a complex and not necessarily dishonorable matter, and it bears some looking into.

There has been very little attention to what Tate actually did in his *Richard II*. Some of what he said about his play is, in fact, ingenuous. Tate was certainly right in asserting that he had almost scandalously *cleaned up* the character and behavior of his Richard.[13] His protestation that he did not, as Shakespeare did, present a "dissolute, unadvisable," arbitrary, and luxurious king was well-founded. The important task is to

11. For details on the censorship and closing of Tate's *Richard II* (retouched as *The Sicilian Usurper*), see Timothy J. Viator, "Nahum Tate's *Richard II*," *Theatre Notebook* 43 (1988): 109–17.

12. For "unpolitical," see Spencer, *Tate*, 84; for "stupidity," see Robert D. Hume, *The Development of English Drama in the Late Seventeenth Century* (Oxford: Oxford University Press, 1976), 222. On "unpolitical," compare the period of "obliviousness" that Harth has to impute to Dryden to keep from imputing Whig meanings to Dryden's "apparently" Whig actions before the end of 1681 (n. 9 above).

13. In the prefatory letter to *The History of Richard II*, Tate quotes "*Quantum mutatus ab illo*" (*Aeneid*, 2.274) to express his sense of how different his Richard II is from those of "*Shakespear* and History." He is aware of how odd this reference to Aeneas's horrified dream of Hector's mutilated body is ("the figure there was alter'd for the Worse and here for the Better"), but he seems to have a real sense of criminality and defacement here: "The Arbitrary Courtiers of the Reign here written, scarcely did more Violence to the Subjects of their Time than I have done to Truth" (sig. A2v).

see what he did do. Tate presented a king who voluntarily resigned his throne—as an act of nobility—in the face of political necessity and the possibility of civil war. More fully than Shakespeare does, Tate presents Richard II as consciously bowing to political-historical necessity and prudence. In the crucial scene, Tate's Richard says:

> let Crowns and Scepters go
> Before I swim to 'em in Subjects blood.
> The King in pity to his Subjects quits
> His Right, that have no pity for their King![14]

Destiny, Tate's Richard says (quite wonderfully), "Is Tyrant over Kings."

This is a complex position. It is reminiscent of Marvell's view of the situation of 1649 in the Horatian Ode. In the context of the Exclusion Crisis, it would seem to suggest, however regretfully, that the King should bow to historical necessity (and exclude the Catholic James from the succession) in order to prevent civil war. As Richard Ashcraft has remarked, the "darker side" of the Whig appeal for popular support was the threat "that civil war would follow if the effort to enact an exclusion bill failed."[15] Tate was certainly not a republican—a brilliant scene he invented for his *Richard II* shows "the rabble" trying to sort out the difference between a "Common-wealth" and a Republic[16] — but it is important to recognize that most Whigs, including Shaftesbury, were not republicans.[17] Where Tate shows both a profoundly political and a very shrewd mind is in recognizing the central role that Parliament had come to have in English politics. This was probably the most enduring legacy of the Great Rebellion, and Tate realized it. His Bolingbroke sends Northumberland "to London, with all speed / [To] Summon a Parliament i' th' Commons Name, / In Order to the King's appearance there." The name that Tate's Richard gives to historical Destiny is not Bolingbroke but "Th' Usurping House." Richard "with free and willing Soul" adopts Bolingbroke his heir at the Parliament. One can now see how complex Tate's "disingenuousness" was in asserting that in composing his *Richard II* he had not "Compil'd a

14. *The History of Richard II*, 39.

15. Richard Ashcraft, *Revolutionary Politics and Locke's "Two Treatises of Government"* (Princeton: Princeton University Press, 1986), 287–88.

16. *The History of Richard II*, 20–24.

17. See Jones, *The First Whigs*, 15; and Tim Harris, *London Crowds in the Reign of Charles II* (Cambridge: Cambridge University Press, 1987), 161–64.

Disloyal or Reflecting Play."[18] Certainly the play was "Reflecting," but as composed by a Whig constitutional monarchist, it was certainly not "Disloyal."

In giving this reading of the political meaning of Tate's *Richard II*, I am clearly drawing on the strategies and, to some degree, the attitudes of John M. Wallace's seminal works on Marvell and on Denham.[19] These works are devoted to altering preconceptions about seventeenth-century figures, about Marvell's "opportunism" in the one case and Denham's "royalism" on the other. I am not prepared to do for Tate's career what Wallace has done for Marvell's, but I do want to do for Tate's *Lear* something like what Wallace has done for "Cooper's Hill." In that analysis, Wallace argues, through a combination of close reading and what I have called "close contextualization," that his view of the political content of the poem at its moment of composition fits the details and the general contours of the work better than the competing, more conservative view of Denham as a Laudian and *jure divino* monarchist. Wallace's argument is an avowedly intentionalist one, and it is conducted with great care, subtlety, and attention to the proportions of the poem as whole. It provides a usable model for thickly contextualized close reading.

Yet Wallace is also one of the propounders of the "Tory" view of Tate's *Lear*. This would not necessarily be theoretically significant—he and I could simply differ in our readings of the work—but I think that there is theoretical significance here. I would argue that the methodology through which Wallace arrives at this reading of Tate's *Lear* is not the same as the methodology through which he arrived at his readings of Denham and of Marvell. This methodological difference is, I think, crucial to the question of how to form a reasonable hypothesis about the political (or other) content of a work. The key distinction is between reading for intention and reading for "application."

Wallace sees "application" as the historically proper (seventeenth-century) word for describing what a reader or auditor does in making a connection between a theme or detail in a text and his or her contemporary world.[20] Wallace is certainly right about the word and the

18. Prefatory letter to *The History of Richard II* (sig. A1r).

19. *Destiny His Choice: The Loyalism of Andrew Marvell* (Cambridge: Cambridge University Press, 1968); "*Cooper's Hill*: The Manifesto of Parliamentary Royalism, 1641," *ELH* 41 (1974): 494–540.

20. See "'Examples Are Best Precepts': Readers and Meanings in Seventeenth-Century Poetry," *Critical Inquiry* 1 (1974): 273–90.

practice, but—because, I think, he was always ultimately reading for intentions—he did not recognize that reading for intentions and reading for "applications" are, in fact and in theory, very different sorts of practices.[21] "Application" could go any which way and loose. There were no rules for "applying" a text. An application could seize on a stray detail or anything else in a text. The praise of application, as Wallace realized, was a cornucopic "more the merrier" principle. The text was a nose of wax. What is odd in Wallace's treatment of this phenomenon is that he never focuses on how contrary it is to reading for intention. When he quotes Bacon speaking of "what pliant stuff fable is made of," he fails to note that Bacon is issuing a caveat, not making a celebration. In fact, Bacon distinguishes in the passage quoted between meanings that a text was "meant to bear" and meanings that "with a little dexterity . . . may be plausibly put upon it." Even George Sandys, an avowed reveller in "the variety of mens severall conceptions," stated that it was proper to limit this variety to conceptions in which *"the principal parts of application resemble the ground-work"*—a potentially important (and usable) interpretive principle.[22]

As we have seen in the case of Stanley Cavell, critics do not always follow their own best precepts or examples.[23] Wallace's treatment of Tate's *Lear* does not follow the example (or implicit precept) of his treatment of Denham's "Cooper's Hill." His "reading" of the play is very brief—it is not the focus of the piece in which it occurs—and is based on an assertion about its intended application. The argument goes as follows: the Exclusion of the Duke of York meant his banishment, so that during the Exclusion Crisis any reference to banishment would "almost certainly" be applied to the Duke's exclusion. Since Tate's play opens with a series of banishments that are "evil and unnatural," the play *must* have been taken as (and have been) a Tory, that is, anti-Exclusion play.[24] Add to this Edmund the Bastard's speculation at one point that he might have royal blood in his veins (5.5.50), a clear invitation to think of Edmund as the royal bastard (Monmouth), and a

21. Compare Alan Roper, "Drawing Parallels and Making Applications in Restoration Literature," in Richard Ashcraft and Alan Roper, *Politics as Reflected in Literature* (Los Angeles: Clark Library, 1989), 51–52. The distinction between intention and application is parallel to E. D. Hirsch's distinction between meaning and significance; see *Validity in Interpretation* (New Haven: Yale University Press, 1967), 8, 57, 62–64.

22. For Bacon and Sandys, see Wallace, "'Examples Are Best Precepts,'" 277 and 275.

23. See chap. 3, pp. 52–54 above.

24. John M. Wallace, "Otway's *Caius Marius* and the Exclusion Crisis," *Modern Philology* 85 (1988): 363–72 (quotations from pp. 363–64).

mention of a "the King's blest Restauration" (5.6.119), and the case is made.[25]

The trouble with this is that it meets the low standard of "application"—any conceivable connection—rather than the more stringent one of intention. The reading of the play suggested is based on a few details and on a key term ("exclusion") that is introduced by the critic and never occurs in the play. The more one looks at the actual details or explicit themes and actions of the play, the less convincing these possible applications seem as indications of intention. The "exclusions" in Tate's play all appear in Shakespeare's, and the fact that Tate quickens the pace of them does not make them any more emphatic. In Tate, the first "exclusion" is, in fact, by Gloucester rather than by Lear, and, as in Shakespeare, there is no sense that the banishments that Lear imposes (on a courtier and his youngest daughter) are in any way forced on him. The moment of the Bastard speculating that "possibly a King might be my Sire" may have provided a momentary *frisson* for Tate's audience, but again it does not much "resemble the ground-work" of the play. It doesn't lead anywhere; it is, to put it mathematically, a point rather than a parallel—which, after all, needs to be a line. Wallace commends Robert D. Hume's comment on this "point," a comment that dramatizes the danger of trying to make a line out of such a point. Hume (followed in this by Michael Dobson as well as by Wallace) sees Tate as deftly touching on "the succession question" (Tate is no longer stupid or unpolitical) in showing "the suppression of a rebellion [that is led] by an illegitimate son."[26] This is all very well. It sounds right (confirming scholarly prejudgments), but it gets Tate's play exactly backward. As we shall see, in Tate even more than in Shakespeare, the Bastard is part of the group that is in power, and it is the *legitimate* son who is involved in a military rebellion.

The most recent full-length treatment of the play follows Wallace's words on Tate rather than his example on Denham.[27] Nancy Klein Maguire takes "the King's blest Restauration" as her title. She speaks of

25. I cite from *The History of King Lear. Reviv'd with Alterations. By N. Tate*, in Christopher Spencer, ed. *Five Restoration Adaptations of Shakespeare* (Urbana: University of Illinois Press, 1965). I have occasionally, where indicated by square brackets, departed from the punctuation of this edition.

26. Hume, *The Development of English Drama*, 350; Michael Dobson, *The Making of a National Poet: Shakespeare, Adaptation and Authorship, 1660–1769* (Oxford: Oxford University Press, 1992), 81.

27. See Maguire, "Nahum Tate's *King Lear*," 30. References to this essay will appear in the text.

reading Tate's play closely (35), but her method is that of application rather than explication. She relies on bits and pieces, often tendentiously described. Although she sees Tate as equivocating "to some degree" (35), Maguire sees the play as basically "part of the Tory counter-propaganda campaign" (30).[28] She wants to see Tate's *Lear* as evoking "the mid-century trauma" (apparently, no right-thinking person could have seen the regicide as other than a "trauma").[29] When Tate has Edmund (after Goneril has already given the command) propose the execution of Lear, Maguire sees Edmund as strategically reinforcing Goneril's command, "in much the same way, perhaps, as Cromwell pushed through the execution of Charles I" (35). That "perhaps" was well thought on. There is no parallel, since what Tate does is to *eliminate* Edmund's responsibility for the order to murder Lear. But the important thing is to bring in, somehow, a reference to Cromwell.[30] Similarly, "Tate's militarized Kent" is described as "perhaps recalling the loyalty and determination of Prince Rupert" (36). Again, much virtue in that "perhaps." Maguire would have done well to note Alan Roper's cautionary remarks about "particular parallels," and his observation that the anti-Whig "parallel of '41 and '81" was recognized, even at the time, as working best only in general terms and not in terms of individuals.[31]

Even on the more general level, when Maguire describes Goneril and company as "disruptive and Whiggish tyrants" (36), she never specifies what makes them Whiggish. She does not show that they *say* anything that alludes to (for example) Shaftesbury's political views. But that does not matter. Tate was a Tory and so the villains must be Whigs. If Maguire is right (following Wallace's suggestion), the whole thrust of the play is toward "the King's blest Restauration." The trouble, however, as

28. Maguire quotes this phrase ("the Tory counter-propaganda campaign") from Tim Harris, *London Crowds*, but it is important to keep in mind that Harris does not see this "campaign" as beginning until late in 1681 (pp. 131ff.).

29. Using a line from *The Second Part of Absalom and Achitophel* to explicate Tate's *Lear*, Maguire asserts that "*like everyone else* at the time, Tate felt that by excluding 'the bright Successor of the Crown,' the nation would re-enact the 1649 'Scene of Woes'" (33; emphasis mine). Apparently there were not any Whigs, let alone republicans. For "the mid-century trauma," see p. 37.

30. An even more bizarre moment occurs earlier in the same paragraph when Maguire suggests that an obvious typographical error ("the poor old King *beheaded*" rather than "bareheaded" in 3.3.39—miscited by Maguire) is somehow relevant to Tate's intentions. The typo is perhaps relevant to *the period's* "political unconscious," and it is uncanny, but it has nothing to do with Tate.

31. "Drawing Parallels and Making Applications in Restoration Literature," 43–44.

Maguire in this case does realize, is that this is not what happens in the play. Moments after the "blest Restauration" is announced (5.6.119), Lear once again renounces rule (5.6.147–50). The "Restauration" never takes place. Wisely, Maguire backs off: "The happy (and Whiggish) agreement to have Cordelia and Edgar rule is, in a sense, elective monarchy rather than divine right" (39). That this "foreshadows the succession of William and Mary" (39) is probably too much to say; it is merely an "application," though Mary was an obvious choice for a Protestant successor. However, the claim that emerges in the final sentence of Maguire's essay—that Tate "hedged his bets" and the play is not straight "Tory propaganda"—is a very important one, however inconsistent with her overall argument.[32]

Before moving toward an "internal" reading of the politics of Tate's *Lear*—the only sort of reading that can ever establish more than a presumption—it might be well to have in mind what a what a genuinely Tory play of the Exclusion Crisis sounds like. Whatever the status of Wikander's view that all Restoration adaptations of Shakespeare were part of a conservative agenda that aimed to portray "all civil unrest as butchery," this view does seem to apply to Henry Crowne's adaptations of the *Henry VI* plays, and especially to *The Misery of Civil War*. The fact that Crowne's title announces his political theme seems nontrivial to me. When a writer provides signposts, I see no reason to ignore them. I can, of course, imagine cases where a critic might show them to be misleading or delusive, but my point is that these are special cases, and need to be argued as such (since Tate entitled his version of *Coriolanus The Ingratitude of a Common-wealth*, Wallace is right, I think, to suppose this might be a guide to its political theme). In comparing a moment in Crowne's *Misery* with a parallel moment in Shakespeare's *2 Henry VI*, Wikander points out that where Shakespeare offers a fellowship (or competition) in grief, Crowne offers the following:

Oh you, who when you suffer by your Kings
Think to mend all by War, and by Rebellion!
See here, your sad mistakes! how dreadfully

32. In *The Making of a National Poet*, Dobson adopts Maguire's reading, with all inconsistencies intact. After treating the play for a number of pages as "determinedly anti-Whig" (83), Dobson then quotes Maguire's sentence on Tate hedging his bets (85). Dobson's more coherent as well as more original treatment of the play is with regard to its domestic and "sentimental" aspects.

You scourge your selves! Learn here the greatest Tyrant
Is to be chose before the least Rebellion.[33]

This is indeed, as Wikander says, a "homily on obedience," or
rather, a homily against disobedience. It echoes the extreme position of
the 1570 Homily "Against Disobedience" in the second book of Homilies.[34] Passive obedience, of the sort that Thomas Pomfret preached in
1683 and that Crowne asserts in the passage quoted, was the normal
Tory position, especially with regard to the lower orders of society.[35]
The other extreme, represented in the late seventeenth century by
Locke and in the mid-sixteenth century by Ponet, Goodman, and
Buchanan, was that tyranny could and should be actively resisted by the
people at large.[36] When, in a late seventeenth-century work, a speech
like the one in Crowne's *Misery* is spoken by a sympathetic character
and supported by the events of the plot, we are on firm ground in
assigning a Tory valence to the work in question. I am suggesting not
that all plays contain such explicit morals but that we should pay attention if they do; that we should attend, in any case, to what is actually
said, and look for sustained and explicitly thematized political views. To
do this, I think, is far preferable—if we are seeking meanings rather than
applications—to relying on bits and pieces of language and plot torn
from their context. The lines quoted from Crowne can serve as a touchstone for the Tory position on the matter of popular resistance to
tyrants: "Learn here the greatest Tyrant / Is to be chose before the
least Rebellion." The rest of this essay will be devoted to showing how
far Tate's *Lear* is from this position.

II

Tate's dedication of the play to his friend Thomas Boteler
does not deal with politics, but it does quote directly, on an aesthetic

33. John Crowne, *The Misery of Civil War* (London, 1681), 44; cited by Wikander,
"The Spitted Infant," 345.

34. For the difference between the 1570 homily "Against Disobedience" and the
Edwardine homily "On Good Order, and Obedience to Rulers," see Essay 7, pp. 170–72,
above.

35. See Pomfret's sermon, *Passive Obedience, Stated and Asserted* (London, 1683).

36. For Ponet, Goodman, and Buchanan, see Essay 7, pp. 173–75, above; for the
radicalism of Locke's position, see Ashcraft, *Revolutionary Politics and Locke's "Two
Treatises of Government."* The radicalism of Locke's position is Ashcraft's thesis.

matter, from Dryden's exactly contemporary *The Spanish Friar,* "which mercilessly ridiculed the Catholic priesthood at a time when the outcry over the Popish Plot was serving Whig interests,"[37] and Tate's verse prologue, most of which is rather innocuous, ends with some mordant lines:

> Morals were always proper for the Stage,
> But are ev'n necessary in this Age.
> Poets must take the Churches Teaching Trade,
> Since Priests their Province of Intrigue invade;
> But We the worst in this Exchange have got
> In vain our Poets Preach, while Church-men Plot.

On the one hand, these lines defend "the Stage" against possible charges of immorality or profaneness; on the other, and this is their primary thrust, they attack intriguing and plotting "Priests." The "Popish Plot" of 1678 was the immediate background of the exclusion movement, and the exclusion party drew its energy from the extent and depth of anti-Catholic feeling among the English populace of all classes. In 1680, as Harth notes, it was the Whigs who were making political use of the Popish Plot; Tory propaganda sought to play down rather than to emphasize the Plot.[38] In the body of the play, Tate includes another gratuitous bit of anti-Catholicism. To Lear's vision of dying bravely "like a smugge Bridegroome" (TLN 2641), Tate adds this comparison: "flusht and pamper'd as a Priest's Whore" (4.4.164).[39] Moreover, in the prologue, the figures being indicted are not simply "Priests" but, by implied logical and grammatical structure, *our* "Church-men": "In vain, our Poets Preach, whilst [our] Church-men Plot." This ambiguity is only a flicker, but it is a definite one, and it certainly does not suggest a Tory context. Only the Whigs had any

---

37. Harth, "Dryden in 1678–1681," 56; see also p. 68.

38. See also Harris, *London Crowds,* 104–11. It was only later, after the fall of 1681, that the Tories made anti-Catholic sentiment part of their propaganda campaign; see Harris, 164–80, 223–24.

39. I cite the Folio *Lear* (F), *The Tragedie of King Lear,* by Through Line Number (TLN) according to the numbering in The Norton Facsimile of *The First Folio of Shakespeare,* prepared by Charlton Hinman (New York: Norton, 1968). Tate had access to both a Quarto and a Folio *Lear.* James Black concludes that after the first act, Tate relied on the Folio. See "Appendix A: Tate's Shakespearean Text," in Nahum Tate, *The History of King Lear,* ed. James Black (Lincoln: University of Nebraska Press, 1975), 97–100. I agree with this general picture, though I think the situation slightly more complicated.

sympathy at all with the idea of extending antipapal feeling to include the English church hierarchy.[40]

But these are still bits and pieces. I have argued for the use of sustained and, if possible, explicitly thematized material in determining the political content of a work. Tate's most obvious "newmodelling" of Shakespeare has been universally noted: his provision of a romantic relationship between Cordelia and Edgar ("that never chang'd word with each other in the Original").[41] His other most prominent change from "the Original" has been almost universally unnoticed: Tate makes Gloucester central to his play—perhaps more so than Lear. That this has not been noticed shows the way in which data that does not fit an established scheme, even when there is a lot of it, is simply invisible. My effort will not merely be to demonstrate that Tate makes this change in emphasis, but (since I think the fact rather easily established) to establish why he does this. I will argue that Tate does this to provide his play with its political thematic. Gloucester, I will argue, is central to the politics of Tate's *Lear*. Moreover, I will suggest that Tate's famous change is not unconnected to his upgrading of Gloucester. Certainly, the additions are narratively related (that Gloucester's line will become part of the royal family may help justify the expansion of Gloucester's role) but I will suggest that the romance too might ultimately be motivated as much by political as by aesthetic considerations, by Tate's concern for social as well as poetic justice.

Shakespeare's play begins with a casual conversation between Kent and Gloucester about the details of the division of the kingdom(s); the Gloucester household comes into the opening subscene only through Gloucester's explanation of Edmund, who has exactly three (short) lines in the exchanges. Tate begins with a strong focus on the Gloucester household. The play opens bumptiously—we realize how quiet Shakespeare's opening is—with Edmund's soliloquy on "Nature." The first angry father we see in the play is Gloucester, and Tate's Gloucester is a figure of towering rage. In Tate's play, Kent's initial action is an attempt to dissuade *Gloucester* from being "rash" (1.1.27). We never get to see Kent the master courtier, only Kent the plain-speaker.[42] Tate's

40. See Harris, *London Crowds*, 81–82, 118–24, 133–34; and Richard L. Greaves, *Secrets of the Kingdom: British Radicals from the Popish Plot to the Revolution of 1688–1689* (Stanford: Stanford University Press, 1992).

41. Letter to Boteler, in Spencer, ed., *Five Restoration Adaptations*, 203.

42. For Kent as master courtier in the opening exchange, see Essay 7 above.

Gloucester is unmitigable and is thematized as such: "Plead with the Seas," he says to Kent, "and reason down the Winds." This Gloucester then, with Kent and "this Light" as "Witnesses," solemnly and formally states "That I discard him [Edgar] here from my Possessions, / Divorce him from my Heart, my Blood and Name" (1.1.33–34). Tate is obviously "modeling" these speeches on those that Shakespeare gave to Lear, but the effect in Tate's play is less to strengthen the parallel between Gloucester and Lear than to make Lear's anger seem merely an echo of Gloucester's. The Lear of Tate's play is closer to Shakespeare's neurotic Leontes than to Shakespeare's terrifying Lear. Tate gives Kent and Gloucester rather than the wicked daughters the lines about "the infirmity of [Lear's] Age" and the worry about Lear's mental stability, and even Cordelia refers to him as "the chol'rick King" (1.1.50–56, 93). Leontes-like, Tate's Lear is sensitive to these charges: "'Tis said that I am Chol'rick, judge me Gods / Is there not cause" (1.1.116–17).[43] Tate's Lear needs rationalizations for his anger and finds one in "The Truth of what has been suggested to Us" regarding Cordelia's "Fondness for the Rebel Son of *Gloster*" (1.1.119–20). In Tate, what has apparently happened to Gloucester helps Lear understand what he thinks is happening to him. Again, Lear follows Gloucester.

The reference to "the Rebel Son of *Gloster*" confirms Maguire's remark about the intense political awareness of Tate's characters.[44] Tate's Lear calls Kent "Traytour" (1.1.158), as Shakespeare's never does, and Tate's Kent describes his protest as "my just Complaint" (1.1.160), a legal-political term. Tate's Burgundy (whom Tate correctly saw as the favored suitor in Shakespeare) speaks of "the breach / Of our Alliance" (1.1.186).[45] Tate's Gloucester shares, quite spectacularly as we shall see, this political awareness. Tate's Lear is again echoing his Gloucester in referring to Edgar as Gloucester's "Rebel Son," since Gloucester had already spoken, in a way that Shakespeare's character never does, of experiencing Edgar's supposed crime as "the sting of disobedience" (1.1.25). Tate ends the opening scene by returning to the Gloucester household, so that the Lear story is entirely framed by that

43. Compare Leontes, 2.3.121–22: "Were I a tyrant, / Where were her life?" in *The Winter's Tale* , ed. J. H. P. Pafford (London: Methuen, 1963).

44. Maguire, "Nahum Tate's *King Lear*," 36. Unfortunately, Maguire makes this observation in the context of an invidious comparison of Tate's characters with "the political innocents in the original text."

45. On Burgundy as the favored suitor, see Essay 7, n. 39 above.

of Gloucester. Gloucester's rage is again emphasized. In one of the final speeches of the scene, Gloucester says of Edgar:

> Fly *Edmund*, seek him out, wind me into him
> That I may bite the Traytor's heart, and fold
> His bleeding Entrals on my vengefull Arm.

This is pure invention and a thoroughly political version of rage. James Black has seen this speech as factitious in raising the issue of treason ("To have Gloster, who will be blinded for treason, refer to Edgar throughout the early acts as 'traitor' is simply irony"), and Black sees the reference to disemboweling as "grotesque" and "in very bad taste."[46] Wikander sees this image as a pictorial emblem and as conjuring up civil war.[47] But a son conspiring against a father was, in fact, a version of treason; like the case of a servant conspiring against a master (or a wife against a husband), it was a clear case of "Petty Treason."[48] Whatever sort of taste we might find Gloucester's image to be in, there is nothing adventitious in the terms of Gloucester's rage. As Foucault has reminded us, violence to the body of the traitor is intrinsic to the conception of treason in early modern Europe.[49] This violence was, it should be noted, especially directed at the internal organs of the body of the (male) traitor, whether "high" or "petty."[50] It was, in fact, directed at precisely those organs that Tate's Gloucester mentions, the "entrails" and the heart: "The traitor is to be . . . hanged by the neck until he be half dead, and then cut down; and his entrails to be cut out of his body and burnt by the executioner." The headsman or hangman was to slice open the chest and cut thence the heart, plucking it forth and holding it up to the

---

46. Black, "Introduction" to Tate, *King Lear*, xxxii–xxxiii.

47. Wikander, "The Spitted Infant," 354.

48. On servants and masters see Essay 7, n. 75 above. On wives and husbands, see Frances E. Dolan, "Home-Rebels and House-Traitors: Murderous Wives in Early Modern England," *Yale Journal of Law and the Humanities* 4 (1992): 1–31; expanded in *Dangerous Familiars: Representations of Domestic Violence in England, 1550–1700* (Ithaca: Cornell University Press, 1994), chap. 1.

49. Michel Foucault, *Discipline and Punish: The Birth of the Prison*, trans. Alan Sheridan (New York: Pantheon, 1979), 3–69.

50. Punishment for treason was gender-differentiated. Women found guilty of treason, whether high or petty, "shall be burned alive"; see Michael Dalton, *The Countrey Justice* (1619; facsimile London, 1973), 215. The punishments described in the text above (and in Foucault) were male prerogatives. The male traitor, either high or petty, suffered the same evisceration; see Dalton, 215.

populace, saying, "Behold the heart of a traitor."[51] The traitor's head was also to be prominently displayed, but this, interestingly, does not get into Gloucester's fantasy. It should be said, moreover, that Tate borrows some of his grotesquerie and "bad taste" from Shakespeare, whose Lear fantasizes, under the guise of revulsion at the non-European Other, about making his "generation messes" (TLN 123), but it is Tate who makes this taste for familial blood political.[52]

The point of making Gloucester thus prominent and of giving him this deeply political sensibility does not emerge until the third and later acts of Tate's play. It is there that the full "Whig" meaning of the play emerges. Yet it is important to see that this orientation permeates the play. Tate's handling of the villains shows this. The most striking features that Tate adds to the presentation of this group are, first, an emphasis on their luxurious frivolity and, second, an expanded treatment of their sexual goals. In Tate's version of Cornwall and Regan's dialogue with Gloucester on their arrival at his house, Tate drops all reference to needing Gloucester's "counsel" and instead develops Regan's "Lay comforts to your bosome" (TLN 1069). Tate's Cornwall says:

> Lay comforts, noble *Gloster*, to your Breast,
> As we to ours, This Night be spent in Revels[;]
> We choose you, *Gloster*, for our Host to Night,
> A troublesome expression of our Love.
> On to the Sports before us. . . . (2.2.45–48)

This is clearly a court on progress, a court demanding proper "Revels." The sense of distinctly courtly entertainment as characterizing Cornwall and company is continued later in the scene. When Lear demands to see "this Daughter" (Regan) who has stocked his messenger, he is told that

51. William Andrews, *Old Time Punishments* (1890; rpt. Toronto: Coles, 1980), 202; see Dalton, *The Countrey Justice*, 215: "The punishment for pety treason is this: The man so offending, shall be drawne and hanged."

52. It is worth noting that drawing and quartering for treason did not disappear with the Restoration. Ten of the condemned regicides were so treated. See Ronald Hutton, *The Restoration: A Political and Religious History of England and Wales, 1658–1667* (Oxford: Clarendon Press, 1985), 134. Hutton provides a vignette similar to that which opens Foucault's book (see n. 49): "One old soldier was still sufficiently alive as his naked body was sliced open to sit up and strike the executioner. A moment later his heart was displayed to the cheering crowd." On October 17, 1660, Evelyn wrote: "I saw not their ['those murderous Traytors'] execution, but met their quarters mangld and cutt and reaking as they were brought from the Gallows in baskets on the hurdle"; *The Diary of John Evelyn,* ed. E. S. de Beer (London: Oxford University Press, 1959), 412.

Regan is "Within, Sir, at a Masque" (2.2.177), that is, at the most distinctively royal and extravagant form of entertainment known to the seventeenth century.[53] Goneril poisons Regan "amidst thy rev'ling Bowls"; Regan has poisoned Goneril "at thy own Banquet" (5.5.101 and 107). Even Oswald is made even more pointlessly elegant in Tate than in Shakespeare. Tate invents three new insults of Oswald for his Kent-Caius—"vile Civet-box" (1.2.27), "dappar Slave" (2.2.28), and "Essence Bottle" (2.2.59)—and Tate's Lear describes Oswald as "A Fashion-fop that spends the day in Dressing" (2.2.254).

The heightened sexuality of Tate's villains consists primarily of two features. First, the attraction of the older sisters for Edmund is developed earlier and further (Regan describes Edmund as "A charming Youth" at 2.2.43 and he receives love letters from both sisters in 3.2; a scene of Regan and Edmund "amorously Seated[,] Listening to Musick" is added, and it is clear that their relationship has been consummated [5.2.6–7]). Second, Edmund's sexuality is made explicit. He is given outright (though politically tinged) lust for Goneril and Regan ("O for a Tast of such Majestick Beauty" [3.2.9]); he is given a Volpone-like, classically oriented lust for Cordelia ("like the vig'rous *Jove* I will enjoy / This *Semele* in a Storm" [3.2.123–24]; and he is given a definite and recognizable sexual philosophy as a happily self-professed "Libertine" (5.5.19).[54] Tate's revisions make us aware of how (oddly?) unconcerned with sex as such Shakespeare's Edmund is. Where Shakespeare's character sees

53. Court masques were perhaps a more prominent feature of the pre- rather than the post-revolutionary Stuart court, but they certainly did exist in the Restoration. See Andrew R. Walkling, "Politics and the Restoration Masque: The Case of Dido and Aeneas," in Gerald Maclean, ed., *Literature, Culture, and Society in the Stuart Restoration* (Cambridge: Cambridge University Press, 1995). I am grateful to Mr. Walkling for sharing with me this essay and some of his other work on the Restoration masque.

54. James Black has suggested that Tate's Edmund is a portrait of a "Hobbesian 'natural man'" as understood in the Restoration. I am agnostic on this matter, since the "libertine" sexual philosophy was so well established earlier in the seventeenth century, with disdain for constancy and praise for variety as its touchstones; see, for instance, Louis I. Bredvold, "The Naturalism of Donne in Relation to Some Renaissance Traditions," *Journal of English and Germanic Philology* 22 (1923): 471–502; and Hugh M. Richmond, *The School of Love: The Evolution of the Stuart Love Lyric* (Princeton: Princeton University Press, 1964). This position might well, however, have taken on an association with "Hobbism" in the Restoration. That the political position of the play as a whole is Hobbesian (which Black does not claim, but Maguire, 37, does) seems to me not to be true. Hobbesian political philosophy was associated with the Tory position. As Ashcraft points out (*Revolutionary Politics*, 571, 293–94), Hobbes was often used against the Whigs, and virtually never by them. This means that if Maguire is claiming that Tate presented Edmund as *both* Hobbesian and a Whig, such a claim is very unlikely.

the choice of sisters as merely a strategic problem, Tate's Edmund opts for "bright Gonerill" on the principle of "dear Variety," since he has already "enjoy'd" Regan (5.2.7–9). Tate makes Edmund a Restoration rake.[55] Charles II's court, of course, was notable not only for its sympathy for Catholicism but also for its outright licentiousness. These features, moreover, were not entirely unrelated, since two of the royal mistresses were Catholic. The crowds of apprentices and others who pulled down brothels in Shoreditch and elsewhere in London in March of 1668 are reported to have shouted that "ere long they would come and pull White-hall down"—"presumably in their eyes," as Tim Harris rather coolly puts it, "the biggest bawdy house of the lot."[56]

The theme of luxury and licentiousness is treated by Tate not only morally and, through implicit allusion, politically, but also, even more remarkably, economically. The analysis is given by Edmund. This puzzles Maguire. "Even the Whiggish Edmund," she says, acknowledges that there is something wrong in the kingdom (37). She is right to be surprised to find Edmund criticizing Regan and company. But this is not what he is doing. His stance toward what he describes is entirely admiring; he is not horrified but envious:

> The Storm is in our louder Rev'lings drown'd.
> Thus wou'd I Reign cou'd I but mount a Throne.
> The Riots of these proud imperial Sisters
> Already have impos'd the galling Yoke
> Of Taxes, and hard Impositions on
> The drudging Peasants Neck, who bellow out
> Their loud Complaints in Vain—Triumphant Queens!
> With what Assurance do they tread the Crowd. (3.2.1–8)

For Edmund, "tread[ing] the Crowd" and imposing yokes on peasant necks are part of what ruling in the grand (French?) style is all about. "The Storm is in our louder Rev'lings drown'd" brilliantly continues the theme of "revelling" that Tate has introduced into the play, and it does so in a passage that not only sees "Rev'lings" as drowning out awareness of physical conditions (the storm) but also, presumably, of social ones, the "loud Complaints" of the "peasants." Holistic social thinking—as when imperial "Riots" are seen as paid for by "Taxes, and hard Impositions" on the laboring classes—is always impressive, but we must ask

---

55. It is interesting that Tate omits Edmund's oddly touching pride, in Shakespeare, at having been "beloved" (TLN 3196).

56. Harris, *London Crowds*, 83.

some specific questions about this passage. First of all, could a "Tory propagandist" have written it? Unless one thinks that we are meant to share Edmund's admiring attitudes here, the answer must be in the negative. "Loud Complaints" have already been identified with a virtuously protesting figure—Kent bellowed his "just Complaint" in vain to Lear—and Edmund's attitude is a recognizably Tory one. Although the Tories did eventually (after 1681) engage in populist politics to take back the streets of London from the Whigs, who were committed to gaining popular support, the Tory aim was always to keep the common people in their place, to "reduce the deluded Multitude to their Just Allegiance."[57] The Tories were never sympathetic to "the Crowd," who were always thought of as "the rabble."[58] Rulers should be able to "tread the Crowd" with "Assurance."

We can be even more specific about Edmund's admiring speech, since the speech itself is remarkably specific. Tate is building on a short passage at the beginning of act 5 of Shakespeare's *Lear* in which Albany speaks of those "whom the rigour of our State / Forc'd to cry out" (TLN 2868–2869). The Shakespearean Quarto also includes in this speech a further reference to "others whome . . . / Most just and heavy causes make oppose" (K3r),[59] but this "rigour" and these "heavy causes" are never specified. Tate alone gives us "Taxes, and hard Impositions." He is so unsympathetic to these that he can hardly maintain the dramatically required admiring tone. This is a topical reference. One of the great revolutions in English taxation was the imposition of the excise by the Long Parliament in 1643. This was a tax on the buying and selling of a number of items, including beer, meat, and salt. The most important general characteristic of the excise duties of this period, as William Kennedy explains, "was that they made the poor man regularly pay taxes."[60] This feature made the excise "a new departure of the most striking kind" because for the century preceding the Long Parliament, the tradition regarding taxation of the poor was exemption.[61] There were riots against regressive taxation in 1659–60, but the Restoration did not remove the excise and, after an initial pause, the number of goods

57. Harris, *London Crowds*, 131.
58. See Ashcraft, *Revolutionary Politics*, 298.
59. I cite the Quarto (Q), *The Historie of King Lear*, from *King Lear 1608 (Pied Bull Quarto)*, Shakespeare Quarto Facsimiles, no. 1 (Oxford: Clarendon Press, 1939).
60. William Kennedy, *English Taxation, 1640–1799* (London, 1913), 66.
61. Kennedy, *English Taxation*, 51, 22.

that it applied to continued to grow.[62] In 1667, Marvell thought the excise "a monster worse than e'er before," and related it to, among other things, the luxuriousness of the court.[63] Moreover, not only did the Restoration regime fail to repeal the hated excise—that on beer was the most important—but it also introduced, as Harris puts it, "another bitterly resented imposition" in the form of the hearth tax.[64] The truly indigent were exempt (the number of households exempted is one of our best guides to the growing extent of poverty in the period),[65] but the hearth tax, like the excise, fell heavily on small landowners, thus, as Christopher Hill somberly notes, "helping the downward march of yeomen and artisans."[66] The Whigs always hated the hearth tax but it was not repealed until 1688, when it was declared (in very Whiggish terms) "a great Oppression to the Poorer sort" and "a badge of Slavery upon the whole People."[67] "Taxes, and hard Impositions" on the lower classes were truly characteristic of the period in which Tate was writing his version of *Lear*, and this economic situation certainly did contribute to the possibility of popular unrest.

It is with regard to popular unrest that Gloucester assumes centrality in Tate's play. When Tate's Gloucester enters in 3.2 (not having heard Edmund's opening speech on treading the crowd), he mentions not only the cruelty that Lear has suffered but also the fact that "the Commons / Repine aloud at their female Tyrants" (3.2.32–33). Significantly, he says "the Commons" here, not the crowd, the multitude, or the rabble. He conceives of this group politically and respectfully. Ashcraft has noted the importance of Locke's defense of the rationality of "the people" in the *Second Treatise*.[68] The Commons, in Tate's *Lear*, call not for a republic but for "the re-installment / Of their good old King." This is not a divagation into popular Toryism. Most of the Whigs, as we have already noted, were not republicans, and to present "the Commons" as

62. Harris, *London Crowds*, 42–45, 61.

63. Marvell, "The Last Instructions to a Painter," lines 124–41, in *Andrew Marvell: The Complete Poems*, ed. Elizabeth Story Donno (New York: Penguin, 1972).

64. Harris, *London Crowds*, 190.

65. Keith Wrightson, *English Society, 1580–1680* (New Brunswick: Rutgers University Press, 1982), 148.

66. Christopher Hill, *The Century of Revolution, 1603–1714* (New York: Norton, 1961), 217.

67. See "An Act for the takeing away the Revenue ariseing by Hearth-Money," in *The Statutes of the Realm* (London, 1819), 6:61.

68. See Ashcraft, *Revolutionary Politics*, 306–7.

faithful to a nontyrannical king can be seen as countering the Tory accusation of popular republicanism.[69] The distress of the Commons at "their female tyrants" is based on the tyranny that they feel, presumably the luxury-supporting "Taxes, and hard Impositions," but economics does not seem to be enough to mobilize the Commons (this seems to have been largely true in the seventeenth century).[70] Gloucester thinks that knowledge of Lear's injuries could be the spark that "will inflame 'em into Mutiny" (3.2.36). He states he fears this—it is the great Tory fear—but Edmund shrewdly knows better. Acting as a kind of agent provocateur, Edmund says of an uprising of the Commons, "'Tis to be hopt, not fear'd." This is a brilliant piece of dialogue on Tate's part. Gloucester is caught. He acknowledges that he has adopted the cause of the repining Commons, the cause of "Mutiny":

Thou hast it Boy, 'tis to be hopt indeed[.]
On me they cast their Eyes, and hourly Court me
To lead 'em on, and whilst this Head is Mine
I am Theirs. (3.2.39–41)

Gloucester knows and accepts the price of leading an unsuccessful popular revolt. He is the figure of revolution in Tate's play. It is, I think, important to Tate that Gloucester takes on this role before his blinding. Tate seems to have been extremely sensitive to and repelled by motives that were purely self-concerned. He saw as an advantage of the "one Expedient" he had hit upon that might actually have improved the original, the love between Edgar and Cordelia, that it makes Edgar's adoption of the "Tom o' Bedlam" disguise "a generous Design" to aid Cordelia "that was before a poor Shift to save his [Edgar's own] Life."[71] Worry about self-interest is perhaps also why the Commons need Lear's grievances as well as their own to "inflame 'em into Mutiny." Tate wants the motivations of the virtuous, whether individuals or whole groups, not to be purely self-interested. For Tate, personal revenge is not a good enough motive for an aristocrat to ally himself with and lead a popular rebellion (the aristocrat does not have to do the initial work of alerting "the Commons" to their situation because, as Locke says, they "have the sence of rational Creatures" and know when they are being op-

69. See Harris, *London Crowds,* 134–38 and chap. 6 passim.

70. See Harris, *London Crowds,* 206 ("collective action against the imposition of taxes was uncommon") and chap. 8 passim.

71. Letter to Boteler, Spencer, ed., 203.

pressed).[72] Gloucester gives himself to a cause, not to self-interest: "I am Theirs." His politics are not "a poor Shift."

Gloucester attempts to bolster the cause by sending Edmund with "Dispatches to the Duke of Combray," an "invetrate" highland enemy of Cornwall's (3.2.46–50).[73] Before continuing Gloucester's story, however, Tate has to return to Lear's (and, in his version, to Cordelia's). Tate skilfully compresses scenes 3.4 and 3.6 of the Shakespearean Folio into one scene (dropping the Fool but keeping virtually all of Edgar-Tom's lines);[74] he adds a scene in which Edgar saves Cordelia from ruffians who are to abduct her for Edmund's sexual pleasure and in which Cordelia finally accepts Edgar's love (3.4).[75] It is important to see that in having the Edgar-Cordelia story culminate here, before the end of the third act, Tate allows himself the possibility of following Shakespeare as closely as he wishes to for the rest of the play. Tate could, after all, have given his play the "Hollywood" ending and saved the acceptance of Edgar by Cordelia until the final moment, but he did not do this. The romantic resolution is tucked into the third act; the final event of the act remains Gloucester's blinding.

I argued in the previous essay that the blinding scene is central to the politics of Shakespeare's play; it enacts and articulates the crucial paradox of "service through resistance." In Tate, the scene is oddly muffled, but the way in which Tate handles it conveys very clearly the difference in the ways in which the two (three?) plays are politically radical. In Tate's play, as in Shakespeare's, Gloucester is spoken of by Cornwall and company as a traitor, but only in Tate's is he also addressed as a "Rebel" (3.5.34). The emphasis in Tate is on immoral authority rather than on

72. John Locke, *The Second Treatise of Government,* par. 230, in John Locke, *Two Treatises of Government,* ed. Peter Laslett, rev. ed. (New York: New American Library, 1965), 466.

73. Combray (later Cambria; see "the *Cambrian* prince" at 3.5.60) is, of course, Wales. Monmouth was in Wales, and this may well have been a reference to the Duke of Monmouth. The association of Monmouth with "Mountaineers" is also plausible, since Monmouth led Scottish troops, especially Highlanders, in putting down the revolt of the Covenanters in June 1679; see Jones, *The First Whigs,* 79–80. I do not think that interpretation should be based on such details, but this possible reference does harmonize with the general political orientation that I see in the play.

74. Tate is following F here in omitting the "mock-trial" of Goneril (see Q G3v-G4r).

75. Though a bit drawn out, this much-maligned scene has some real power and poetic distinction. The culminating line, "Come to my Arms, thou dearest, best of Men" (3.4.93), is truly beautiful, and Cordelia's oath, beginning "By the dear Vital Stream that baths my Heart" (3.4.97–102), is too lovely, too well-written, and (dare I say it) too Shakespearean to be merely sentimental. It resonates, for instance, with much in *Cymbeline.*

personal cruelty; Cornwall does not do the blinding himself but instead
has his "Slaves" do it ("Slaves, perform your Work, / Out with those
treacherous Eyes"). Tate misses much of the force of the servant's
intervention in Shakespeare's scene by having both of Gloucester's eyes
put out at once. In Shakespeare, the servant intervenes at a moment
when he can still do some practical good. The theme of "service through
resistance" remains in Tate's version, but it is not, even in this scene, his
focus. Tate's emphasis is not, like that of Shakespeare and the Marian
resistance theorists, on the moral duty of the individual, regardless of
class or status, to attempt to oppose wickedness wherever it appears.[76]
Tate's emphasis is on the resource of popular rebellion.

Shakespeare never gives his Gloucester a meditation on the experience
of blindness. Tate, probably drawing on Milton (in both *Paradise Lost*
and *Samson*) does do this,[77] but the remarkable feature of the speech of
this sort that Tate writes for Gloucester is not its Samson-like self-pity
but its sudden un-Samson-like turn to political activity. Following the
sentiments of Shakespeare's Gloucester (TLN 2503–4, on the "benefit"
that "wretchednesse" has "To end it selfe by death"), Tate's Gloucester
says, "Yet still one way th' extreamest Fate affords, / And even the Blind
can find the Way to Death" (3.5.82–83). The turn comes a line later.
Tate's Gloucester, again like Shakespeare's Lear rather than Shakespeare's Gloucester, decides not to "go gentle": "Must I then tamely
Die, and unrevenged?"[78] As in Shakespeare, the question is how to
respond to tyranny. Where the response of Shakespeare's Gloucester to
"Tyrants rage" (TLN 2505) is the Senecan one of frustrating "his [the
tyrant's] proud will" by putting oneself out of the reach of it through
suicide, Tate's Gloucester immediately recognizes the political uses of his
condition:

> I will present me to the pittying Crowd,
> And with the Rhetorick of these dropping Veins
> Enflame 'em to Revenge their King and me. (3.5.86–88)

76. See Essay 7 above.

77. "No more to view the Beauty of the Spring, / Nor see the Face of Kindred, or
of Friend" (3.5.80–81) seems to echo *Paradise Lost* 3.40–47, while "Shut from the Living
whilst among the Living; / Dark as the Grave amidst the bustling World" (77–78) seems
to echo *Samson Agonistes*, lines 79, 99–105. See *John Milton: The Complete Poems and
Major Prose*, ed. Meritt Y. Hughes (New York: Odyssey, 1957).

78. See Dylan Thomas's villanelle, "Do not go gentle into that good night," in
Collected Poems (New York: New Directions, 1957), 128.

This determination is clearly based upon Regan's politically shrewd analysis, in Shakespeare, that "It was great ignorance, Glousters eyes being out / To let him live" because "where he arrives, he moves / All hearts against us" (TLN 2394–96). In Shakespeare, Gloucester "moves" hearts simply by being in his condition of victimization; there is no intention involved. It is the moral process (metaphysicalized in *Macbeth*) by which "pity" becomes a political force.[79] What is spontaneous, mute eloquence in Shakespeare's play is "Rhetorick" in Tate's, a presentation that is calculated to "move." The mutilated body here is not a symbol of the horrors of civil war but a call for the overthrow of tyranny, for the "Glorious Mischief" of a justified popular rebellion (3.4.89). It is part of Tate's presentation of "the Commons" that he sees the "Crowd" as not only compassionate but also as needing something as extreme as "the Rhetorick of these dropping Veins" to "Enflame 'em." This is the second time this latter phrase is used. The first time is when Gloucester pretends to fear that knowledge of Lear's injuries will "inflame 'em into Mutiny." Tate seems to share Locke's view that the people, rather than being constantly mutinous, "are more disposed to suffer, than [to] right themselves by Resistance."[80] It takes a powerful moral force to put them into motion.

Tate's "expedient" of pairing Cordelia with Edgar serves to eliminate France from the play. There is no invasion in Tate's *Lear* (except, that is, the "invasion" of the state that, for Locke, tyranny constitutes).[81] Not only is France eliminated by the (virtuous) love-plot, but Gloucester's dispatches to "the Cambrian Prince" are intercepted by Regan and Cornwall. The war in Tate's *Lear* is entirely a popular rebellion. The reason that Gloucester goes to Dover, in Tate, is only to jump off the cliff there—after he has done his rhetorical task. In setting up the plot

79. See the famous "naked babe" passage in *Macbeth* in which (in Macbeth's visionary analysis) "Pity" becomes an apocalyptic force. See *Macbeth*, ed. Kenneth Muir (London: Methuen, 1984), 1.7.21–25.

80. Locke, *The Second Treatise*, par. 230; ed. Laslett, 466.

81. Locke, *The Second Treatise*, par. 239; ed. Laslett, 474. It is interesting that the statute abolishing the hearth-tax (see n. 67 above) speaks of the king restoring the people's "Rights and Liberties which have beene *invaded* contrary to Law" (emphasis mine). I am not sure why Wikander thinks that the invasion of England by France was "Shakespeare's innovation" in the Lear story, so that in eliminating it, Tate "returns to the sources of Shakespeare's play" ("The Spitted Infant," 354). The French invasion is extremely prominent in *The True Chronicle History of King Leir and his three daughters;* see *Narrative and Dramatic Sources of Shakespeare*, ed. Geoffrey Bullough (New York: Columbia University Press, 1978) 7:337–402.

in this way, Tate can be seen as continuing the process of radicalization that Shakespeare began in revising the Quarto version of the play into the version that appears in the Folio.[82] There is no reason to think that Tate, with the two versions of *Lear* in front of him, and working closely with them, could not have noticed the differences that Taylor, Urkowitz, and other modern scholars have. Both Taylor and Urkowitz argue that after act 3, the Shakespearean Folio version of *Lear* "encourages an audience," as Taylor puts it, "to forget [the French invasion] by systematically removing verbal and visual reminders of the French presence, so that Cordelia seems to lead not an invasion but a rebellion."[83] By eliminating France entirely, Tate carries this process to its next logical step.

By eliminating France, moreover, Tate eliminates any suggestion that a French connection could be virtuous. France, not without reason, was the great bugaboo of the Whigs. It was synonymous with popery and arbitrary power—with unlimited monarchy.[84] It is possible, in other words, that the love story was created by the politics. The elimination of France may have been at least as important to Tate as the provision of romance. The shift from a French invasion to a popular rebellion, moreover, was not, for Tate, merely a choice of horrors. Tate goes out of his way to present his popular rebellion as positive. In the scene following the blinding of Gloucester, Regan's meditations on defending her possession of Edmund against Goneril's encroachments are disturbed by "Shouts" offstage and the "hasty Entrance" of an Officer announcing "A most surprizing and a sudden Change" (4.1.32). This surprising change is not, as in Shakespeare, a moral and psychological transformation ("never man so chang'd" says Oswald of Albany [TLN 2270]) but a sociopolitical one.[85] Instead of "the Army that was

---

82. See Gary Taylor, *"King Lear:* The Date and Authorship of the Folio Version," and "Monopolies, Show Trials, Disaster, and Invasion: *King Lear* and Censorship," in Gary Taylor and Michael Warren, eds., *The Division of the Kingdoms: Shakespeare's Two Versions of "King Lear,"* (Oxford: Clarendon Press, 1983), 351–451 and 75–119. Clearly, I accept the "two-text" hypothesis, the view that holds that the first Quarto and first Folio texts of *King Lear* are separate and distinct realizations of the material by Shakespeare (see Essay 7, n. 1 above).

83. Gary Taylor, "The War in *King Lear," Shakespeare Quarterly* 33 (1980): 27–34; see also Steven Urkowitz, *Shakespeare's Revision of "King Lear"* (Princeton: Princeton University Press, 1980), 71–74.

84. Ashcraft, *Revolutionary Politics,* 205–7.

85. Tate does preserve Oswald's description of Albany, but this scene with Regan is structurally parallel to the scene with Oswald and Goneril in Shakespeare. Tate moves the description of Albany to later in act 4.

Landed" (TLN 2171), we hear that "The Peasants are all up in Mutiny" (4.1.33). Interestingly, Regan also finds this change surprising. "On what Provocation," she asks. The answer is Gloucester:

> At last day's publick Festival, to which
> The Yeomen from all Quarters had repair'd,
> Old *Gloster*, whom you late depriv'd of Sight,
> (His Veins yet Streaming fresh) presents himself,
> Proclaims your Cruelty, and their Oppression,
> With the King's Injuries; which so enrag'd 'em,
> That now that Mutiny which long had crept
> Takes Wing, and threatens your Best Pow'rs. (4.1.36–43)

This is again very careful in its details. It amply repays close, contextualized reading. "Publick Festival[s]" were the "normal" occasions for apprentice and other uprisings.[86] The "Bawdy House Riots" of 1668 (in which the "mob" tore down brothels) took place during the Easter Holidays.[87] London was the most active scene of such uprisings, and the mention of "Quarters" suggests (perhaps oddly) an urban setting. It also suggests that the London "crowd" or "mob," as Valerie Pearl and others have shown, was much more organized and articulated than the derogatory terms assert.[88] The characterization of the "mutineers" as "Yeomen," moreover, is also interesting and surprisingly accurate. Only recently have historians come to recognize that "it should not be assumed that crowd activity in seventeenth-century London was the preserve of plebeian elements," but rather "was often engaged in by people who are perhaps better termed 'the middling sort,'" for whom "Yeomen" is a good designation.[89] The "Provocation" that Gloucester provides also bears examination. First of all, as he planned, he "present[s]" himself as a kind of emblem of the results of tyranny; he then articulates the meaning of his self-presentation: "your [Regan and Cornwall's] Cruelty" and then "their [the people's] Oppression." Restoration is not the central idea of this mutiny. Only in the next line, very weakly

---

86. See, *inter alia*, Buchanan Sharp, *In Contempt of All Authority: Rural Artisans and Riot in the West of England, 1586–1660* (Berkeley and Los Angeles: University of California Press, 1980); David Underdown, *Revel, Riot, and Rebellion: Popular Politics and Culture in England, 1603–1660* (Oxford: Oxford University Press, 1987).

87. Harris, *London Crowds,* 82–91.

88. Valerie Pearl, "Change and Stability in Seventeenth-Century London," *London Journal* 5 (1979): 3–34; J. A. Sharpe, "The People and the Law," in Barry Reay, ed., *Popular Culture in Seventeenth-Century England* (New York: St. Martin's, 1985), 244–70.

89. Harris, *London Crowds,* 17.

connected syntactically to the foregoing list ("With the King's Injuries")
is Lear mentioned. In Tate as in Shakespeare, Regan gives voice to
conservative political philosophy, but the difference of focus between the
two plays is nicely captured by the difference between the outrage of
Shakespeare's Regan at "a pezant stand[ing] up thus" (TLN 2154) and
the outrage of Tate's Regan at "this Monster of Rebellion" (4.1.46).

Tate wants to include everything that is in Shakespeare's Gloucester
in his play, but the two playwrights' differing conceptions of the character sit awkwardly together. Tate's Gloucester, having used his "Rhetorick" successfully, can proceed to Dover with his plan for suicide, but
this seems far less appropriate to him than to Shakespeare's figure.
"Revenge, thou art afoot" (4.2.11) is much closer to the true voice of
Tate's character. Tate retains the remarkable plea for "Distribution" that
Shakespeare gives Gloucester (TLN 2255–2256; 4.2.54), but adds re-
unions with Cordelia and with Kent.[90] The latter is the more important
in the play because it becomes part of the revolution plot. Gloucester
exhorts Kent to throw off his disguise because "There's business for thee
and of noblest weight." The "business" is that "Our injur'd Country
is at length in Arms" and needs a military leader (4.2.100–103). The
yeomen, the crowd, the peasants are "Our . . . Country." Kent agrees
to "Head these Forces," so "this Monster" will not be "many-
headed."[91] Tate keeps Shakespeare's mock-miracle and retains the
Gloucester-Lear dialogue at Dover almost verbatim, but he continues his
own vision with the report of an officer to Edmund on "the Posture of
the Enemy":

> The banisht *Kent* return'd, and at their Head;
> Your brother *Edgar* on the Rear; old *Gloster*

90. Judy Kronenfeld's "'So Distribution Should Undo Excess, and Each Man Have
Enough': Shakespeare's *King Lear*—Anabaptist Egalitarianism, Anglican Charity, Both,
Neither?" *ELH* 59 (1992): 755–84, is another example of conservative use of the charge
of anachronism to discredit the possibility of a radical dimension in a Renaissance text. As
Scodel does with Donne's third Satire (see Essay 6, n. 37 above), Kronenfeld imports "the
ubiquitous mean" (763) into Shakespeare's *Lear*—it is one of those notions that must be
there. Like Maguire on Tate's *Lear*, Kronenfeld has the good sense to pull back from the
strong form of the argument that she initially asserts (Scodel is never committed to such
a strong form). The strong form of Kronenfeld's argument is that to hear a socially radical
meaning in "Distribution" in Gloucester's speech is "totally ahistorical." The Anabaptists,
etc., who are acknowledged but dismissed, somehow couldn't really have existed (or
mattered). *Utopia*, which at least seems to advocate communism, could not have been
written in the sixteenth century. Surely there is no such poem (see Essay 1, p. 25 above).
91. See Christopher Hill, "The Many-Headed Multitude," *Change and Continuity
in Seventeenth-Century England* (Cambridge: Harvard University Press, 1975), 181–204.

(A moving Spectacle) led through their Ranks,
Whose pow'rfull Tongue, and more prevailing Wrongs,
Have so enrag'd their rustick Spirits. (5.2.15–19)

Even Tate's heroic Gloucester cannot actually fight in the battle, but where Shakespeare's figure sits in silence (onstage) through the battle, Tate gives his Gloucester a soliloquy—quite a powerful one. It mostly consists of Gloucester's frustration at his enforced passivity, but in line with the character that Tate has developed, it turns toward action. "Forth / To th' open Field," Tate's Gloucester resolves, and explains his decision with the following remarkable image:

Yet the disabled Courser, Maim'd and Blind,
When to his Stall he hears the ratling War,
Foaming with Rage tears up the batter'd Ground,
And tugs for Liberty. (5.3.13–16)

The passion for Liberty could hardly be more strongly—or more positively—articulated. A popular rebellion led by injured aristocrats certainly sounds like the "darker side" of the Whig appeal for popular support.[92]

It might be said that the fact that the popularly embodied and aristocratically headed rebellion in Tate's *Lear* does not succeed in the battle means that Tate did not ultimately countenance popular rebellion, even for the best of causes.[93] I do not think that we can draw this conclusion. The rebellion, as we have seen, is very sympathetically presented. The reason that Tate does not allow the rebellion to succeed has to do, I think, less with his politics than with his desire to follow Shakespeare. As far as possible, within the limits of his major changes, Tate tries to retain Shakespeare's plot. Tate wants the deaths of Goneril and Regan to result from jealousy over Edmund (though Tate engineers the deaths differently) and he wants to retain the duel between Edgar and Edmund. Most of all, he wants Lear and Cordelia sent off to prison and slated for execution (by Goneril rather than by Edmund—this is truly, I think, an improvement).[94] Tate wants Edgar and Albany to rescue Lear and Cordelia in a "lucky" minute (5.6.39) in order to be

92. See n. 15 above.
93. See Wikander, "The Spitted Infant," 355.
94. In Shakespeare, no clear reason is given why Edmund needs to have Lear and Cordelia murdered. He has one very vague line about his need to "defend" his "state" (TLN 2915–16).

able to assert, ultimately, that "there are Gods, and Vertue is their Care" (5.6.97). Politically, the meaning of this assertion of "poetic justice" might be that the goals of a justified popular revolution will succeed even if the revolution itself does not. It is important to recall, as I noted earlier, that Tate's play does not end with "the King's blest Restauration" (5.6.119). Lear abdicates again, getting it right this time, and the play ends with the rule of the king's daughter and her husband—who was a major participant in the rebellion.

To experience a work like Nahum Tate's *King Lear* with what Empson wonderfully calls "a clean palate" involves giving up a good many preconceptions.[95] First and foremost, it involves not continuously punishing the work for not being Shakespeare's version of the story or Shakespeare's language. The same sort of scorekeeping that inhibits the appreciation of Tate's play makes it difficult for many persons, perhaps especially Shakespearean scholars, to appreciate the power of, for instance, Peter Brook's film of *King Lear*, and generally from enjoying any innovative or daring production or offshoot of Shakespeare. To recognize that Tate's play is not Tory propaganda involves just the sort of exercise that Empson had in mind in his controversy with Rosemond Tuve. It means putting aside, or at least holding lightly, for the duration of a first reading, what one expects the work to be or to mean on the basis of one's prior knowledge of the author, the period, or the genre. *Nil admirari*—never to be surprised—should hardly be a critic's ideal. Particulars will never alter one's generalizations if the particulars are never examined closely enough to reveal their distinctive shapes. It may be highly improbable for Nahum Tate's *King Lear* to be a thoughtful and well-written Whig drama, but the important question is not whether this is probable but whether it is true.

95. See William Empson, "George Herbert and Miss Tuve," *Kenyon Review* 12 (1950): 738; and see Essay 1 above.

Index

Compositor: Braun-Brumfield, Inc.
Text: 10/13 Galliard
Display: Galliard
Printer: Braun-Brumfield, Inc.
Binder: Braun-Brumfield, Inc.

8113